Seeking Ezekiel

Also by David J. Halperin

The Merkabah in Rabbinic Literature

The Faces of the Chariot:
Early Jewish Responses to Ezekiel's Vision

Seeking Ezekiel

Text and Psychology

David J. Halperin

The Pennsylvania State University Press
University Park, Pennsylvania

Library of Congress Cataloging-in-Publication Data

Halperin, David J. (David Joel)
    Seeking Ezekiel : text and psychology / David J. Halperin.

        p.   cm.
    Includes bibliographical references and index.
    ISBN 0-271-00947-0 (cloth).—ISBN 0-271-00948-9 (pbk.)
    1. Ezekiel (Biblical prophet)—Psychology.   2. Bible. O.T.
Ezekiel—Criticism, interpretation, etc.   I. Title.
BS1545.2.H355   1993
224'.406'019—dc20   92-33568
                                                                              CIP

Published by The Pennsylvania State University Press, Barbara Building, Suite
C, University Park, PA 16802-1003

For Rose
My friend, my companion, my love

Contents

Preface

I am not a psychoanalyst, nor have I received formal training in psychology. My education and my expertise are in philology and history; their primary subjects have been the Hebrew language and the history and literature of ancient Judaism. My acquaintance with psychoanalysis derives from reading in the works of Freud and his followers, conversations and correspondence with psychiatric professionals, and personal experience as an analytic patient.

The readers of this book, I assume, will include Bible scholars and psychologists. I also assume that these will not be its only readers. I have therefore taken pains to make the book accessible to all interested persons and to write so that the only prerequisites for understanding my arguments are curiosity, an open mind, and perhaps a certain measure of patience. I have avoided technical language wherever possible, and I do not presuppose a knowledge of Hebrew. Much of the book, to be sure, is given over to discussions of the minutiae of Hebrew philology and Bible scholarship. But I have tried to make these discussions intelligible to the nonspecialist, and always to keep before the reader's eyes the broader aims that my analyses are intended to serve.

I intend to make a case for the psychoanalytic perception of human nature and for its value as a tool for understanding literary creations of the remote past. I do not mean thereby to assert the validity of every doctrine in the Freudian system, far less to arbitrate the disputes among the various psychoanalytic schools. My interpretations of Ezekiel rest upon a limited number of premises, shared by most psychoanalytically oriented psychologists. In order to find this book persuasive, the reader must be prepared to grant at least the plausibility of these premises.

Specifically, I presuppose that we humans are capable of unconscious as well as conscious thought; that our unconscious determines, or at least influences, much of our conscious thought and our behavior; that dreams,

and by implication hallucinations, may be expected to express unconscious thoughts in symbolic form; that our unconscious thoughts very
often concern our sexual and aggressive impulses, particularly those we
are not willing to admit to ourselves; that events and emotions of our early
childhood have profound influence on our adult ideas and behaviors; that,
as children, we have sexual desires for our parents (and vice versa); and
that we may disown feelings that are uncongenial to us by projecting them
onto other beings, real and imaginary.

Those who regard these assertions as too fantastic even to be worth
entertaining will necessarily remain unconvinced by my arguments. But if
the reader is prepared even provisionally to admit that they may be thinkable and to consider without prejudice how well (or poorly) they work to
explain the difficult ancient document that is the subject of our investigation, he or she may eventually be moved to grant that their explanatory
power gives them some claim to truth. If psychoanalytic premises permit
us to make good sense of passages in Ezekiel that have driven earlier
commentators to despair—as I believe they do—this will itself be powerful warrant for their soundness.

Many have helped me with this project. In October 1987, I presented a
very early version of my argument to a faculty seminar in psychoanalytic
theory, organized by the University of North Carolina's Program in the
Humanities and Human Values, under the direction of Warren Nord and
Susan Landstrom. The warm support and plentiful help I received from
the participants encouraged me to continue to develop and formulate my
ideas.

Approximately one year later, members of the Society for the Religion
and Culture of the Ancient Mediterranean—a small group of Southeastern
scholars—read an early draft of this study and provided me with criticism
and suggestions. I have profited also from responses to presentations given
before the North Carolina Psychoanalytic Society (January 1991) and the
Psychology and Biblical Studies Consultation of the Society of Biblical
Literature (November 1991). I am particularly grateful to Wayne G. Rol-
lins for organizing the latter session and to Adela Yarbro Collins and
Walter Wink for their formal responses to my presentation.

Adela Collins, Allen Dyer, Daniel Merkur, Mortimer Ostow, and Robert Segal graciously read early drafts of the book and made detailed and
very useful comments. Robert Daniels, of the UNC Anthropology Department, read a draft of my section on the menstrual taboo and helped me

sharpen my understanding of the problems bound up with it. My colleagues in the Department of Religious Studies, Jack M. Sasson and James H. Sanford, offered suggestions and directed me to sources of which I had been unaware, as did John Boswell, M.D., of the Psychiatry Department.

Michael Fishbane, Victor R. Gold, and Judith Van Herik read the completed work and proposed improvements. Judith Van Herik, in particular, improved my title out of all recognition. It is to her I owe the title the book currently bears.

UNC's University Research Council provided me with funds to employ research assistants, and I was singularly fortunate in those I found to assist me. Early in the development of the project, June Williams Hurt did preliminary research scrupulously and well. Dexter Hall and Pamela E. Kinlaw carefully read drafts of the book and made extremely perceptive and important comments. On more than one occasion, as the reader will see from the index, I have profited from their insights into the text; I have at times found it appropriate to quote their comments verbatim. They did all of the research tasks I assigned them with outstanding creativity and skill, and their participation has greatly enriched the book.

As the manuscript approached its final stage, I was helped in the preparation of the reference list by my students Emily Downing Ball, David S. Langdon, Diana Merelman, and N. Michelle Stem. Bonita Samuels, of the UNC Institute for Research in Social Science, kindly lent her time and her computer to the task of printing out a final draft. Michael J. Cowan, Blair P. Gormley, Tracie Y. Lee, and Kristian Rhein helped me prepare the index; Julie Daniel typed it for me.

I am grateful to the editors at Penn State Press: Philip Winsor, always ready with an encouraging word and a well-considered suggestion; Cherene Holland, who guided the book from manuscript to press; and Andrew B. Lewis, who brought enormous care, sensitivity, and intelligence to the task of copyediting the manuscript.

The UNC Department of Religious Studies provided me with every possible support—not least, a friendly collegial context in which to think and work. Frederick O. Behrends (UNC Department of History) has been a constant friend and intellectual companion; so, through the wonders of BITNET, has Marc Bregman (Hebrew Union College—Jewish Institute of Religion, Jerusalem).

Rose Shalom, M.D., was always ready to guide me through the unfamiliar world of medical literature, to help me locate pertinent sources and interpret them once I had found them. A skilled and caring psychiatrist, she has heard the ideas presented in this book since I first began to formulate them, and her responses have often influenced the shapes they were to take. She has been my friend; she has been my companion; she has been my love; she has been my wife. I am more thankful to her than I can possibly say.

Note on Citations

For the purpose of directing the reader toward secondary sources (and, on occasion, editions of primary texts), I have used the system of citation recommended in Mary-Claire Van Leunen's *Handbook for Scholars* (New York: Alfred A. Knopf, 1978).

At the end of the book, the reader will find a reference list, which replaces, and to a great extent corresponds to, the bibliography that would normally be found in a book of this sort. The items in the list—books, articles, sometimes individual pages or clusters of pages—are numbered sequentially. Bracketed numbers within the text direct the reader to the appropriate items in the reference list. Thus, in the first pages of the book, "[410]" indicates that full bibliographic information on the opening epigraph is to be found at item 410 of the reference list, "[28]" points to item 28, and so forth.

Quotations given in English from sources cited in the reference list under foreign-language titles are my own translations. Unless otherwise indicated, all translations of Biblical passages are my own.

Introduction

> Now, before we can do any kind of justice to our
> forefathers, —a matter, be it remembered, of no
> moment to them, for they have gone to their
> reward, but . . . of considerable importance to
> us . . .
>
> —George Lyman Kittredge,
> *Witchcraft in Old and New*
> *England* [410]

The Book of Ezekiel has long been recognized as one of the stranger documents in the canon.

It is the work, supposedly, of one Ezekiel son of Buzi, a priest, carried away captive from Jerusalem to Babylonia in the first of two deportations (597 B.C.). Its central concern is the city and Temple Ezekiel left behind. The first half of the book pounds across the idea that the city, drenched in blood and sin, is doomed, for its Temple has been corrupted beyond hope of reform. True to the prediction, both city and Temple are destroyed. In the book's second half, the seer promises their restoration and turns his fury on such foreign powers as Tyre and Egypt.

All this is cast in prophetic rhetoric, often gruesome and occasionally obscene, yet powerfully effective throughout. It is backed up by bizarre visions and pantomimes. Ezekiel must perform strange operations on his own body. He must lie paralyzed. He is told, until he protests, to bake his bread with human excrement. His tongue is bound, and his dumbness only leaves him when the Temple is at last destroyed. Yet, this "dumbness" notwithstanding, he is extraordinarily fluent. His fellow exiles, God tells him, respond to him as to "a love-song, finely sung to a pretty tune. They hear your words, but do not do them. Yet when it comes—and it is coming—they will know that a prophet has been among them" (33:32–33).

A love-song? Most moderns will find little love in these dreadful images of unforgivable sin and relentless catastrophe. The thought of sexuality evokes in its author a vindictive loathing, which turns traditional erotic themes into a puritan pornography of revenge. Beyond question, the book is powerful. Yet we may be inclined to see its power as that of dementia and to apply to Ezekiel the words of another prophet. "The man of the spirit is mad" (Hosea 9:7).

"Mad" is a vague diagnosis. In 1946, Edwin C. Broome tried to refine it. He accepted the book's claim that it was the work of the prophet Ezekiel— priest of Jerusalem, later of Babylonia—and supposed that the oddities of the book were the oddities of the historical Ezekiel. He approached these peculiarities from a psychoanalytic perspective and unified them with a clinical diagnosis. They were, he argued, symptoms of paranoid schizo-phrenia [28].

Scholarly response to Broome's paper was less than enthusiastic. The biblicist Carl Gordon Howie and the psychiatrist Ned H. Cassem pre-pared full-dress refutations of it [49,143]. Most others have either ignored it entirely or taken for granted that Howie or Cassem or both had demol-ished it. Bernhard Lang, writing in 1981, summed up the consensus: "Broome's work requires no further refutation. It is to be noted more as a curiosity than as a serious contribution to the understanding of the prophet" [184].

This consensus is mistaken. Broome's article indeed contains much that can be refuted and must be discarded. His bumptious diagnosis, even if correct, offers little help in understanding Ezekiel or his book. But he also offers important and provocative insights that open the door to fruitful inquiries into what lies behind the text. To dismiss Broome's paper as a "curiosity" is to slam this door, needlessly, in the face of scholarship.

I propose to reopen Broome's door and to pass as far as I safely can into what lies beyond. The centerpiece of my argument will be a reexamina-tion of one of Broome's suggestions: that the act of digging through a wall, described in Ezekiel 8:7–12, is a symbolic representation of sexual inter-course. I believe that this interpretation is correct and that it can and should be developed considerably further than Broome does. I elaborate this point in Chapter 3.

Two prior chapters are necessary. In Chapter 1, I summarize Broome's argument and examine the responses to it by Howie, Cassem, Stephen Garfinkel, Ellen F. Davis [49,60,92,94,143], and (briefly) others. The purpose of this chapter is in part polemical. I undertake to defend Broome, which will involve attacking his attackers. But the controversy over Broome's article will also serve as an introduction to broader methodological issues. Not everyone will grant that psychoanalytic methods can legitimately be applied to biblical texts. Skepticism on this point, and Broome's failure to anticipate and to respond to it, accounts for much of the ridicule and neglect Broome has received. If I expect a psychoanalytic approach to the Bible to be taken seriously, I cannot evade the methodological questions it raises.

In Chapter 2, I examine the immediate context of Ezekiel 8:7–12: the Temple vision of chapters 8–11. In the course of a trance journey to Jerusalem, the prophet witnesses a series of "abominations" being performed in the Temple, and he predicts their consequences. Scholars have long recognized that this text is riddled with problems from beginning to end and have offered a wide variety of solutions. I contend that the most effective solution is to acknowledge the authenticity of Ezekiel 8—but as a description of Ezekiel's inner landscape rather than of anything that actually went on in the Temple. This lays the ground for the argument in Chapter 3, that this landscape can be most effectively mapped in psychoanalytic terms.

Here again, I have a twofold aim. I intend to anticipate and to head off one of the most widespread objections to psychoanalytic interpretation; namely, that it offers abstruse and farfetched explanations for phenomena that can be accounted for in more straightforward ways. By showing that "straightforward ways" lead us into confusion, I hope to predispose the reader to look favorably upon Broome's way—and mine—of viewing 8:7–12.

At the same time, I intend Chapter 2 as more than a prolegomenon to Chapter 3. My purpose is not to explore Ezekiel's psychic reality in isolation, but to show how it interacted with the physical and social realities that surrounded him. My theory of what lies behind 8:7–12 is a part of a larger theory of the reality underlying the entire vision of chapters 8–11. I intend my analyses of the detail and of the ensemble to confirm and enrich one another; not just to clarify one specific detail of Ezekiel's vision, but to explain the behavior that is reflected in the whole.

If the literary context of 8:7–12 is chapters 8–11, its psychic context extends to other parts of the book. In Chapter 4, I examine this context. Hidden behind the imagery of 8:7–12, I suggest, is the same pattern—frantic loathing of female sexuality—that is expressed openly in chapters 16 and 23 and more covertly in Ezekiel's behavior at the death of his wife (24:15–24). Examination of these latter passages will confirm my interpretation of 8:7–12, just as 8:7–12 helps explain the horrid intensity of chapters 16 and 23.

This material will permit us to pursue our investigation in a fresh direction. I believe I can detect something else, something yet more primary and important, beneath Ezekiel's relatively straightforward hatred of the female—a deep and erotically charged ambivalence toward a dominating male figure. Ezekiel, I argue, tended to displace the positive elements of his ambivalence onto his God, its negative elements onto other real or imaginary males. Yet he could not carry out this split with absolute consistency. Realization of this fact will allow us to explain some of the strangest and theologically most troubling elements of the Book of Ezekiel.

My argument to this point will suggest a fresh solution to the old problem of Ezekiel's dumbness, which will explain why his dumbness should have ceased with the destruction of the Temple. I will elaborate this solution in my final chapter.

My approach to Ezekiel may well seem wildly radical and superconservative at once. On the one hand, my approach to the biblical materials is entirely nontheistic. I take for granted, for example, that the wrath of Ezekiel's God is in fact Ezekiel's own unconscious rage. On the other, I advocate a respect for the Masoretic Text, a reluctance to correct or dissect the book, and a willingness to take its statements about itself at face value, that might please the most rigid fundamentalist.

Further, I argue that it is possible to recover Ezekiel the man from behind Ezekiel the book and, indeed, to know that man rather intimately. Not everyone will concede that such a feat is possible with a person who has been dead for more than 2500 years. This is a legitimate and indeed essential skepticism, and I fully accept the responsibility of satisfying those who hold it. I ask only that the issue not be decided in advance, on the basis of abstract considerations of what can and cannot be done with an ancient text, but in the light of my specific arguments.

My reconstruction of Ezekiel's inner and outer worlds entails proposals for the solution of a wide range of long-recognized problems, great and small. If enough of these proposals fall flat, they will properly discredit the framework in which they are propounded. But the more that are judged successful, the harder it will be to accept them and yet deny the framework. In the nature of things, there is no way that any portrait of the man Ezekiel can be tested against its original. But if such a portrait coheres with itself and gives sense to the text of the Book of Ezekiel that it did not have before, I believe it has a claim to be accepted as a truthful depiction of the man as he really was.

This leads me to the last, and perhaps the most painful, point I must make in this introduction. Ezekiel "as he really was"—as I imagine him—is very far from being a lovable person. He emerges in these pages as an extreme exemplar of a morbidity that afflicts many and perhaps all human societies. This sickness, it may be argued, has effected the subjection and humiliation of the female half of our species. It has surely poisoned the pleasures and comforts of sexuality for women and men alike. Ezekiel himself, through the influence of his book, perhaps did as much as anyone to infect Western culture. It is hard to contemplate this pathology without revulsion, harder still to imagine so hideous a system of delusion dominating one of the great figures of the Bible. It is hardest of all to accept this portrait of Ezekiel and still think of him as a moral or religious authority.

Yet if it is true that the sickness discussed here has tainted the relations of men and women the world over, it is also true that we are at last learning to crave release from it. Perhaps, in this struggle, Ezekiel may serve as our guide. He was vulnerable as we are; and surely he suffered his disease to a degree beyond that of most humans who have ever lived. He was gifted as we are not; and his extraordinary literary genius allowed him to express his pain in images of ghastly luminosity, which, once absorbed, are all but impossible to forget. Psychoanalytic consideration of his aberrations cannot and should not teach us to like or admire them. But it may show us how deeply and dreadfully human they are. In contemplating Ezekiel's illness, we may perhaps come to contemplate how, in better circumstances, he might have found healing. This may in turn lead us to contemplate how we ourselves may be healed. If so, psychoanalytic study of Ezekiel's personality, unpleasant as it perhaps may be, will not be in vain.

1
Broome and His Critics

A heretic said to Rabbi Abbahu: Your God is a
jokester. For he says to Ezekiel, *Lie on your left
side;* and then again, *Lie on your right side* [Ezekiel
4:4–8].

—Babylonian Talmud, Sanhedrin 39a

If Broome's paper received a chilly reception from Bible scholars, psychoanalytic writers have not been a great deal friendlier. Few even mention his
ideas; and they normally take care to distance themselves from them.

Thus, the distinguished psychoanalyst Jacob Arlow mentions the view
(supposedly held "by many authors") that Ezekiel was psychotic, only to
dismiss it. "Such long range diagnosis is hazardous and not particularly
illuminating." He himself, as we shall see, agrees exactly with Broome's
interpretations of two passages in Ezekiel. Yet he does not seem to have
been aware that Broome had earlier proposed them [310]. Yorick Spiegel's
anthology of articles on psychoanalytic interpretation of the Bible (published in 1972) does not include Broome's piece, although it does appear in
the bibliography [396].[1] Daniel Merkur gives Broome credit for his contribution, but criticizes his diagnosis and makes clear that he regards Arlow's
discussion as superior [370].

By and large, Bible scholars have blamed Broome for doing too much
with the data and doing it badly, whereas psychoanalytic writers appear to
have blamed him for not having done enough. There is some justice in

1. It is perhaps also worth noting that Broome's article is not listed in the *Chicago
Psychoanalytic Literature Index.*

both complaints. We will therefore need to survey Broome and his critics with the aim of learning from all sides. We must begin by setting Broome against his background. For we will not understand the importance of his work and the objections to it unless we grasp what it was that Broome innovated, and what it was he left undone.

1. Klostermann

Broome was not the first to notice that Ezekiel was a rather peculiar man. Nor was he the first to try to explain Ezekiel's peculiarities with a medical or quasi-medical diagnosis. That idea can be traced back at least to a paper published in 1877 by August Klostermann. Some of the stranger features of the book, Klostermann proposed, could be best explained as symptoms of an illness. Ezekiel himself understood that illness as having made his body into a living embodiment of prophecy [173].

The "illness" that Klostermann identified, with the aid of one Dr. Bartels, was something called "Katalepsie oder Starrsucht" [176]. He formed his picture of this disease from three medical reports from the years 1850 to 1875 that described a nervous illness whose most prominent symptoms were paralysis and loss of speech. The symptoms set in mysteriously and, after some hours or weeks or months, just as mysteriously went away. They were, Klostermann thought, very suggestive of the puzzling "dumbness" reported of Ezekiel, which also seemed to come and go without clear reason (3:24–27, 24:25–27, 33:21–22). Further, like the "cataleptic" patients Klostermann had read about, Ezekiel suffered from a feeling of being "bound"—now by Yahweh (4:8), now by an unspecified "they" (3:25). Thus immobilized, he had to lie on one side for 390 days, on the other for 40 (4:1–8).

The parallels did not end here. A fifteen-year-old Austrian girl ("Judenmädchen," Klostermann calls her) also had among her symptoms occasional shaking and howling and a limited ability to eat [393]. Compare this with Ezekiel 4:10–11, 6:11, 12:17, and 21:6–7 and 14 (= 21:11–12 and 19 in the Masoretic Hebrew Text). A sixty-year-old British laborer suddenly went into a trance, "his arms outstretched, his legs fixed, the whole body rigid and immoveable."[2] So Ezekiel, "bound," must set his face against a

---

2.   Klostermann quotes the English original [176].

representation of Jerusalem he has inscribed on a tile and prophesy against it, his arm bared and presumably outstretched (4:7). The Englishman's paralysis, like Ezekiel's (assuming some direct link between 24:15–24 and 24:25–27), set in shortly after his wife's sudden death. A few days before his paralysis, he experienced visual and auditory hallucinations: "[H]e saw various colours and heard various sounds, sometimes the firing of guns." Similarly, the paralysis reported in Ezekiel 3:25–27 was preceded by his fantastic vision of the divine chariot (the *merkabah*, as the rabbis were later to call it), with its rainbow-like colors and its auditory components (1:1– 3:15) [125]. It seemed reasonable, then, to suppose that Ezekiel suffered from catalepsy, the only disadvantage being that no one knew what catalepsy was.

Klostermann did not intend his diagnosis to disparage Ezekiel or to cast doubt on his divine inspiration. Quite the contrary, Klostermann set himself to rescue "poor Ezekiel"[3] from the derogation of Bernhard Duhm and Julius Wellhausen. These scholars, as Klostermann perceived them, insisted on treating Ezekiel as a theological way station along prophetic religion's downward slide into Judaism, not as a God-inspired human being. If one is to read God in history, says Klostermann, one must know the men of God. This demands that we utilize the possibilities the Book of Ezekiel offers for comprehending Ezekiel as a human individual [174]. Klostermann's diagnosis of Ezekiel's illness is to be taken as a part of this theological project.

But there is an objection to this proceeding, which did occur to Klostermann. Surely one might say that to the extent that Ezekiel's behavior is made intelligible as symptomatic of a natural illness, its divinely inspired character is diminished. Klostermann replies to this that catalepsy is not a natural disease. "The medical authorities themselves acknowledge that they cannot account for [its symptoms] by factors that operate in the material constitution, that are accessible to their research." One such authority, a Professor Brücke, had repeatedly examined the cataleptic Austrian girl and had proposed that it was some dream-image, an "obscure conception [*dunkle Vorstellung*]," that had occasioned the rigid positions her body assumed [394].[4] If (Klostermann argues) a physician can thus resort

---

3. "Der arme Ezechiel," he calls him at the very beginning of the article.

4. Neither Klostermann nor Joseph Skoda (Klostermann's source for the girl's case [393]) gives a first name for this "Prof. Brücke." I assume the reference is to Ernst Brücke (1819– 92), who was later, as head of the Vienna Physiological Institute, to exercise a formative influence on the young Sigmund Freud. (Freud named one of his sons after Brücke and, near

to a "psychic element" to explain a modern occurrence of the disease, why should we refuse to attribute the obvious coherence of Ezekiel's symptoms to "an idea which God had planted in his soul"? Surely "another active intelligence" was operating within Ezekiel, independent of Ezekiel's own free activity or even of his understanding. For Klostermann, this "other intelligence" could be none other than God [177].

It would be outside the scope of this book to trace the scholarly world's reactions to Klostermann. Bernhard Lang has, in any case, surveyed much of the response, in a chapter appropriately entitled "Der kranke Prophet" [184]. Many scholars, Lang points out, are unwilling to agree that Ezekiel was sick at all. Most of those who do agree do not seem to have gone significantly beyond Klostermann in explaining what the illness was. Lang admits that in looking for the causes of the illness he has nothing to say that is materially different from what Klostermann had said a hundred years earlier: Ezekiel experienced a "Kulturschock" in exile, he was unsuited to the marshy climate of Babylonia, he was frustrated at not being able to exercise his priestly office, he was isolated among his fellow exiles [184].

I have the impression that most of those who accept Klostermann's claim that Ezekiel suffered from some illness are unwilling also to accept Klostermann's corollary: that the illness was an expression of an intelligence outside of and unknown to Ezekiel's consciousness. They seem more inclined to treat it as if it were akin to diabetes: a disabling malady that just happened to him, about whose meaning it is pointless to ask. Ezekiel's prophetic activity is an object of inquiry, precisely to the extent that the pathological features can be excluded from it [15,71].

In the decades that followed the appearance of Klostermann's article, Freud and his followers found what could be seen as validation for Klostermann's premise that an illness can indeed be a manifestation of an intelligence that seems alien to the individual's consciousness. How Klostermann responded to their work, or whether he had even heard of it—he died in 1913, when Freud had a certain international reputation but had not yet become a household word—I do not know. To my knowledge,

---

the end of his life, remembered him as "the greatest authority that ever acted upon me" [327,346,347].) The young Brücke's opinion on this case, as reported by Skoda (1852), may thus be of some interest for the prehistory of psychoanalysis. The phrase "dunkle Vorstellung," which Klostermann repeats from Skoda (and he from Brücke?), is evidently a technical term of mid-nineteenth-century medicine. Neither I nor my research assistant, Pamela E. Kinlaw, have been able to trace its precise meaning.

none of the other students of Ezekiel's peculiarities found a way to apply psychoanalysis to them; until, in 1946, Broome published "Ezekiel's Abnormal Personality."

2. Broome

Broome's basic argument was that certain puzzling features of the Book of Ezekiel could be correlated and rendered intelligible, if only they were taken at face value as symptoms of a recognizable mental illness. To describe this illness, Klostermann's "catalepsy" was no longer adequate.[5] Newer terms must be introduced: "catatonia," "paranoia," "schizophrenia," "psychosis" [28].

No one feature of the Book of Ezekiel, Broome was careful to point out, can by itself justify any of these drastic diagnoses. "Evidence for any mental abnormality is cumulative, and this is true of Ezekiel" (page 278). One must "rely upon the mass of this evidence, as well as its congruent and consistent character" (page 282). Even a piece of evidence that by itself "is insignificant, and can be eliminated by textual criticism," takes on its true importance in conjunction with other data that point in the same direction (page 283). This claim—that Broome's chain is stronger than its weakest and perhaps even its strongest link—is important, because much of the criticism directed at Broome implicitly denies or disregards it.

What, then, is this evidence? Broome opens his case with the old problem, which occupied Klostermann, of Ezekiel's immobility (3:24–4:8). "That this mutism, immobility, and feeling that bands were placed upon him (either by Jahweh or by the people) is a characteristic a [sic] psychotic experience is hardly questionable." Either the Jews tied Ezekiel up or they did not. If they did not, he was obviously hallucinating; if they did, it was because he was out of his mind and dangerous. "In either event he was psychotic" (page 280).

We already note here the style of Broome's argumentation, as well as his tendency to shoot himself in the foot. For once he has acknowledged the possibility that Ezekiel's "binding" was in fact executed by his fellow exiles (as 3:25 might suggest), he can hardly treat it as a symptom of

---

5. Broome nevertheless acknowledged Klostermann as "the pioneer," whose "article is still worth reading" (page 278).

psychosis. There are, after all, other reasons why a prophet with an unpopular message might be physically abused. But Broome's concession is unnecessary to begin with. It is very difficult to read 4:1–8 and believe that immobility is imposed on Ezekiel by some external force. When, without any obvious compulsion, a man is reported to have lain on his left side for 390 days (or even, with the Septuagint, 190), and on his right side for 40, it is hardly farfetched to suppose that psychic disturbance may have been involved.

Just as pointless, and considerably more irritating, is Broome's re-arrangement of the text into the sequence 3:15, 3:24, 4:4–5, 4:8, 3:26. This innovation, for which Broome supplied no evidence, had no effect but to expose him to ridicule [143]. It is so gratuitous, so completely unnecessary to his argument, that I half suspect he advanced it in the belief that he could not establish his bona fides as a Bible scholar without at least one arbitrary textual operation.

Broome is back on firmer ground when he points out that the acts Ezekiel is supposed to have performed while "bound" confirm that this state was pathological. They were all, he thinks, hallucinatory (page 281). One of these acts is "the rather revolting procedure in regard to the cakes, utilizing human dung for fuel—an act reminiscent of the soiling properties of the anal-sadistic state of regression" (page 281, referring to 4:9–15). Another is Ezekiel's shaving his own head and beard with a sharp sword, which is "of course symbolic of the castration wish and fancy, while the beard and hair of the head suggestive [sic] of genital hair growth" (page 289, referring to 5:1–4).

The process of "displacement upward," from the genital hair to the head and beard, is a commonplace of Freudian psychology. Non-Freudians may find themselves wondering irritably what is so "of course" about it. Broome's critics, as we shall see, did not overlook this opportunity to ridicule his self-assurance on this point [93,143]. I postpone my defense of Broome and here note only that the Mishnah (Sanhedrin 8:1) describes the displacement process quite explicitly. "From what age might [a boy] be classified as *a stubborn and rebellious son* [and thus subject to the legislation of Deuteronomy 21:18–21]? From the time when he sprouts two hairs, until he has grown a full beard." This "full beard," the Mishnah goes on to explain, is in fact "the lower [so-called beard] and not the upper; but the sages spoke in pure language." This passage is of course from a time much later than Ezekiel's. But it will encourage us to be open to the possibility that, when Ezekiel imagines himself ordered to take a "sharp sword" to his "beard" (Ezekiel 5:1), he may have unconsciously intended the "beard" between his legs.[6]

As for "the rather revolting procedure in regard to the cakes," Broome actually understates his point; 4:12 plainly implies that Ezekiel is to use human excrement as an ingredient in his cakes. The preposition used here (be-, "with") is to be contrasted with that in verse 15 ('al, "upon"). The change is significant: God responds to Ezekiel's horrified plea that he had never before eaten filth (verse 14), not only by substituting animal excrement for human (verse 15, explicitly), but by allowing him to use it in its normal function as fuel rather than as a part of his food.[7]

The next item on Broome's agenda is the merkabah vision (pages 282–83). In the introduction to the vision (1:1–3), Broome finds evidence of Ezekiel's grandiosity. Following a line of interpretation that goes back to Origen—and includes Klostermann—Broome explains the "thirtieth year" of 1:1 as a statement of Ezekiel's age. It is characteristic of Ezekiel, Broome thinks, that no chronology matters to him but his own. In the same way, Ezekiel insists that "the word of the Lord came expressly to me, Ezekiel" (1:3). Broome finds the same kind of self-importance expressed in the unpublished autobiography of an anonymous paranoid schizophrenic, who plays much the same role for Broome that the cataleptic British laborer and the Austrian "Judenmädchen" do for Klostermann. Unfortunately, the evidence in 1:1–3 for Ezekiel's self-importance is so dubious—Broome's intepretation of the "thirtieth year" is very uncertain, whereas much of the "grandiosity" of 1:3 rests on an arbitrary textual emendation[8]—that Broome himself is inclined to dismiss it as insignificant. Once again, he appears to have shot himself in the foot.

The merkabah itself reminds Broome of the "influencing machines" found in the fantasies or hallucinations of modern paranoid schizophrenics. "Like Ezekiel's throne chariot, these 'influencing machines' defy

6. The ša'ar haraglayim (literally, "hair of the feet") of Isaiah 7:20, which seems to have influenced Ezekiel here [104], is usually taken to be the pubic hair [12,53,80,134, 156,158].

7. Jacob Arlow interprets the passage in a way very similar to Broome's, understanding it to mean that Ezekiel is trying to introject God by eating excrement. Arlow gives Ernst Kris credit for the suggestion; he is clearly unaware that Broome had made a similar one a few years earlier [310].

8. From "to Ezekiel" ('el yeḥezqel) to "to me, Ezekiel" ('elay yeḥezqel). On the other hand, Broome takes seriously the Masoretic Text's difficult (indeed, unparalleled) hayoh hayah, which he translates, "came expressly." Perhaps he has a point when he sees it as expressing Ezekiel's "feeling of self-importance, the conviction that it was all meant for him personally" (page 283).

description and are difficult for the subject to diagram" (pages 285–86). They presumably express the paranoid's sense of being dominated and persecuted by unseen forces.

Broome does not try to explain all of Ezekiel's details. But, he suggests, the prominence of fire reflects "the nameless terror of the paranoid" (page 283). The ferocity of the faces of the "living creatures" similarly points to anxiety, and perhaps fear of being devoured. Broome stresses that, as *ḥayyot*, the "creatures" are at least grammatically feminine,[9] and, apart from their wings, appear to be nude. (Broome does not cite evidence for this, but it is perhaps a legitimate inference from 1:11.) This perhaps reflects Ezekiel's own desire to exhibit himself, running to and fro (1:14)— which, once again, suggests anxiety.

Eyes are particularly prominent in the vision. At its beginning and its end we find the "eye of *ḥashmal*" (1:4, 27; cf. 8:2), the meaning of which is unclear but which points to "a glowing substance of some sort" (page 283).[10] In between are the eyes of the wheels (1:18). "All eyes are staring at Ezekiel, haunting him, pursuing him, accusing him" (page 284). This last sentence owes a great deal to Broome's imagination. Yet we cannot deny it a certain plausibility. Why should someone have a vision of eyes, if these eyes have no role with regard to him? Staring is a natural role to suppose.

Finally, Broome calls attention to the hallucinations of water (1:24) and then light (1:27–28), which suggest that Ezekiel is reliving the birth trauma. Like an infant, he then collapses, helpless (1:28).

We must acknowledge that Broome's analysis of the *merkabah* is highly speculative, and that he has no way to verify any of his suggestions. He can do no more than point to what he takes to be their inherent plausibility. But we must remember, too, that he is not wantonly muddling a perfectly clear text with psychoanalytic jargon. He is using an unconven-

---

9.   In a footnote, Broome appears to back away from this observation, pointing out that the *ḥayyot* become masculine cherubim in Ezekiel 10. But, he thinks, this does not affect his suggestion that the nudity of the *ḥayyot* reflects Ezekiel's own "paranoid exhibitionism" (page 284).

10.   Carl Gordon Howie insists, against Broome, that there is not "one whit of reason for taking חשמל [*ḥashmal*] to be another larger eye" [143]. He overstates considerably. In 1:4 and 27, *'en (ha)ḥashmal* is normally translated "color of *ḥashmal*," the meaning "color" for *'ayin* being clearly attested in Proverbs 23:31. This was surely Ezekiel's conscious intent. But there is no reason to deny that the more common meaning of *'ayin* ("eye") may have been present to his unconscious, and that it may have influenced his selection of the word. Certain *Hekhalot* texts, at any rate, understand *'en haḥashmal* as a staring, accusing eye [128]. Their authors have perhaps recovered Ezekiel's original unconscious intent.

tional tool to make sense of what has been long acknowledged one of the Bible's most abstruse and impenetrable visions [125].

Broome offers other "symptoms" to confirm his diagnosis. Characteristically paranoid, Ezekiel hears voices that announce threatening messages (pages 286–87). He is convinced certain specific individuals are persecuting him and is only too glad to name names (page 290, referring to 8:11, 11:1). His delusions of grandeur recur in the power he grants himself to resurrect the dry bones (chapter 37) and in his undertaking to legislate the future of Judaism. ("The meticulous and fanciful detail" of chapters 40–48, says Broome, "is dear to the paranoid.") Like a modern paranoid schizophrenic, he feels unpleasant physical sensations, notably of pricking: 2:6 speaks of a "sensation of stinging in the posterior regions," expressed as "briers" and "thorns" and "scorpions"; 3:8–9 of "a nail-like pain, seeming to drive inward into the brain," which "is not unusual in schizophrenia" (pages 287–88).[11]

Most interesting are the hallucinations in which Broome finds sexual symbolism. The scroll that Ezekiel imagines himself ordered to eat, in 2:9–3:3, is a disguised representation of a penis. "Ezekiel is regressing to what Freud calls the oral stage—but perverted" (page 288).[12] And, in 8:7–11,

> Ezekiel sees first a small hole in the wall, is then told to dig in the wall, does so, and finds a door, presumably as the result of his digging a small tunnel. He enters, and sees the "creeping things," etc., portrayed on the walls of the small chamber. In the midst of all this are seventy elders of Judah, and in the midst of them, one Jaazaniah ben Shaphan; each held a censer smoking in his hand. Even by itself this "dream" is suggestive; in conjunction with what has gone before, it is almost diagnostic. The digging, the little door, and the small room are symbolic of the act of coitus, but the experience is abominable to Ezekiel now that his "feeling that he is a woman" makes it so. (Page 289)

11. The interpretation of *shamir* (RSV "adamant") that underlies this last claim seems very dubious.

12. Arlow makes the same point, at rather greater length—again, apparently unaware that Broome had made it before him. But Arlow carries it considerably further than does Broome. He correlates this "fellatio-impregnation fantasy," of "introjection of Jehovah and the divine phallus," with the fascination with God's loins expressed in 1:27–28. Further, by suggesting that the scroll represents God's feces as well as his penis, Arlow links this vision with the eating of excrement in 4:12–15 [310].

"In conclusion," writes Broome, "we find that Ezekiel exhibits behavioristic abnormalities consistent with paranoid schizophrenia. . . . 1. Periods of catatonia. 2. The 'influencing machine.' 3. A narcissistic-masochistic conflict, with attendant phantasies of castration and unconscious sexual regression. 4. Schizophrenic withdrawal. 5. Delusions of persecution and grandeur" (pages 291–92).

It is surprising to learn, after all this, that Ezekiel's "religious significance is by no means impaired by our diagnosis of a paranoic condition." Broome does not try to explain or justify this claim, other than by appeal to the authority of William James.[13] It accords so poorly with the trend of his argument—which will hardly allow a boundary to be drawn between Ezekiel's psychopathology and his religious perceptions—that I cannot help viewing it as a contrivance to soothe the religious feelings of the readers of the *Journal of Biblical Literature*. As such, it fully deserves Howie's acid summation: "It is, therefore, not impossible to accept Ezekiel as a great religious, social, and political leader even though he was mentally sick" [143].

Lang sums up the difference between Klostermann's and Broome's approaches to Ezekiel by saying that Freud came in between [184]. There is no question that he is right. Yet it is important to understand precisely what significance Broome's "Freudianism" has. It is not merely that Broome has substituted a twentieth-century psychiatric nomenclature ("paranoia," "psychosis," etc.) for Klostermann's old-fashioned "catalepsy." That, by itself, would be trivial. Nor is Broome's frequent use of sexual interpretations, which would no doubt have appalled Klostermann, the key point.

Rather, Broome has tried to incorporate Freud's crucial insight that the symptoms of a psychogenic illness are meaningful, that they are the deliberate creations of an intelligence that is the subject's own, yet paradoxically outside his conscious awareness. They are not afflictions that come from the outside and hem him in, leaving him only the choice of how to maneuver within them and how to interpret them for his life. *His disease is him;* and its symptoms communicate to the attentive listener things about him that he himself would rather not know.[14]

13. The reference is presumably to lecture 1 in *The Varieties of Religious Experience*, to which Judith Van Herik kindly drew my attention.
14. Ironically, the devout Klostermann, who sees Ezekiel's catalepsy as a manifestation of an outside intelligence working through the prophet, is much closer to Broome than are his

At his best, Broome is that attentive listener, unraveling the unconscious concerns symbolically expressed in Ezekiel's manipulations with a sword, his sensation of swallowing a scroll, and—as we shall see in much more detail later on—his hallucination of digging through a wall into a chamber filled with unspeakable creatures.

These concerns, as Broome conceives them, are not very exalted. I have no doubt that this partly explains the icy hostility with which Bible scholars have received Broome's work. The idea of a "sick prophet" is, by itself, tolerable enough. Even "pathological elements" may be acceptable, as long as they are safely impersonal and external to Ezekiel's character. It is by no means un-prophet-like for Ezekiel to have had auditory and visual hallucinations and "peculiar feelings in his throat, as if he had swallowed down a parchment roll with a sweet aftertaste (2:8–3:3)," even if Klostermann must therefore designate him "der Kranke" [175]. It is quite another thing for him to have had unconscious fantasies of swallowing a penis.

And Broome is not always at his best. Even where his exegesis is plausible—which, as we have seen, is not always the case—he too often contents himself with recording rather than interpreting what he perceives as a symptom. Where we might hope for a coherent picture of Ezekiel's psychic life, and the interactions of his conscious and unconscious selves, we get a collection of tics brought together under the heading "paranoid schizophrenic." As a result, Broome's article reads like a series of note cards, indifferently arranged.[15]

It will now be clear why the psychoanalysts have not exactly hailed Broome's paper as a breakthrough. It is not that they perceive anything grotesque or farfetched about his exegeses of individual passages. On the contrary, Arlow is prepared not only to entertain but to extend two of Broome's more daring suggestions (see notes 7 and 12 to this chapter). But Arlow also, as we have seen, rejects Broome's "long-range diagnosis" as "not particularly illuminating" [310]. Daniel Merkur states more explicitly his objection to any diagnosis of Ezekiel as psychotic: "Because psychosis is, by definition, socially dysfunctional, the diagnoses are paradoxical. In order to account for the religious data, a diagnostic category is innovated—socially functional psychosis—whose existence is otherwise undemon-

more rationalistic successors [15,71], who treat Ezekiel's disease as an impersonal pathology. Writing before Freud had formulated his conception of the unconscious, Klostermann had little alternative but to identify the outside intelligence with God. Broome had another option.

15. In summarizing Broome's paper, I have found that his arguments actually do come across more clearly and forcefully if one rearranges their sequence.

strated" [371]. In place of the psychoanalytic understanding of Ezekiel that both Arlow and Merkur attempt, Broome has contented himself with a diagnostic label. Since we have no clinical responsibility toward Ezekiel, this label is not of the slightest use.

I would make the point yet more sharply. With his psychoanalytic interpretations of various passages of Ezekiel, Broome has advanced the Freudian enterprise. To the extent to which these interpretations are valid—and I believe that many, though not all, will stand against the criticism they have received—they may be credited to Broome as an achievement. But, with his diagnosis, he abandons and indeed betrays the enterprise. For its effect must be to distance us from Ezekiel: *we* are normal, *he* was a paranoid schizophrenic.

This is not what Freud intended when he undertook to use psychoanalysis as a tool for understanding great personalities of the past. On the contrary, its purpose, "in narrowing the gulf which separates the perfection of the great from the inadequacy of the objects that are its usual concern," is to demonstrate that all are "subject to the laws which govern both normal and pathological activity with equal cogency."[16] Ezekiel acted as he did, fantasized as he did, hallucinated as he did, not because he was so much different from us "normal" folk, but because he was so much the same.

Broome's failure, from the psychoanalytic viewpoint, is one of omission. He did not sustain Freud's insight that the "normal" individual and the "pathological" are kindred beings. He therefore could find no way to integrate, in accord with this insight, his exegetical perceptions.

But, from the viewpoint of the Bible scholars who have considered Broome's work, his failure is far more absolute. Not only was he unable to make proper use of his discoveries; he had no real discoveries to begin with. The psychoanalytic critique of Broome encourages us to build on his achievement better than he himself could. The biblicist critique urges us to deny his achievement, and therefore to build nothing on it. This criticism will exclude not only Broome, but any psychoanalytic approach to the Book of Ezekiel—including my own. I thus cannot proceed further without having examined its merits.

---

16. So Freud begins his essay, "Leonardo da Vinci and a Memory of His Childhood" [341]. It is difficult to read Freud's analysis of the memoirs of the psychotic Schreber without having a sense of his deep respect for the profoundly disturbed individual he is discussing [345]. Little respect of this sort is visible in Broome's article, despite the unconvincing effort at conciliation with which it concludes.

3. Howie

The first full-dress refutation of Broome appeared in 1950, as part of "Psychological Aspects of Ezekiel and his Prophecy," a chapter in a monograph by Carl Gordon Howie [143].

Howie devotes the bulk of his discussion to a point-by-point refutation of Broome's interpretations of specific passages from Ezekiel. He begins, however, with a methodological consideration: it is futile to try to psychoanalyze someone long dead. For a comparable undertaking nowadays, after all, one needs "a relatively complete case history of family and social background" and "at least six interviews." Further, a diagnosis of insanity must be made according to the standards of Ezekiel's own culture; for Ezekiel's "strange words and ideas may not have been important deviations from 'the norm' established for that time" (page 74).

In this last point, we may perceive a note of apologetic, a reaction to what Howie takes to be an accusation that the prophet Ezekiel was a lunatic. It is perhaps an effective protest against Broome's diagnostic label, which we have already seen to be the most dubious part of Broome's argument. We must admit, further, that how Ezekiel's contemporaries perceived his peculiarities is a matter of some consequence. If they had rejected him as a madman, his isolation would surely have aggravated whatever psychological problems he started out with [392]. Yet even if we grant Howie this point, Broome's position does not thereby collapse. It is possible to imagine that his explanation of the dynamics underlying Ezekiel's visions would be equally valid whether or not one could perceive them as the norm for Ezekiel's society. We shall see, however (in Chapter 4), that it is possible to defend Broome's claim that Ezekiel was abnormal, even by the standards of his own time.

Howie's individual criticisms of Broome are often well taken. He completely demolishes, for example, Broome's use of Ezekiel 1:1-3 to demonstrate the prophet's grandiosity. Successes of this kind, no doubt, led Lang and others to suppose that Howie has shown Broome's position to be entirely baseless. But they are only part of the story.

To begin with, Howie's criticisms are not always fair. He sometimes misrepresents or exaggerates Broome's positions. He inaccurately represents Broome as saying that *ḥashmal* "was probably a great bronze eye," and that "the repetition of the inaugural vision of chapter 1 in chapter 10 is typical of the recurrent phantasies experienced by such people." He rightly dismisses Broome's arbitrary rearrangement of chapters 3 and 4,

but he misleadingly presents this gratuitous tinkering as if it were fundamental to Broome's thesis.[17]

Two unspoken assumptions underlie much of Howie's refutation. First,
Howie ignores Broome's protest that his argument is cumulative and proceeds to isolate each of his points and pick them off one by one. He
thereby disregards the possibility that individual observations that seem
trivial or dubious may nonetheless fit together into a convincing pattern.
Second, he appears willing to accept psychoanalytic explanation only as a
last resort. Should any plausible alternative exist, it must be adopted not
only in preference to the psychoanalytic explanation, but in complete
exclusion of it. He does not consider that a psychoanalytic interpretation
may be useful even in the presence of a reasonable alternative if there are
some features of the phenomenon that the alternative will not readily
clarify or if it, unlike the alternative, allows several distinct phenomena to
be brought together into a coherent picture.

The limiting effect of these assumptions will become clearer if we watch
Howie at work (page 77):

> The rather difficult terms סריבים[18] (briers) and סלונים (thorns) are
> forced into the pattern. They are said to represent the stinging,
> pricking sensation commonly experienced by those in this [para-
> noid] state. One wonders if the man who is able to propose this
> theory has ever heard of figurative expressions used both in ancient
> and in modern times.
>
> Of course, with Freud sex is the basic drive in human life, and
> Broome certainly follows "the party line" completely. Eating of the
> scroll (2:9–3:3) represents the worst sort of sexual perversion, a
> conclusion largely drawn from the shape of the scroll. Obvious and
> important symbolism known to be connected with the scroll is
> overlooked. Worse yet is the symbol of the sword (Ez. 5), which
> betrays the prophet's desire to castrate himself. In ancient times the
> sword represented the destruction of warfare, not of emasculation.

17. Concerning Howie's misrepresentation of Broome's interpretation of *ḥashmal* and the
repetition of the vision of chapter 1 in chapter 10, contrast Howie, *The Date and Composition of
Ezekiel*, pages 72–73, with what Broome actually wrote in "Ezekiel's Abnormal Personality,"
pages 248n. and 290. Concerning Broome's rearrangement of the text of Ezekiel, Howie
writes: "Should scholarship finally succumb to such subjective treatment of textual material,
we might soon have well worked out 'case histories' for many ancient figures" (page 74).

18. Masoretic Text סָרָבִים (*sarabim*). The misspelling, which occurs three times, is
Howie's, not Broome's.

The warped sexual makeup of the prophet is further revealed by the sexual act of digging a hole in the wall and beholding abominations of an unbelievable kind (8:7–13). Why could not the digging of such a hole represent no more than the vision of a common process which was actually carried out in chapter 12? We are rather disappointed that a Freudian explanation of the removal (cf. Ez. 12) has not been given us, for that would have been most interesting.

To which one may reply, in Broome's defense: It is hardly likely (to answer Howie's sarcastic query) that Broome had never heard of figurative expressions. But it is one thing to invoke this term, and another to explain why Ezekiel chose certain particular expressions—being pricked by thorns, sitting on scorpions—to convey the point that his people would oppose him. Surely it is plausible that these images, and not others, came to his mind because they accorded with certain idiosyncratic perceptions of his.

To see the scroll of 2:9–3:3 as representing a penis does not require us to disregard its other symbolic meanings. We need not, for example, question the conventional view that Ezekiel has put into plastic form Jeremiah's perception that God's "words were found, and I ate them, and your words became joy and gladness to me" (15:16) [298]. But neither Jeremiah nor any other prophet imagined himself actually presented with a scroll that he had to take into his mouth. We must explain why Ezekiel, and Ezekiel alone, translated Jeremiah's words into a hallucination of this physical act. Why not suppose that a sexual suggestion implicit in the shape of the scroll may have had some influence?

Obviously Ezekiel uses the sword to represent the destruction of warfare (5:12). But this does not explain why he turns his own sword[19] on himself, in an action that strongly suggests self-mutilation. The point he goes on to make in 5:1–12 does not, after all, require him to shave himself. He does not need his own hairs to chop, burn, and so forth; other objects, such as the grains mentioned in 4:9, would have done just as well. This suggests that the act of shaving had some meaning for Ezekiel that is not explicated in the text. And, if we try to explain this meaning by invoking

19. Or, perhaps, a razor that he imagines to be a sword for the purpose of his pantomime. The Hebrew text of 5:1, unlike most English translations, will allow the possibility that *ḥereb ḥaddah* and *ta'ar haggallabim* are in apposition, and that Ezekiel actually "took" a barber's razor. So Greenberg translates: "You, man, take a sharp blade, a barber's razor take in hand . . ." [104].

the influence of Isaiah 7:20 (see note 6 to this chapter), we are back to the
question of why Ezekiel should have felt impelled to turn his body into an
objectification of Isaiah's image.

Let us grant, for the sake of argument, Howie's rather curious assertion
that digging holes in walls was a "common process" in Ezekiel's time. (It is
hard to imagine who, aside perhaps from a burglar, would have had use for
such an operation.)[20] What need was there to apply this "process" to a
visionary wall? A man who can fly hundreds of miles to Jerusalem should
have no difficulty walking through a wall if he wants to. If Ezekiel imagines himself digging through the wall, it must be because the act of digging
itself has some significance for him. Further, as we will see, there is
something very strange about the digging described in 8:7–8, which supports Broome's contention that this significance was sexual.

Howie's comments on the *merkabah* vision are revealing. It is "very
improbable," he thinks, that it is an "influencing machine." Howie's alternative? "This vision is extremely hard to understand, and we must admit
that the exact nature of the *merkabah* is beyond explanation. So cryptic is
the whole passage that one does well to avoid drawing definite conclusions. It is probable that the whole vision would be explicable if we knew
more about the circumstances under which Ezekiel experienced it" (page
76). So: psychoanalytic explanations must yield not only to alternatives
that have actually been formulated but to those that *might* be formulated if
only we had more information. Laboring under such a handicap, it is no
wonder they do not make a better showing.

4. Cassem

The second refutation of Broome was published in 1973, as an article devoted entirely to that purpose [49]. It is of particular interest, for its author,
Ned H. Cassem, has had a long and distinguished career as a psychiatrist.[21]

---

20.   Exodus 22:1 uses the root *ḥtr* (Ezekiel's verb for digging) to describe burglary. So,
perhaps, do Jeremiah 2:34 and Job 24:16. Yet, as we shall see in Chapter 3, the two latter
passages can be plausibly understood to use "digging" as a metaphor for sexual activity, and
thus to confirm Broome's interpretation of Ezekiel 8:8. In the Excursus to this book, I take up
Howie's challenge and tentatively offer a Freudian explanation of Ezekiel 12.

21.   He wrote his critique of Broome, however, at a very early stage of that career, when
he had barely completed his residency [316]. It would be interesting to know if he still stands
by all the views he expressed in 1973.

Cassem does not seem to have been aware of Howie's critique, published twenty-three years earlier. He does not refer to it and marvels that no one had previously tried to respond to Broome's contentions. "Perhaps no one has known quite what to say" (page 60).

His strategy is different from Howie's. Although he summarizes Broome's arguments (page 63), he does not attempt a point-by-point refutation. "We are told, incidentally, that all these symbols are so manifest in their meanings that they 'speak for themselves' "—plainly implying that he (Cassem) does not find them anywhere near so obvious. This is of course no disproof. Still, given Cassem's psychiatric training, his failure to see Broome's conjectures as inherently plausible does carry some weight.[22]

Instead, Cassem concentrates his attack on Broome's methodology. He raises four objections. First, Broome's exegesis of Ezekiel is hyperliteral; it does not grapple with the question of what Ezekiel's words meant in their ancient Near Eastern context, not to mention the problem of how the Book of Ezekiel came into being and the extent to which it reflects Ezekiel's own words. Second, Broome applies his principles inconsistently. If he is going to psychoanalyze Ezekiel, why doesn't he do the same for other Old Testament prophets who had visions, not to mention Paul (Acts 9), Stephen (Acts 7:55), and the author of Revelation? And why does he say nothing of the sexual imagery of Ezekiel 16? Third, Broome ought to have clearly identified the presuppositions that underlie his argument on such vital questions as "whether a transcendent being exists, whether he reveals himself to men, whether he has revealed himself in some very special way to some particular men (e.g. authors in the canon or 'mystics'), and so on" (page 67). Fourth, since Broome has not tackled the question of how the Book of Ezekiel relates to the man Ezekiel, or what conventions the man Ezekiel might have used to express himself,[23] he has no basis for undertaking a psychoanalytic study.

The first and fourth of these points, which seem to me barely distinguishable, are a fuller and more effective statement of Howie's methodological objection. It is a legitimate objection, it applies to my own efforts as well as to Broome's, and I will be obliged to take it up.

Cassem's second point, by contrast, seems almost frivolous. Even if the

22. Yet Jacob Arlow—himself hardly wanting in psychiatric expertise—independently reached two of Broome's interpretations.

23. "No psychiatrist has, for example, accused Martin Luther King of having had hallucinations because of his famous speech 'I Have a Dream' " (page 68). This is, as we will see, not the only place where Cassem assumes that Ezekiel stands "accused" of something or other.

other sources he cites offered the same scope for psychoanalytic interpretation as does Ezekiel—which I do not believe they do[24]—Broome can
hardly be blamed for not having treated each and every one of them in one
article. One has to start somewhere; why should Broome not have started
with Ezekiel?

The complaint that Broome did not take Ezekiel 16 into account is
particularly strange. Cassem is right on this point; but what this means is
that Broome's case is in fact *stronger* than Broome stated it to be, and that
Broome omitted important evidence in its favor. We will presently rectify
this omission.

What of Cassem's third objection? It seems clear enough that Broome's
approach to the biblical visions is fundamentally nontheistic. He follows
the tradition of psychoanalytic writers, from Freud onward, that insists on
treating the experiences and perceptions of the religious with the utmost
seriousness and respect—for they are unquestionably real, albeit distorted
[342]—but without the belief that any transcendent or superhuman deity
stands behind them. Perhaps Broome should have stated his premises
explicitly; perhaps he should not have muddled them with his final apologetic plea that Ezekiel's abnormalities do not detract from the religious
value of his message. But they are not very hard to guess at. Cassem's own
remarks show that he understood them well enough.

Throughout his article, Cassem (like Howie) adopts a tone of lofty
irony, which at times degenerates into flippancy.[25] He jeers at Broome's
"almost heroic naivete" (page 68), and finally refuses to grant Broome's

24.   Cassem's invocation of Acts 7:55, 9, and "the Tabor experience" is odd: none of the
visions he mentions is described in the words of the person who supposedly experienced it, as
Ezekiel's visions at least claim to be. (Or is Cassem perhaps thinking of the first-person
version of the "Tabor experience" in 2 Peter 1:16–18, which nearly all scholars regard as
pseudepigraphic?) Cassem's comments on Revelation are worth quoting: "Ezekiel is singled
out as psychotic because of his use of bizarre and obscure language. Yet from any common-
sense point of view, one would have to admit that Ezekiel makes far more sense than, and in
fact is the pinnacle of lucidity when compared to, Revelation. However, we find no bevy of
authors claiming that the Johannine school responsible for the production of this latter
remarkable work were, in fact, the earliest known colony of schizophrenics." Note the logic:
if Ezekiel was schizophrenic, the author of Revelation must have been schizophrenic; *therefore*
the whole Johannine school must have been schizophrenic; *therefore* they must have consti-
tuted a schizophrenic colony. The effect of this contorted argument is that Broome is made to
appear responsible for the grotesque image of a Johannine schizophrenic colony, and thus
made to look ridiculous. It is unfortunate that Cassem allowed his argument to descend to
this level.

25.   "Accustomed as he was to lying in various positions for days at a time, Ezekiel
seemed amply suited for the analytic couch" (page 63).

thesis the slightest respect.[26] It is impossible to believe he is writing entirely *sine ira et studio*.

Perhaps it is Broome's implied atheism that has so nettled him. Or, perhaps, it is the belief that Broome's motive was to degrade and insult Ezekiel. Thus, Cassem speaks of Broome's "quest for clues to clinch the indictment for psychosis" (page 63); and claims that "one is tempted to accuse Jeremiah and Isaiah of equally 'perverse' unconscious meanings when they report the word of Yahweh who puts words in their mouths" (page 66).[27]

It is odd to hear a psychiatrist speaking of an "indictment" of psychosis, "accusations" of unconscious perversities. Against this, we must insist that analyzing mental disturbance in Ezekiel is in no way tantamount to declaring him an unworthy human being. The opposite is closer to the truth. When we grasp the extent of Ezekiel's inner torment and the magnitude of his struggle, and when we recognize his struggle as akin to our own, we will be able to achieve empathetic understanding of those features of his character that otherwise repel us. We will necessarily be moved, not to deride him as a lunatic, but to acknowledge him as our brother in pain.

5. Garfinkel

Two recent articles (1987, 1989) by Stephen Garfinkel propose yet another counter to Broome's analysis [92,94]. The argument of both articles—advanced more boldly in the second than in the first—is that the historical Ezekiel had some familiarity with Akkadian literature and that direct influence of Akkadian incantation texts may be detected in at least two passages of the Book of Ezekiel. Garfinkel tries to demonstrate this by examining Ezekiel 2:6, in which God tells Ezekiel that "thorns and thistles surround you, and you sit upon scorpions," and 3:25–27, which introduces the theme of Ezekiel's dumbness.

Both passages are generally acknowledged as problematic. Both, as we have seen, figure in the list of "symptoms" by which Broome diagnoses Ezekiel's paranoid schizophrenia. Garfinkel therefore supposes that by

26. "One might accuse this paper of being a *reductio ad absurdum* and therefore unfair. However, it is impossible to reduce Broome's argument any further in the direction of absurdity than it already is." Cassem's self-defense is less than accurate; see note 24.

27. See also note 23.

explaining them as derived from Akkadian literary sources he has under-
cut Broome's psychological model for understanding Ezekiel's peculiarities
and put a literary model in its place. He makes this claim only parentheti-
cally, though in extremely emphatic terms, in his first article.[28] But the
focus of his second article is a polemic against any effort to understand the
Book of Ezekiel in psychological terms. The article's title—"Another
Model for Ezekiel's Abnormalities"—makes clear that Broome's paper is
the main target of Garfinkel's challenge.

What exactly is his challenge? Garfinkel offers a few criticisms, familiar
to us from Howie, of Broome's method. "Psychiatric evaluation without
in-depth interview, discussion, and testing, is methodologically questionable, if not foolhardy." Questions concerning Ezekiel's psychology can
only be answered by "inference," and therefore should not be asked at all.
The evidence Broome invokes, Ezekiel's eating the scroll and his operation
with the "sharp sword," may be given interpretations more appropriate
than Broome's [93]. (Garfinkel never quite says what they are.) And the
dumbness and paralysis of 3:25–27, like the thorns and thistles and scorpions of 2:6, are susceptible to an alternative interpretation: Ezekiel is not
describing his own symptoms, but borrowing details from Akkadian incantation texts.

We must now ask: Has Garfinkel in fact established some link between
the Akkadian texts and the passages of Ezekiel? If so, is the link to be
explained, as he supposes, by direct literary influence? If this is again
granted, will it show that speculations about Ezekiel's psychology (whether
or not along the Freudian lines favored by Broome) are false or irrelevant?

Not everyone will grant that the resemblances between the relevant
passages of Ezekiel and the texts Garfinkel cites are strong enough to bear
the whole of Garfinkel's argument. But Garfinkel has certainly made a
reasonable case for a relationship of some kind. He quotes, for example, a
text in which a divine "hand" is supposed to have afflicted the unfortunate
speaker, with the result that his mouth is "seized" and he is "tongue-tied."
This collocation of the god's "hand" with the individual's dumbness does
suggest, as Garfinkel says, the relation of Ezekiel 3:22 to its sequel. Other

28. "If the material adduced here does nothing more than offer a literary, rather than
psychological, model against which to measure Ezekiel, the comparison will be very much in
order. This approach rules as irrelevant—not correct or incorrect—psychological evaluations
of Ezekiel based on Ezek. ii 6. It is not so much an 'unwillingness of students of Ezekiel to
admit to the prophet's abnormality' [Broome] that is at issue here, but rather the appropriateness, or even the possibility, of raising the question at all" [95].

Akkadian texts link paralysis with dumbness, much as Ezekiel does. And, when the speaker in a popular poem of the seventh century (*Ludlul bēl nēmeqi*), complains of imprisonment in his house, along with his mutism and paralysis, we might almost imagine we are hearing the Ezekiel of 3:22–5:12 [92].

Garfinkel thus expands the range of potential literary associations for Ezekiel's experiences from the Bible into Akkadian literature. This is, of course, problematic. Part of the plausibility of looking to Jeremiah 15:16 for the source of Ezekiel's edible scroll, or to Isaiah 7:20 for his razor, is that we may reasonably imagine Ezekiel reading Isaiah or Jeremiah. It is not quite so easy to think of him reading Akkadian incantations or the *Ludlul bēl nēmeqi*. To be sure, it is possible to imagine how images from these sources might have reached him. My own proposal (see Chapter 3), that Ezekiel had some awareness of the content of the myths of Tammuz and Ishtar, assumes no less than Garfinkel's that Ezekiel was not insulated from his cultural surroundings in Babylonia.[29] But the existence of formidable linguistic barriers between Ezekiel and his supposed sources must give us pause and encourage us to consider whether some model other than literary dependence may not explain Garfinkel's data just as well.

Let us assume that Garfinkel is right to consider the resemblances between Ezekiel and the Akkadian sources significant, and right again to suppose that Ezekiel was familiar with certain themes of Akkadian literature and translated them into afflictions of his flesh. This "literary model" will not replace the "psychological model." For no sooner do we grant the "literary" explanation, than we start looking for some way to render Ezekiel's proceeding psychologically intelligible. Let us grant that Ezekiel, following in Jeremiah's footsteps, sought some way to concretize the ingestion of God's sweet word or, inspired by a still earlier prophet, turned Isaiah's razor on himself. What might have driven him to concretize, in a similar way, the complaints and boasts of heathen sorcerers?

This question occurred to Garfinkel. He points out that the texts he cites speak of adversary relationships: the speaker is pitted against demons, or against unfriendly humans. Ezekiel might therefore have found them peculiarly relevant to his own confrontations with the skeptical and hostile exiles.

This view is at least thinkable. Whether one finds it convincing will

---

29. I am aware, of course, that not all scholars have accepted the Book of Ezekiel's claim that its author was living in Babylonian exile. I will take up this point explicitly in Chapter 2.

depend on whether one finds this situational analogy so overwhelming that it might reasonably be supposed to have driven Ezekiel to model his prophetic life after books of idolatrous magic. My point here is not that Garfinkel's conjecture is wrong, although I think it is. The very constraint he feels to advance it shows that his literary model does not allow him to dispense with speculation about Ezekiel's motives. (What *might we infer* from what we understand of Ezekiel's historical situation about the motives that *might have induced him* to behave as he supposedly did?) Willy-nilly, Garfinkel finds himself forced into the realm of psychological inference from which he has earlier warned us away.[30]

Unlike Broome, Garfinkel does not offer his psychological speculation with awareness of and responsibility for what he is doing. Again unlike Broome, he works from a psychology that is straightforward and common-sensical, knows nothing of unconscious motivation, owes nothing to Freud. For the many who disbelieve the Freudian representation of human nature, this is to Garfinkel's advantage. The argument implied in such a judgment is entirely legitimate, once its premise is granted. Freudian psychology is wrong; Broome rests his argument on Freudian psychology; therefore Broome must be wrong. But Garfinkel does not make this argument (nor, as far as I am aware, do any of Broome's other critics). His argument, instead, seems to be the following: Freudian psychology *may* be right; but it is impossible to make a psychological statement of any kind, Freudian or otherwise, about Ezekiel; therefore Broome is irrelevant. *This* argument Garfinkel cannot consistently maintain.

The question that exercised Broome—what manner of human being stands behind the Book of Ezekiel, and what led that human being to perceive and to act as he did—cannot be dismissed as "irrelevant." Any answer given to it, Garfinkel's as well as Broome's, will necessarily be based on inference. Since the dead no longer exist, we cannot possibly know them except by inference. To deny for that reason "the appropriateness, or even the possibility, of raising the question at all" is to deny the appropriateness or possibility of any history that treats its actors as recognizable humans.

Garfinkel's "literary model," then, does not spare us psychological hypothesizing. It demands a fair amount of hypothesizing of its own about Ezekiel's direct or indirect familiarity with Akkadian incantations. Do we really want it? Surely we can find some other way of accounting for the

---

30. I here anticipate a point which I develop more fully in section 7.

resemblances Garfinkel has noted—without requiring Ezekiel to have been conversant with Akkadian literature, and with a potential for providing a more persuasive account of what Ezekiel's experience (or imagined experience) of dumbness and paralysis might have meant to him.

Garfinkel himself calls attention to such an alternative. Perhaps Ezekiel and the incantation texts both speak of psychogenic afflictions to which individuals in sixth-century Babylonia believed themselves prone, and which therefore befell them? Curiously, Garfinkel seems to have no difficulty believing that the incantation texts describe ailments from which people actually suffered. He does not hesitate, any more than Broome did, to apply modern medical terminology to these ailments: "motor (ataxic) aphasia," "sensory (auditory) aphasia." He offers no clear reason, except perhaps his programmatic aversion to "inference," why we should not similarly trust the Book of Ezekiel to report its author's actual experience of illness.

"At first sight," Garfinkel writes, "invoking parallels from incantation texts might seem to support a medical interpretation of the phenomena described. However, I suggest that the medical descriptions are a function of the model (i.e., the incantation texts), and that the prophet put the 'medical' data to a different usage. Therefore, this portion of the text of Ezekiel may be seen primarily as a literary borrowing, without the application of any psychological or medical conditions described" [93]. This is the closest Garfinkel comes to weighing the merits of the alternatives, and he draws back from doing so. In the passage quoted, we observe, his "Therefore . . ." hangs upon nothing more substantial than his own "I suggest."[31]

My own view is that Garfinkel's "first sight" was his keener sight. We do best to suppose that Ezekiel described, as truthfully as his conscious awareness permitted, a disability that his unconscious imposed upon him, which will demand elucidation in psychoanalytic terms. Others in his

31. In "Of Thistles and Thorns," Garfinkel writes: "J. V. Kinnier Wilson, who categorizes *Maqlû* as 'one of the main textbooks of Babylonian psychiatry,' reflecting the illusion of its author/speaker, explains that this portion of *Maqlû* typifies the speaker's paranoia. The Akkadian passage is presented [here], however, with the assertion that even if *Maqlû* were proven to be an article from an ancient psychiatric journal, we would gain no evidence for determining Ezekiel's psychological make-up. At most we are able to show only his familiarity with incantation literature and his reworking of several of its themes or texts" [95]. Garfinkel's unwarranted shift from the claim that literary dependence is *a thinkable alternative* to shared pathology (which is certainly true) to the claim that it is *the preferable alternative* is a fundamental maneuver of both this article and "Another Model for Ezekiel's Abnormalities."

environment, Garfinkel has shown, shared this disability.[32] We cannot show, but may be permitted to imagine, that their sufferings had causes similar to his. In this respect, as in others, Ezekiel may provide an important clue to the social and psychological pathologies of the world in which he lived.

6. Davis

Garfinkel's claim, that psychology is irrelevant to the understanding of the Book of Ezekiel, is echoed in a recent monograph by Ellen F. Davis, *Swallowing the Scroll* [60]. Her formulations differ from Garfinkel's, and her approach is "literary" in a far more profound and thoroughgoing sense than his. Broome is only incidentally a target of her attack. She neither offers to refute, nor even acknowledges his specific arguments. But the thrust of her presentation is to undermine, not only Broome's particular assertions but the legitimacy of the questions that evoke them.

Davis distinguishes two lines of approach to the book's problems, which she traces back to the Jewish commentators of the Middle Ages. The first of them

> suggests that the solution lies in whatever can be determined about Ezekiel's personal disposition. Most modern studies which share the same perspective evoke psychological phenomena or the particular interests and obsessions bred by the priesthood. But the second . . . points in quite a different direction, suggesting that this style of prophecy may be a response to external circumstances which created difficulties for Ezekiel in establishing his message as authoritative. (Pages 29–30)

Davis's monograph is a brief for the second approach. The conditions of the Babylonian Exile, she believes, demanded that prophecy shift from the oral to the written mode of expression, that it transform itself from public speech into literary text. Ezekiel was the great agent of this transformation; and this transformation shaped his book.

---

32. I will make a comparable suggestion in Chapter 5, with reference to the author of Psalm 137.

Many of Davis's observations are sound and thought-provoking, and much of her case is plausible. I will need to quarrel with her specific proposals only where they contradict my own—as does her explanation of Ezekiel's dumbness (see Chapter 5). I do not, of course, share her preference for external and socially oriented modes of interpretation over those emphasizing the internal and the psychological. But as long as her preference is left as such, there is no reason to object. Ezekiel was both an individual and a social being. Both approaches are legitimate, and both must be taken into account. No one scholar can ask or answer all the questions. Each has the right to deal with the ones he or she finds congenial.

Davis, however, does not content herself with exercising that right. From her initial stance of developing a fruitful alternative to psychological approaches, she shifts to a polemic exclusion of such approaches. ("Privatistic," she calls them.) By the end of her book, she is claiming to have "already argued that Ezekiel's first-person narrative yields little information about the prophet as an individual" (page 76), and to have "argued" that Ezekiel is not a "distinct personality" but an "almost transparent vessel of the divine word" (pages 134–35).

But the reader who works back through the book in search of Davis's "arguments" for these propositions will find them sparse to nonexistent. She says, correctly but without any great consequence, that no account of Ezekiel's personality thus far propounded has won universal consent (page 47). To David Noel Freedman's characterization of the Book of Ezekiel as a "spiritual diary," she offers a baffling rejoinder: "The fact that Ezekiel's whole book is composed from a first-person perspective sharpens the issue. For if that makes it a spiritual diary, then it is doubtful whether Ezekiel can legitimately be called a prophet at all" (page 67).[33]

Broome is dismissed in two ironic sentences:

> This [psychological] tradition reached its acme in a "case study" by Broome, who diagnosed the prophet as a paranoid schizophrenic showing symptoms of catatonia, alalia, delusions of persecution and grandeur, narcissistic masochism, sexual regression and gender

33. What can Davis mean by a prophet "legitimately" so called? Is this a person who has actually received some message from a transcendent deity? In the passage I have just quoted, Davis talks as if "the divine word" is something real and external to Ezekiel, for which Ezekiel can be an "almost transparent vessel." These passages point to a theological agenda underlying Davis's scholarly argument, which may suggest a reason for her sharp rejection of the psychoanalytic approach.

confusion, psychotic withdrawal. While Broome's confidence in
the exegetical power of medical science is exceptional, even so
responsible a scholar as Gunkel resorts to explanations such as
nervous derangement or an irrepressible unconscious for antics and
images whose purpose or meaning is unclear (e.g. binding, dumbness). (Page 66)

Davis thus insinuates, in a not-very-straightforward manner, that
Broome was something less than a responsible scholar. Yet she offers no
evidence for this, beyond her apparent belief that anyone who holds views
like Broome's *must* by definition be irresponsible. She speaks sarcastically
of Broome's "confidence in the exegetical power of medical science." But
she does not explain why it is wrong to think that medical science, by
expanding our knowledge of the sufferings the human species can experience, may help us understand the suffering of one human individual.

Beyond this, as far as I can see, Davis offers nothing like an argument
for why everyone should share her preference for social or literary models.
She only asserts and reasserts, in varying language, her aversion to psychological interpretations. She finds psychological questions uncongenial, and
therefore refuses to ask them. By the end of her study she has discovered,
unsurprisingly, that she has found no answers for them.

7. Jaspers, Goodenough

There would be no point in surveying every reference to Broome in the
scholarly literature of the past forty-five years. Most writers who mention
him simply repeat the verdicts of Howie and Cassem. Others, whose
viewpoints lead one to expect they will be well disposed toward Broome's
work, seem not to have been aware of it. Thus, Kelvin Van Nuys, writing
in 1953, remarks that "the Freudians would probably like to interpret [the
eating of the scroll] as a sexual symbol." He is sympathetic to this interpretation, although he does not believe that it exhausts the meaning of the
image [280]. He shows no sign of being aware that one Freudian had done
just what he proposes, only a few years earlier, in the pages of a distinguished journal.

The responses of psychoanalytic writers—Jacob Arlow, Daniel Merkur
[309, 370]—have already been mentioned. The coolness with which they

have received Broome's central claim is, as we have seen, essentially justified. Yet it has had the melancholy result that Broome, rebuked for his
excesses by scholars to whom his perspective is alien, gets little credit for
his insights from those to whom it is congenial.

There is one more contribution, however, that deserves our close attention. Among the vast writings of the great psychologist and philosopher
Karl Jaspers is a short paper entitled "Der Prophet Ezechiel: Eine
pathographische Studie" [152]. This article is not and indeed could not
have been a response to Broome's, for it originally appeared, in Germany,
in 1947. But it points the way to the response we must give to Cassem's
criticism, implicitly repeated by Garfinkel, that Broome moves too
quickly from the Book of Ezekiel to the man Ezekiel.

Like Broome, Jaspers categorizes Ezekiel as a schizophrenic. His grounds
are essentially the same as Broome's. But his argument is broader in scope,
less detailed and precise. Jaspers calls attention (as Broome does not) to
Ezekiel's strange excitements (6:11, 21:11), his extraordinary use of panto-
mimic actions, and—particularly important—his extraordinarily extended
and unabashed use of sexual images (chapters 16, 23). He suggests that two
phases of Ezekiel's illness can be detected, separated from each other by the
destruction of the Temple. This illness, he proposes, may be partly to
blame for some of the less attractive characteristics of Ezekiel's prophecies:
their dogmatism, their lovelessness, their priestly pedantry (pages 18–21).

Jaspers is sensitive to precisely those methodological questions that troubled Cassem. He affirms, though with appropriate qualifications, that
there is something about schizophrenia that may be expected to have
remained the same from the ancient world to our own. The material at
hand for psychological analysis, he admits, is sparse; yet no other biblical
prophet offers anything comparable. Indeed, it is a matter for some amaze-
ment that antiquity should have provided any material that yields itself so
well to study from the viewpoint of psychopathology.[34]

Most striking, Jaspers anticipates and reverses Cassem's claim that we
cannot begin to ask about Ezekiel's psychology until we have cleared up
the critical problems posed by his book. How, for example, can we judge
whether or not the book is a unity? Surely, on the basis of a set of expecta-

---

34. In his *General Psychopathology* (to which Daniel Merkur kindly called my attention),
Jaspers expresses a judgment that might almost seem to echo the views of Broome's critics:
"Where there is insufficient material, pathography becomes ridiculous (e.g. pathographies
concerning Jesus or Mohammed)" [354]. Jaspers apparently exempted Ezekiel from this
judgment.

tions about the "spirit" of the materials it contains. But these expectations will necessarily be shaped by our judgment about what sort of human being Ezekiel was; and it is precisely a psychological investigation that may enable us to make this judgment. We may therefore regard such an inquiry as an important preliminary to literary-critical study of the book, and not as a luxury to be postponed until after the results of literary-critical investigation are assured.

From this perspective, let us reexamine the preconditions Cassem [49] sets for any psychoanalytic study of Ezekiel. "I would consider certain information absolutely essential: who said it (was it one man, two men, two or more men with a redactor?), just what he really said (i.e., in the sixth century B.C.) or did, what his written or spoken behavior meant in its ancient Near Eastern cultural context, and what it meant in its canonical context, i.e., the major prophetic tradition" (page 64). And, again: "Are we talking about one man? Do we possess a single unified account unaltered from its basic form and content? What was it he really said or did? What did it mean in the context it was written? etc. Only the exegete is equipped to answer these questions" (page 68). Consequently, "there is nothing to be gained from psychological analysis of scriptural personalities where basic exegetical work has not been done" (page 69), and "whenever hermeneutics precedes exegesis, the result is invariably fantasy" (page 65).

Cassem's demands sound reasonable enough.[35] The problem is that it is impossible to conceive that they will ever be met. No one who reads Walther Zimmerli's commentary on Ezekiel can fail to be impressed by the painstaking care with which he separates the various layers of composition, assigns portions of the text to this one or that, and shows the relation of these layers to one another [297]. But let the reader then turn to Moshe Greenberg's commentary and consider Greenberg's effective critique of Zimmerli's assumptions and conclusions [104,118]. The reader may side with the one or with the other. My point is not that Greenberg is right and Zimmerli wrong—although it will be clear that my own perspective is much akin to Greenberg's. The point is, rather, that we are not likely to come away from examining the work of these two great scholars with much optimism that we are now or ever will be able to arrive at the sort of consensus that Cassem would regard as an "absolutely essential" platform

---

35. Zimmerli makes essentially the same points: "[T]he book has undergone a considerable later editing" and cannot be equated with the actual words of Ezekiel; further, it is highly stylized, and cannot be treated "simply as a description of a biographical situation" [298].

for the launching of psychological inquiries. Unless some unimagined breakthrough occurs, therefore, such inquiries will have to be deferred forever.

It might be argued that this is the only realistic course. But to say this is to despair of knowing what sort of human being stands behind the Book of Ezekiel, and thus to abandon vital questions that a humanistic reader will ask about the book. It is also, if one is prepared to be consistent, to abandon the very investigations into the origins and composition of the book that Cassem declares essential.

Jaspers has shown why. Whenever we declare a certain passage the work of a secondary writer or of a redactor, we rest our decision on a prior judgment of what kind of man Ezekiel was: the kind of man, that is, who could not or would not have uttered those words. The long-standing debate over whether Ezekiel could really have lived in Babylonia (as his book claims)—what is that but a question of plausibility? And what is this plausibility but psychological? The question is, at bottom, whether we can imagine that Ezekiel, living in Babylonia, could so totally have ignored the circumstances of himself and his fellow exiles and concentrated instead on faraway Jerusalem. Perhaps, or perhaps not. Our answer will depend on our tacit image of Ezekiel's psychology. Shall we not seek to replace that tacit image with an explicit one?

Consider another example. Ernst Vogt, in the course of what is to be presumed an "objective" literary analysis of Ezekiel's vision of the polluted Temple, argues that Ezekiel 8:2–3a must be an interpolation. For we cannot imagine that the figure of the man who seizes Ezekiel's hair could have vanished entirely from the rest of the vision if he were an original part of it; nor, in fact, can we grasp the role he plays to begin with. The power of the spirit should be sufficient to carry Ezekiel to Jerusalem in 8:3, as it is sufficient to return him to Babylonia in 11:24. The "man's" action is thus "not only bizarre and incomplete, but also superfluous" (*nicht nur bizarr und unvollständig, sondern auch überflüssig*) [283].

This argument is fair enough, as long as we think we know what Ezekiel can expect to experience. Change this expectation, suppose that the figure of a man grasping his hair may have had some particular meaning (perhaps unconscious) for Ezekiel, and it is no longer *überflüssig*. No dream analyst, after all, will deny the authenticity of a feature of a dream because the action of that dream, considered as a creation of the conscious mind, seems not to require it. The analyst will assume it belongs to the dream and will ask what it can tell us that the rest of the dream cannot. Our critical judgment about the authenticity of the text therefore depends on our psychological judgment of Ezekiel, as much as the reverse.

If we bind ourselves to Cassem's methodological strictures, then, we will find ourselves trapped in a vicious circle. We cannot judge the authenticity of supposedly Ezekielian material until we have grasped Ezekiel's psychology; and we cannot determine Ezekiel's psychology until we can show exactly what material is Ezekielian. The way out of the circle is to refuse to approach Ezekiel step-by-step—first exegesis, then hermeneutics, to use Cassem's terminology. We must prepare ourselves instead to oscillate between textual and historical inquiries on the one hand and psychological inquiries on the other.

These psychological inquiries cannot be carried out, as Howie and Garfinkel rightly observe, by interviewing Ezekiel or by subjecting him to testing. If such opportunities were open to us, we would surely not fail to grasp them. But they can never be. Our choice is not between secure and insecure methods of assessing the character of the human being(s) that created the Book of Ezekiel, but between insecure methods and none at all. Shall we refuse, on principle, to recognize that the visions and declarations that bear Ezekiel's name may offer clues to a personality that is painfully twisted, yet coherent and intelligible? Shall we declare, on principle, that we can never know anything about what the man Ezekiel was like—and then betray, every time we make a judgment about the authenticity of words and actions attributed to him, that we think we know exactly what he might or might not have said and done? If we sometimes imagine that we can hear a voice crying to us from the book's pages, in a language psychoanalysis has taught us to understand, shall we assume it must be our hallucination? Or shall we make our best efforts, feeble and uncertain as these efforts must be, to hear it?

Writing of Philo of Alexandria, E. R. Goodenough suggests how a voice from antiquity may be heard:

> Our interpretation must always be a paraphrase, behind which is a resolution of Philo into an entity common to him and to us, human nature. This, I must insist, again impossible though it is in the fullest sense, is our only approach to Philo. For unless human nature is a constant, however different may be our conditioning in different ages, we can never understand any figure out of the past. Mere words are in themselves the most deceiving things. . . . That is, Philo the man must be understood before his language can fully

speak to us. This implies a very circuitous approach to the problem, and is, as I have stated it, quite paradoxical. Philo's inner mind and life must determine the meaning of his language, but his language is our only approach to that inner mind and life. This is the essential difficulty of writing the history of ideas, and on this rock hopes of objectivity must be wrecked. Our only recourse is a sort of shuttle: we study the words with all possible contemporary evidence until we get an insight into the man, then with that insight return to the words with new criteria for their meaning, and so on back and forth. It is a spiral which reaches Philo himself only at infinity. But we have no other method, and we do not help ourselves by refusing to recognize it. The test before which any final picture of Philo must stand or fall is a double one: is it in accord with Philo's own statements understood in the language of his day, and does it make a convincing human picture out of those statements? For behind Philo's writings stood a human being, one who will appeal to a reader increasingly because his personality lives on in his works. [101]

Our version of Goodenough's shuttle must be something as follows. We should begin to work *as if* we can trust the Book of Ezekiel to be what it claims to be, and *as if* we can trust "human nature" as we know it from ourselves and from other accessible cultures to guide us to the Middle Eastern "human nature" of the sixth century B.C. Where these premises yield satisfying results—where they help us unravel acknowledged exegetical and historical cruxes in the book, correlate its various features into a coherent whole, and in so doing shape a recognizable human portrait of the author—we may judge that they have proved themselves. Where they do not, we learn that they must be modified.

Goodenough's reservations—"impossible though it is in the fullest sense," "on this rock hopes of objectivity must be wrecked"—apply fully to the present study. Ezekiel, too, can be reached only at infinity. That is no reason for us to restrain ourselves from reaching out to him.

In this effort, we do not need to commit ourselves to the more dubious aspects of Broome's thesis, above all his useless diagnosis. Our aim is not to categorize Ezekiel but to understand him. Nor need we follow Howie's defensive assertion that, judged by the standards of his own times, Ezekiel may have been quite normal. We will see in Chapter 4 that there is direct evidence that Ezekiel's contemporaries found his behavior to be, if not pathological, at least troubling, and that, on the point in question, most modern psychiatrists would agree.

For all his errors and excesses, Broome deserves the honor he himself gave to Klostermann, of being the pioneer. I hope to have shown that reports of his demolition are greatly exaggerated. We are free to follow the path he has laid out, toward the discovery of the human Ezekiel.

2
The Abominations in the Temple

It is specially worthy of note that every memory
returning from the forgotten past does so with
great force . . . and puts forward an irresistible
claim to be believed, against which all logical
objections are powerless.

—Freud, *Moses and Monotheism* [342]

1. Ezekiel 8–11: The Text and Its Problems

"In the sixth year, in the sixth month, on the fifth day of the month"
(September, 592 B.C. [105]), Ezekiel sits in his house, the "elders of Judah"
in attendance. A luminous human form appears to him and holds him
transfixed. A "spirit," meanwhile, "lifted me up between earth and heaven
and brought me to Jerusalem in visions of God" (Ezekiel 8:1–3). Some
time later, the spirit again lifts him up and brings him back to Babylonia,
"in the vision, in the spirit of God; and the vision I had seen lifted off me.
And I spoke to the exiles all the words of Yahweh that he had shown me"
(11:24–25). So begins and ends one of the most remarkable and problematic visionary complexes in the entire book.

In between, the prophet has seen the Temple of Jerusalem desecrated by
a string of "abominations," each worse than the one before. An "image of
jealousy, that incites jealousy," stands at the northern inner gate of the
Temple court. Seventy elders of Israel burn incense to images of unspeakable creatures inside a mysterious chamber. Women sit weeping for "Tammuz." A group of men stand outside the Temple and prostrate themselves
toward the rising sun (8:3–18).

Vengeance follows. A band of human-like beings passes through Jerusalem and slaughters the entire population, except for those "who sigh and cry over all the abominations that are done in their midst," and who have been set apart by a mark on their foreheads (chapter 9). One of these beings, the one who has made the mark, is sent to burn the city with coals of fire (10:2, 7). The glory of Yahweh, until now resident in the Temple, leaves the bronze cherubim on which it has been encamped and mounts a chariot carried by animate cherubim. These Ezekiel now recognizes as the "living creatures" he had earlier seen in his vision of the *merkabah* (10:3–4, 18).

The chariot pauses in its departure at the east gate of the Temple (10:19), where it and Ezekiel encounter a band of sinful Jewish leaders. Ezekiel prophesies against them, with the result that one of them, Pelatiah ben Benaiah, drops dead (11:1–13). There follows an oracle, its relation to its context uncertain, which appears to defend the religious status of Ezekiel's fellow exiles against the arrogant claims of the Jerusalemites (11:14–21). The chariot, Yahweh's glory on it, leaves Jerusalem and settles on "the mountain to the east of the city" (11:22–23). And Ezekiel is returned to Babylonia.

Like the rest of the Book of Ezekiel, this vision offers an ample crop of textual, lexical, and exegetical difficulties, many of which will occupy us in the coming pages.[1] But it also offers a set of special problems, which we may sum up under the following heads:

1. To what extent are chapters 8–11 a unity? If they contain secondary material, how are we to distinguish the layers of this material, and how are we to locate the original nucleus?
2. To what extent does this section of the book—or, depending on how one answers the preceding question, the original nucleus of this section—reflect actual events taking place in Jerusalem, in the last decade of the existence of the kingdom of Judah?
3. Precisely what are the "abominations" these chapters describe? (This question remains valid regardless of the answers we give to questions 1 and 2.)

---

1. In considering these difficulties, I have made regular use of the commentaries of G. A. Cooke (1936), Walther Zimmerli (1969), and Moshe Greenberg (1983; to chapters 1–20 only), which I consider the great Ezekiel commentaries of our century. I have also consulted William H. Brownlee's commentary on Ezekiel 1–19; it is not in the same league as the others, but is useful because of its recent date (1986) [31,56,104,297].

4. What was the nature of Ezekiel's experience, and what was his role in the events he describes? Most obviously, if he was physically in Babylonia, how did he know what was going on in the Jerusalem Temple? How could he have brought about Pelatiah's death in Jerusalem?

To the first question, scholars over the past century have answered, nearly unanimously, that chapters 8–11 are *not* a single, unified, composition. The most obvious indication of this is perhaps in 11:1–13. If the sinners of Jerusalem have all been massacred in chapter 9, who are these people Ezekiel is now prophesying against? But there are other problems as well. We have already noted that 11:14–21 has no apparent relevance to its context. The movements of the divine glory, as reported in 9:3 and in chapter 10, are extremely confusing [110]; and chapter 10 seems throughout both disjointed and corrupt.

Walther Zimmerli, in accord with his normal proceeding, reduces chapters 8–11 to a "basic text," considerably shorter than the corresponding text that now appears in our Bibles [302]. Even Moshe Greenberg, who normally seeks ways to endure the tensions within the text instead of reducing them by critical manipulations, finds the tensions within chapters 8–11 difficult to bear. He tentatively defends the anomaly of the sinners in 11:1–13 having survived the massacre of chapter 9: "One might suppose that, in a vision, temporal sequence need not be observed." But he plainly finds this unconvincing. He concedes that 11:1–13 and 14–21 were originally independent, and that perhaps "the evil cabal at the start of ch. 11 belonged to a different, parallel vision" [110].

Joachim Becker defends the unity of these chapters in the framework of a hypothesis that the entire Book of Ezekiel is a pseudepigraph [17]. His efforts demonstrate how hard it is convincingly to resolve the tension introduced by 11:1–13. The whole question of how the men of 11:1 can have survived the slaughter is, he claims, irrelevant. It pursues the false goal of making some sort of realistic sense out of the vision, and does not recognize that apocalyptic writers need not be bound by the rules of factual logic ("ein apokalyptisierender Verfasser nicht alle Gesetze der Tatsachenlogik zu beachten braucht"). But this is plainly unconvincing. It is precisely a pseudepigraphic writer, composing at his ease and in complete freedom from dictation by his sources, who may be expected to produce a meticulously logical and ordered "vision." (The animal apocalypse of 1 Enoch 85–90 is a good example.) If the unity of Ezekiel 8–11 is at all to be defended, it cannot be along the lines proposed by Becker.

In what follows, I will attempt my own defense in the context of a psychological approach to the vision. I must concede that I cannot push the argument to its extreme; for I cannot view 10:9–17 as anything but an exegetical paraphrase of 1:15–21, written perhaps long after Ezekiel's time, inserted into chapter 10 by its author or some later editor [124]. But I think I was far too radical when I claimed that chapters 8–11 are "so overlaid by repeated interpretations and expansions that it is almost impossible to distinguish the original, or to separate the several layers that were later added" [126]. A far greater portion of these chapters may be granted to Ezekiel than scholars have normally supposed, provided we are willing to approach without arbitrary preconceptions the question of the psychic reality that underlies them.

The second question, of the reality of the practices described in Ezekiel 8, is bound up with the historical issue of the extent and the effectiveness of the religious reform that 2 Kings 23 attributes to Josiah, king of Judah (640–609 B.C.). It is bound up, also, with the question of whether the Book of Ezekiel can be properly understood in its ostensible historical context (the beginning of the sixth century). If Josiah indeed purged the Jerusalem Temple of alien cults, as 2 Kings claims he did, and if his reforms survived his death—how could this Temple have been home to sun worship and lamentations for Tammuz less than twenty years later? But if no such things were going on in Jerusalem under Josiah's successors, how could a prophet living in the last days of the Judean monarchy have claimed that they were?

Thus it was that Charles Cutler Torrey, arguing for the long-term success of Josiah's reform, held it to be a necessary consequence that the sixth-century setting of Ezekiel is a redactional fiction. Originally, Torrey believed, the book was a pseudepigraphic prophecy set in the time of Josiah's grandfather Manasseh (687–42), whom 2 Kings 21:1–9 accuses of having introduced much of the idolatry that Josiah later eliminated [272]. James Smith offers a similar argument, but differs from Torrey in that he regards the book as a genuine prophecy from Manasseh's age [240,248]. But the argument is more often made in reverse. Ezekiel 8, it is held, indeed reflects the religious situation of the early sixth century. Therefore Josiah's reforms must have lapsed under his successors, of whom 2 Kings tells us that they "did that which was evil in the eyes of the Lord" (23:32, 37, 24:9, 19) [24,46,207,235].

Yehezkel Kaufmann takes the paradoxical stand of simultaneously affirming the text's authenticity and denying its accuracy. The Book of Ezekiel, Kaufmann says, is precisely what it claims to be, the work of a sixth-century Babylonian exile. Yet its depiction of the goings-on in the Temple is "pure fantasy" [162,163,166,167]. We shall presently take a closer look at Kaufmann's hypothesis, consider why most scholars have found it implausible, and cut a fresh path toward accepting it.

The "abominations" themselves (to take up the third question) have naturally fascinated students of the history of Israel's religion in its ancient Near Eastern context. The tiniest details have generated substantial controversies. What, for example, is the "branch" (*zemorah*) of 8:17, and why should Yahweh find it intolerable that the Jews "send it to their nose" [103,244,246,258]? (The rabbinic tradition that the word *'appam*, "their nose," was originally *'appi*, "*my* nose," further complicates the issue [199].) Torrey saw here a reference to the Persian rite of the *baresma*, and used it as evidence for the late date of Ezekiel; he and Shalom Spiegel debated the point at great length [272]. The mysterious "image of jealousy, that incites to jealousy" (if that is the correct translation of *semel haqqin'ah hammaqneh*, 8:3), has incited similar, though less voluminous, discussion [269].

The most important scholarly debate, however, has concerned the meaning of the ensemble. Thus, for example, Theodor Gaster argued ingeniously that all of the rites fit together into a Canaanite ritual for the autumnal equinox, the liturgy for which has survived in a Ugaritic text [96]. W. F. Albright saw no such coherence in Ezekiel's description, although it did not occur to him, any more than it did to Gaster, to question its accuracy. Instead, he inferred that it is "a valuable description of Syro-Mesopotamian syncretism," combining the worship of the Mesopotamian fertility god Tammuz and other Syrian and Mesopotamian elements with "a syncretistic cult of Egyptian origin" (the reptiles and beasts of 8:12) [4].

More recently, William H. Brownlee has seen in Ezekiel 8 an account of an equinoctial ritual enacting the resurrection from the underworld (represented by the chamber of 8:7–12) of Yahweh-Tammuz in the form of the rising sun (so 8:16). Ezekiel, digging his way into this "underworld" (8:8), was unwittingly playing a part in the ritual. The elders, Brownlee thinks, had earlier sealed themselves into the chamber with bricks, planning to dig themselves out at "the moment of resurrection of Yahweh as Tammuz" [33].[2] Whatever one may think of this theory, it is to be noted that Brownlee

2. Marco Nobile seems to have advanced a similar theory [220].

has put his finger on the embarrassing question (which we will presently take up again) of how the elders managed to get into a sealed chamber. He has also raised, perhaps without meaning to, the question of how they must have reacted to the sight of Ezekiel burrowing into their sanctum.

Scholarly responses to Ezekiel 8—of which I do not pretend to have given more than a sampling—generally suppose that it constitutes a precious testimony to the syncretic Yahwism of pre-Exilic Judah, and thus indirectly to the religions of the surrounding cultures. But those who deny the accuracy of the chapter's portrayal of the religion of Jerusalem are no less obliged to account for its details. We shall presently see how one skeptic (Kaufmann) acquits himself of this duty, and how we may improve upon his proposals.

This brings us to the fourth question, which is in many ways the most difficult. Ezekiel, supposedly in Babylonia, has provided a vivid and circumstantial—though not necessarily accurate—description of cultic "abominations" perpetrated in Jerusalem. He names names: Jaazaniah ben Shaphan (8:11), Jaazaniah ben Azzur (11:1), Pelatiah ben Benaiah (11:1, 13). He even, if 11:13 is to be believed, brings about Pelatiah's death with his prophesying. Just what is the experience that allows him, in reality or in imagination, to do these things?

If belief in the accuracy of Ezekiel's description has often led scholars to trust the book's claim that it derives from the early sixth century, this same belief has provoked a certain distrust of the book's claim that its prophecies were uttered in Babylonia. To have known so clearly what was going on in Jerusalem, some scholars have argued, Ezekiel must have been on the spot (if not in Jerusalem, at least in Palestine). The book's references to Babylonia will then be editorial retouchings of an originally Palestinian prophecy [32,183,241]. More traditionally minded scholars have, in response, sometimes toyed with the idea that Ezekiel was clairvoyant. He thus not only could see the "abominations," but knew of Pelatiah's death the instant it occurred [184,242].

Howie represented his predecessors as choosing between these two options. ("Those who did not admit the possibility of clairvoyance denied that the prophet was in Babylon.") He himself preferred a third path. Ezekiel 8, he proposed, describes "religious practices which had been common in Judah since the death of Josiah. . . . Ezekiel's information undoubtedly came primarily from the memory of similar scenes during his residence in Palestine and late news of these religious trends received via some sort of grape vine." Pelatiah died in Jerusalem while Ezekiel was in Babylonia. Ezekiel later heard of his death. He supposed, in retrospect, that it had been caused by his own visionary activity, and added a note describing it to his account of the vision [144].

Yehezkel Kaufmann, meanwhile, mounted a trenchant attack on both the "Palestinian prophecy" and "clairvoyance" theorists. The whole problem, according to Kaufmann, is misconceived. We do not have to explain how Ezekiel saw what he saw and knew what he knew; for he saw nothing, knew nothing, imagined all. "Ezekiel has seen things that never happened; this is the key to the understanding of the rest of his visions" [163]. To the problems posed at the beginning of this chapter, Kaufmann offered a particularly drastic solution. The merits and the flaws of his solution will occupy our next four sections.

2. Ezekiel 8–11: "Things That Never Happened"

Ezekiel's account of the Temple abominations, Kaufmann writes, "can be controlled and must be tested by the writings of Jeremiah. For while Ezekiel was wafted to Jerusalem by the spirit in 'visions of God,' Jeremiah walked its streets daily." He normally had free access to the Temple (chapter 35). When he was restrained on one occasion from entering it, he was able to send his scribe Baruch in his place (36:4–10). Yet in passage after passage where we would expect him to condemn the Temple abominations if he knew of them—most strikingly, the Temple sermon of 7:1–15—we find only silence. Jeremiah "never sees what Ezekiel 'saw,' nor does he ever reproach the people for practicing in it the abominations mentioned in Ezekiel 8 . . . [which] can only mean they were not present in his time" [162].

The author of the Book of Lamentations, at the opposite pole from Jeremiah politically, agrees with him on this point. The Temple is God's "footstool" (2:1), unblemished by idolatry [162]. The Deuteronomistic author of 2 Kings implies the same. True, he does not state explicitly that the Temple under Josiah's successors was innocent of alien worship. This would hardly suit his intent to show that the fall of Judah was Yahweh's just punishment for its wickedness. But, although he dutifully intones the cliché that each of the kings who followed Josiah "did that which was evil in the sight of Yahweh," he never accuses them of lapsing into Manasseh's idolatry. Like Jeremiah (15:4), he blames the calamities that befell Judah after Josiah's death on Manasseh's sins themselves, "which Yahweh would not pardon" (2 Kings 21:10–16, 23:26–27, 24:3–4, 20). If the writer had known of some dramatic relapse after Josiah's death of the sort implied by Ezekiel's vision, why would he have kept silent about it?

Ezekiel's details of idolatry in the Temple, says Kaufmann, must therefore be "pure fantasy."

> Their fantastic nature is clearly evident in 8:7ff. Seventy elders (cf. Num. 11:16) are in a temple chamber whose door is walled up. (How, then, did they enter?)[3] It appears at first that they are all together making offerings to pictures on the walls, but it then develops that the prophet sees what each man does "in darkness, each in his image-rooms" (vs. 12).[4] They say, "YHWH does not see us; YHWH has left the land"; if so, then, why do they act in darkness? Why do they gather surreptitiously in this God-forsaken temple? It is plain that Ezekiel sees shadows, not living beings; the entire vision is but a "parable." He specifies one man's name (vs. 11); hence it seems likely that the fantasy has some basis in a report of what took place somewhere in Jerusalem. One thing is certain: this was not the cult practiced in the temple, or the prevalent cult of the people of Jerusalem. Ezekiel who was carried to Jerusalem by his hair in a vision sees these things, but Jeremiah who frequented the temple and its courts does not. What Ezekiel really sees are shadows out of the past. He had heard in his youth of the dreadful abominations that took place in the temple during Manasseh's time. Ghosts of that time now rise before his eyes; they are still there, haunting the city and the temple. Retribution still clamors for satisfaction, and its claim will not be met until the city and temple are destroyed. [163]

For the "problem" of how Ezekiel knew of Pelatiah's death, Kaufmann has no patience at all. "The commentators have gratuitously verified Pelatiah's death, though it is not clear why this detail of the vision of 8–11 should be regarded as more real than the slaying of all the inhabitants of the city and its burning by celestial beings. We know nothing more than

---

3. We recall Brownlee's response to this excellent question [33].
4. *'Ish behadre maśkito.* We will presently return to the question of how this phrase is to be interpreted.

that Pelatiah died in the vision; here Ezekiel's word slays, in 37:4ff., it revives—both times in a vision" [163].

At one stroke, Kaufmann resolves the question of the historical reality underlying Ezekiel's visions of Jerusalem ("They are products of an exuberant imagination and have no historical worth"), along with that of their implication for the locale of Ezekiel's activity ("They prove, if anything, that Ezekiel never left Babylonia" [163]). Given that what he says about the fantastic and implausible character of Ezekiel 8–11 is obviously true, we would expect his matter-of-fact skepticism to have ended the debate, or at least to have redefined its agenda.

Yet, remarkably, Kaufmann's views on this issue have been largely ignored. They deeply influenced Kaufmann's translator, Moshe Greenberg; Michael Fishbane follows them, albeit with some hesitation; Morton Smith and George C. Heider have tried to come to grips with them; and Robert P. Carroll has at least acknowledged their existence [48,79,110,115, 138,252].[5] But most scholars have neither bowed to them nor argued against them, but simply ignored them.

What flaw is there in Kaufmann's arguments that might explain why they have been so neglected? We may imagine three possible objections: that the thoroughgoing success Kaufmann attributes to Josiah's reform is inherently implausible; that he uses the evidence of Jeremiah in a selective and uncritical way; and that he does not satisfactorily explain how a "pure fantasy" could have generated the intense conviction evident in Ezekiel 8–11.

We will see that the first two objections, while legitimate, are superable in terms of Kaufmann's own argument. The third is not. Until we have found some way to account for the compelling power of a delusion over both its originator and at least some of those around him, Kaufmann's proposals will remain unconvincing, and the problems he tried to solve will remain in place.

3. Josiah's Reform: Historical Considerations

A religious reformation is likely to have long-lasting effects only to the extent that it corresponds to the prior inclinations of the people it is

---

5. James M. Ward seems to follow the position of Kaufmann and Greenberg, without explicitly referring to them [286].

supposed to be reforming. It does not matter very much if it uses violence to achieve its goals, as long as it does not have to use continuous organized violence to maintain them.

Considered by this criterion, the religious reform promoted in second-century Judea by Antiochus Epiphanes was a failure. The Seleucid government knew that it was a failure, and began to retreat from it even before Antiochus's death [260]. The counterreform of the Maccabees, though hardly less violent than Antiochus's had been, was enough in accord with the religious inclinations of the Palestinian Jews that it did not need endlessly to force itself on them.

In considering Josiah's reform, we must ask if we are to envision Manasseh in the role of Antiochus, imposing unpopular foreign cults on an unwilling people. Josiah's reform will then have allowed his people's natural religious bent to reassert itself. Or was Josiah himself the persecuting tyrant, bent on stamping out hallowed religious practices, which would then be bound to emerge again under his less zealous successors?[6]

If we are to respond sensibly to this question, we must recall that Josiah's reformation was in fact a package of reforms, which may have served different purposes and encountered different responses. The account of the reformation in 2 Kings 23:4–20—the essential truthfulness of which has seldom been questioned[7]—suggests that it had at least three aspects [206]. Josiah is represented as purging non-Yahwist worship from Jerusalem and its environs, but also as taking action against Yahwist shrines in other parts of Judah (verses 8–9), and even proceeding against sanctuaries of what had once been the Northern Kingdom (verses 15–20).

Historians have naturally been disposed to look to something other than pure piety as an explanation of Josiah's motives. His centralization of the cult in Jerusalem may have helped him concentrate power in his own hands and bolster Jerusalem's economy as well. Until fairly recently, many scholars supposed that he was also in effect declaring his independence from the decaying Assyrian Empire by banishing the cults that Manasseh had introduced under Assyrian pressure. His crusade against the sanctuaries in what had once been the Northern Kingdom was presumably legiti-

6. I am much indebted to my research assistant, Dexter Hall, for her help in thinking through the issues discussed in the remainder of this section, and in gathering and organizing the materials relating to them.

7. There is, however, substantial debate over whether it is possible to detect some pre-Deuteronomistic document in the narrative as it stands [142,198].

mized by the Deuteronomic demand for centralization of worship.[8] But it may be read as defiance of the Assyrians, who nominally ruled the territory [52,142].

If we could take it as proven that the essence of Josiah's cultic reforms was a declaration of independence from an oppressive foreign power, we would have a very strong case for seeing Josiah as having played Judah the Maccabee to Manasseh's Antiochus. The plausibility of Kaufmann's view, that the reforms were popular and therefore successful in the long term, could then be taken as demonstrated. Unfortunately, however, J. W. Mc-Kay and Morton Cogan have strongly challenged this hypothesis, arguing that there is no evidence that the Assyrians imposed their religion on subject peoples [54,205]. We cannot rest any deductions on it. Josiah's outrages against Yahwist shrines in Judah and in the North, moreover, can hardly have been popular anywhere outside Jerusalem. We may expect them to have aroused traditionalist opposition that even Deuteronomy's rhetoric could not soothe. If their effects lapsed after Josiah's death, we would have no reason to be surprised.[9]

The question of the sanctuaries outside Jerusalem, however, is not relevant to Ezekiel 8. To suppose that this chapter could accurately describe the post-Josianic Temple—that the worship there might be presumed to have reverted to something like what it was under Manasseh—we must postulate something more than the conservative loyalties of rural clergy and their followers. We must posit a popular and extremely tenacious Judean paganism or syncretism. We must imagine, at the very least, that (as George C. Heider puts it) the people of Judah "incorporated large portions of the Canaanite 'old-time religion' into the Yahweh cult, whether through syncretism of the Canaanite gods with Yahweh, or (as I think more likely) by at least a nominal subordination of the other gods to Yahweh" [136]. Is such a picture plausible?

Kaufmann's *Religion of Israel* argues throughout that it is not. The prophetic and Deuteronomistic denunciations that might seem to lend it some support are in fact grotesque exaggerations, ideologically motivated, of a

---

8. Deuteronomy 12:1–28. I do not mean here to prejudice the question of whether the *book* of Deuteronomy, in some form akin to the one in which we now have it, was an inspiration for the reform [142,197,217]. It is possible to imagine that Josiah was familiar with the demand embodied in this passage in some other form.

9. Greenberg, following an earlier view of Kaufmann's, indeed supposes that these shrines were revived [115].

marginal reality.[10] Kaufmann's thesis, indeed, is controversial. But the recent studies of Jeffrey H. Tigay have dramatically confirmed it, at least with respect to late seventh- and early sixth-century Judah [264,265].[11]

Tigay meticulously examined seals, ostraca, and other ancient extra-biblical materials that attest ancient Israelite and Judean personal names. Of those names that contain within them the name of a deity, he found that in the overwhelming majority of cases Yahweh is that deity. The divine names that occur in the others do not, with one exception, belong to the gods whom the Bible accuses the Israelites of having worshiped. In many of these cases, it is very likely that the parents did not know the meaning of the names they gave their children.[12]

The salutations used by ancient Israelite and Judean letter-writers, such as the authors of the famous "Lachish letters" (contemporary with Ezekiel), invoke Yahweh and only Yahweh. Votive inscriptions and prayers for blessing are more problematic. Inscriptions from Kuntillet 'Ajrud, in the northern Sinai, seem to invoke Yahweh's 'asherah (whatever that may mean) along with Yahweh himself. But Tigay's conclusion seems indisputable, at least for the time and place with which we are concerned: inscriptional evidence would never lead us to "imagine that there existed a significant amount of polytheistic practice in Israel during the period in question" [267].

Jeaneane D. Fowler, in an exhaustive study of ancient Hebrew personal names from both biblical and extrabiblical sources, comes to essentially

10.   Tigay finds a modern analogy in the "Jews for Jesus" movement, which has stirred up indignation and controversy among other Jews out of all proportion to its actual extent and influence. "It is the theological significance of the issue, not the statistical picture, which makes it loom so large to those concerned about it" [268].

11.   The reviewers' most consistent criticism of Tigay's work is that he inappropriately generalizes about all of Israelite and Judean history on the basis of evidence deriving from the last fifty years of the kingdom of Judah. Nearly all concede that within these limits of time and place his arguments are compelling [19,59,74,160,214]. (Herbert Niehr's grounds for dismissing Tigay are wholly unclear to me [219].) These are, of course, precisely the period and the locale that concern us.

12.   Tigay found six people who shared the name "Pashhur" with the priest mentioned in Jeremiah 20, and with two individuals from early Second Temple times (Ezra 2:38, Nehemiah 10:4). The name is Egyptian, a compound with "Horus." But did the parents of the Pashhurs know this, any more than modern parents who name their son "Isidore" know that they are calling him "gift of Isis"? Baal, who *is* frequently named in the Bible as a competitor of Yahweh, appears as a compound in six names, all but one of them from Samaria. But *ba'al* is also a common noun, meaning "master" or "husband," and Hosea 2:18 suggests it could be used in the North as a title for Yahweh. If so, the Samarian "Baal" names would have to be removed from the non-Yahwist category.

the same conclusion as Tigay [83]. Nahman Avigad reinforces it from a different direction, pointing out that Hebrew bullae from Ezekiel's time tend to avoid decorative art, presumably under the influence of the Second Commandment [13]. Archaeological and onomastic evidence, in short, could hardly be less encouraging for Heider's picture of "old-time religion" in ancient Israel.

The evidence will not, to be sure, exclude the far more modest proposals of Hans-Peter Stähli and Mark S. Smith. These scholars have argued that solar representation of the divine was an integral and traditional feature of Yahweh's cult. The indignation expressed in Ezekiel 8:16 will then have reflected a less traditional perspective on this solar piety, neither more nor less "Yahwist" than that of the worshipers it denounces [249,258].

This hypothesis is plausible enough. But, applied to Ezekiel 8, it requires singling out one of the "abominations" and ignoring the rest. To credit the vision as a whole, we must postulate a pagan reaction of major proportions in the very center of Judean Yahwism.[13] In the light of what we have seen so far, this would be, to put it very mildly, unexpected.

4. Josiah's Reform: The Evidence of Jeremiah

Certain passages from the Book of Jeremiah, however, have suggested to many scholars that such a reaction did in fact happen.

Three parallel texts (7:30–34, 19:1–13, 32:26–35) share a complaint that the Jews are burning their children to death in sacrificial rituals in the Hinnom valley outside Jerusalem—which, Yahweh claims, "I did not command, nor did it come into my mind" (7:31). The recipient of the sacrifices is called Baal in 19:5, Molech in 32:35 [55,82,138,210]. Two of these passages make the further charge that the Jews have polluted God's house with their abominations (7:30, 32:34).[14]

The Jews are elsewhere accused of pouring out libations in honor of "the queen of heaven," in the cities of Judah and the streets of Jerusalem (7:16–20). Even as refugees in Egypt, after the fall of Jerusalem, they continue

13. "The picture of the temple depicted in Ezek. 8 suggests that Josiah's reform had no effect at all on Jerusalem's cultic life and raises the question whether 'reform' is the right word for the Deuteronomistic story of Josiah" (Robert P. Carroll [46]).

14. The word used for "abominations," shiqqusim, is not the one used by Ezekiel. These passages nonetheless give the impression of supporting Ezekiel's accusations.

this practice and fiercely defend it (chapter 44) [252]. Judah's gods are as numerous as her cities, Jerusalem's altars for Baal as numerous as her streets (11:9–13) [24].

These passages and others suggest (or can be understood to suggest) that paganism was alive and well in Jeremiah's Judah. It is arbitrary to suppose that they all date from the time before Josiah's reformation.[15] How can Kaufmann discount this evidence, and then claim to use Jeremiah's alleged silence as a control on the statements of Ezekiel?

Kaufmann's use of Jeremiah is vulnerable in another way. It assumes that the Book of Jeremiah and "the writings of Jeremiah" are the same thing. This position may well be arguable; it certainly is not the current consensus. For most of this century, scholars have distinguished different genres of material within the book (poetry, biographical narrative, prose discourses). Most have thought it unlikely that these are all the work of the historical Jeremiah. Other writers, most scholars believe, have had a hand in the book, including at least one Deuteronomistic author/editor of Exilic times or later [26,45,73]. Jeremiah may indeed have walked Jerusalem's streets daily, as Kaufmann says. The creators of his book need not have done the same. Kaufmann's argument from silence, based as it is on the book as we have it, is bound thereby to lose some of its impact.

These two lines of criticism tend to undermine one another, in that the most dramatic evidence for Judean paganism occurs in passages that are often attributed to the Deuteronomistic redaction. This is true of the passages that speak of the Hinnom valley sacrifices, and of chapter 44's vivid dialogue between Jeremiah and the worshipers of the "queen of heaven" [138,252]. It would be unfair, however, to respond to these arguments simply by setting them against each other. We must take each one, give it its maximum force—assume, for example, that the Hinnom passages indeed reflect concerns Jeremiah had, at the times they claim he had them—and see the worst that it can do to Kaufmann's argument.

Let us begin with the Hinnom passages (7:30–34, 19:1–13, 32:26–35). The Book of Jeremiah provides no historical context for the first.[16] The sequel to the second (19:14–20:6) suggests a setting in the reign of Jehoiakim (609–598 B.C.) [25]. The third is set in the last days of the kingdom of

15. Jeremiah 1:2 claims that Jeremiah began to prophesy five years before the reformation.
16. Which led Torrey to advance a rather unconvincing argument that it dates from before the reformation [273].

Judah. *If* these passages reflect messages that Jeremiah delivered in Jehoia-kim's reign and at the end of Zedekiah's, and *if* they denounce contempo-rary evils, we must conclude that the human sacrifices in the Hinnom valley, banned by Josiah (2 Kings 23:10), were revived after his death.

But do they in fact denounce contemporary evils? Careful reading of 32:26–35, with particular attention to verse 31, suggests that the writer intends to provide an overview of the atrocities committed in Jerusalem "from the day it was built until the present." Since the purpose of this overview is to explain why Yahweh is going "to remove [Jerusalem] from my presence," it naturally consists of hostile generalizations. The children of Israel and Judah have *never* done anything but offend Yahweh with their evildoing; Jerusalem has *never* been anything but a cause of divine irrita-tion (verses 30–31). The author consequently fixes upon the most sensa-tional misdeeds in Jerusalem's history—the desecration of the Temple under Manasseh, the child sacrifices of Manasseh and his grandfather Ahaz—and generalizes them to the city's entire past [116,166].

As for 19:1–13, it is hard to deny the force of Kaufmann's observation that Topheth (the location of the Hinnom valley sacrifices) appears to be deserted, that Jeremiah is obliged to bring his audience with him when he preaches there (19:1), and that he does not begin to address the people at large until he returns to the Temple (verse 14).[17] It follows that the passage represents Topheth, as Kaufmann says, as a sin of the past [162,166].

The same can be said of 7:30–34. Verse 30's picture of the defiled Temple will hardly accord, as Carroll remarks, with the Temple sermon of verses 1–15 [46]. As Kaufmann says, the latter passage presupposes that "the sanctity of YHWH's house is intact insofar as it is not polluted by the sin of those who enter it" [162]. The call for repentance in that sermon, which does not mention any cultic sins worse than burning incense to Baal (verse 9), will not suit the idea that its hearers were publicly sacrificing children in the Hinnom valley. We must suppose that, like its two parallel passages, 7:30–34 speaks in retrospect of the whole grisly history of the Hinnom valley and does not claim to describe contemporary reality. Or else we must date the passage substantially earlier or later than verses 1–15, treating it either as a pre-reformation prophecy of Jeremiah's (so Tor-

17. We may add that verse 12 threatens that Yahweh will make all of Jerusalem "like Topheth," which may be taken to mean, desolate and defiled as Topheth is. But this point is not by itself decisive, since the threat could also be understood to mean that the city will be made into a great fire pit. (This is evidently the meaning of *tofteh* in Isaiah 30:33, and it will suit *tofet* in Jeremiah 19:12.)

rey), or as the creation of a later redactor, perhaps based on 19:1–13 and 32:26–35. Whichever we choose, it is hardly evidence for large-scale public paganism in post-Josianic Jerusalem.

What of "the queen of heaven" (7:16–20, chapter 44)? For Kaufmann, her cult is a perfect illustration of what Judean paganism really was: "a forlorn and debased worship, without benefit of temple, altar, or clergy . . . which some old women performed with the help of their relatives." Only Jeremiah's ideological prejudices could inflate this "vestigial idolatry" into "a grave sin and impurity of national proportions" [162,166]. Kaufmann surely overstates his case. Yet it is hard to avoid the impression that the cult of the "queen" had fallen on bad times when Jeremiah knew it. Once, her worshipers nostalgically claim, the kings and princes of Judah practiced her cult, with full public support. But now—since Josiah's reform, presumably[18]— she is neglected; and "We lack everything, and perish by sword and famine" (44:17–18).

Josiah had suppressed the hilltop sanctuaries outside Jerusalem. Passages from Jeremiah imply that people continued to visit them for purposes of piety (17:1–4) and romance (13:27). The latter passage makes its point particularly vivid: "Your whoring! Your rutting! / Your wanton affairs! / On the hills, in the fields / I have seen your indecencies. / Ah, woe to you, Jerusalem! / Will you never be clean?" (Bright's translation [25]).

Surely, scholars have reasoned, these frolics must have been pagan rites [27,69,235]. But why? There is nothing inherently polytheistic about sex, even outside the bounds one normally associates with biblical morality [279]. A country shrine is hardly a bad place for a rendezvous—especially if it is no longer much frequented.

Jeremiah may be presumed to have seen the matter differently. From Hosea, he had learned to represent pagan worship as sexual promiscuity (Hosea, chapters 1–3; Jeremiah, chapter 3). Reversing the equation, he supposed that sexual promiscuity was *prima facie* evidence of pagan worship. This is why, in 2:20–25, Jeremiah's denunciations of his contemporaries' freewheeling sexual behavior lead him to the accusation that they have "gone after the Baals," whereas they insist, no doubt truthfully, that they have done no such thing (verse 23).

---

18.   Morton Smith questions this conventional understanding of the passage. He suggests that it refers to a cancellation of non-Yahwist cults, which he hypothesizes to have taken place during the final siege of Jerusalem [252]. But he does not advance any compelling support for his suggestion, and it remains at the level of a plausible alternative. Were it not for the problem of finding some context for Ezekiel 8, it is not clear that Smith would have felt any need for it.

Surely this is the context in which we are to view the accusation of 2:28 (repeated and extended in 11:9–13), that Judah's gods are as numerous as its villages. Plainly, if Tigay's data are any indication, none of these supposed deities was thought worth naming a child after.

The Temple sermon of 7:1–15, to which I have already referred several times, may similarly give us a context for interpreting the repeated claims that the Jews are burning incense or pouring out libations to Baal or some other gods (1:16, 7:9, 11:17, 18:15). Yahweh declares that he will protect the Temple, and consequently its devotees, only if they mend their ways. "Will you steal, murder, commit adultery, swear falsely, burn incense to Baal, go after other gods whom you have not known, and then come and stand before me in this house and say 'We are saved'—so that you can go on doing all these abominations?" (7:9).

We need not assume that burning incense to Baal was any more common an occurrence than murder. The author of 7:1–15 (whether Jeremiah, or some Deuteronomist) tests the Jews' conduct against a code of behavior that is apparently drawn from some ethical digest akin to the Decalogue, if not the Decalogue itself [44]. Not astonishingly, he finds them wanting. With rhetorical exaggeration, he represents them as failing utterly. The Decalogue had prohibited "other gods," so he accuses them precisely of going after "other gods." Surely there must have been some substance to this accusation; surely some people did burn incense or make libations in suspicious circumstances. But the passage hardly encourages us to believe in a massive slide into paganism by the people of Judah.

Most important for our purposes, it plainly has not entered the author's mind that the Temple itself can have been home to pagan worship. The briefer parallel in 26:1–6 is equally silent on this point.

Further, Josiah's purge of the Temple could hardly have been reversed without the collusion of his successors. Yet, although the Book of Jeremiah is filled with hostile comments on the last kings of Judah, it nowhere accuses them of having brought idolatry into the Temple. This is not one of the sins for which Jehoiakim is going to be "buried with the burial of an ass" (22:13–19), "his carcass cast out to the heat of the day and the frost of the night" (36:27–31). Nor is Zedekiah told that he must clean the "abominations" out of the Temple if the city is to be spared (38:14–23).

In the entire Book of Jeremiah, 7:30 and 32:34 are the only texts that can be construed to support Ezekiel's portrait of the polluted Temple. We have seen it likely that both, like 15:1–4, look back to the time of Manasseh.

This is, of course, Kaufmann's argument from silence. If we suppose that the Book of Jeremiah is, as he assumes, "the writings of Jeremiah" himself, the argument is quite overwhelming. But suppose we deny this assumption? Suppose we go to the extreme of declaring the book an accumulation of anonymous sources brought together by Exilic (or even post-Exilic) Deuteronomists? What will be the effect on Kaufmann's case?

The consequence is that we will have to restate his argument as follows: The Deuteronomistic author(s) of 2 Kings know of no massive idolatry after Josiah that might account for Jerusalem's downfall; and the Deuteronomistic author(s) of Jeremiah are similarly ignorant. To their silence, we must add that of Lamentations. We must add, as well, the absence of pagan elements from Judean personal names [83,264,265].

The argument is, no doubt, weaker on this premise than it was when Kaufmann presented it. But it remains impressive enough. All that stands against it are the hallucinations of Ezekiel 8–11; some of which, like chapter 9, are openly fantastic. Nothing in our examination of Josiah's reform, or of the pertinent texts in Jeremiah, has given us any ground for believing there is a substrate of truth in these hallucinations.

We are back, therefore, with the question of why scholars refuse to follow Kaufmann in dismissing Ezekiel's testimony.

5. The Problem Redefined

The answer must lie in the power of Ezekiel's conviction, and his apparent belief that his contemporaries would share it.

Zimmerli remarks, in what can be taken as an indirect response to Kaufmann, that Ezekiel "undoubtedly seeks to point to things which really happened in Jerusalem. Only so does the accusation which justifies the ensuing judgement upon Jerusalem carry real weight" [303]. It is hard not to agree. Let Ezekiel's imagination be as "exuberant" as we like; we are left with the problem of how its creations could have generated the conviction evident in Ezekiel 8–11, or how they could have failed to bring Ezekiel ridicule and discredit from the exiles (11:25), who would have known perfectly well they were false.

The question has so far received no satisfactory answer. Kaufmann's invocation of ghosts from the age of Manasseh [163] is more poetic than convincing. Greenberg wrestles with the problem at greater length but with no greater success [115]. Morton Smith suggests a less sympathetic way out of the impasse: "If Ezekiel did lie about his opponents' practices— well, the prophets of his time had a reputation for lying, so it is not unlikely that one or two examples of their art should be preserved" [252]. But Smith obviously recognizes this solution as inadequate, for he devotes the rest of his article to trying to buttress Ezekiel's testimony. It was easy enough for Torrey, who denied Ezekiel's existence, to deny as well that Ezekiel 8–11 could describe the post-Josian Temple [273]. For those who believe in the man, it is harder to reject his report.

No wonder, then, that Kaufmann himself wavers. The mention of Jaazaniah ben Shaphan in Ezekiel 8:7–12, he thinks, suggests that "the fantasy has some basis in a report of what took place somewhere in Jerusalem" [163]. Greenberg follows him on this point. "Private and clandestine pagan cults certainly seem to have existed," he remarks, basing himself on Ezekiel 8:12 as well as on passages from Jeremiah [115]. "The public pagan rites of ch. 8 belong historically to the age of Manasseh; the secret cults of vss. 10–12 are another story and may have been practiced in Ezekiel's time" [110]. But how can one isolate these three verses from the rest of the chapter?

We must add that Kaufmann's treatment of the death of Pelatiah, impressive as it seems at first sight, has its difficulties. For, Kaufmann to the contrary, there *is* a reason "why this detail of the vision of 8–11 should be regarded as more real than the slaying of all the inhabitants of the city and its burning by celestial beings" [163]. In chapter 9, not one but all of the sinners of Jerusalem are slain. In chapter 37, which Kaufmann also compares with Pelatiah's death, not one but all of the dried-up skeletons are revived. Given the incredible powers Ezekiel is prepared to grant himself, why should he turn modest in 11:13? Why should he restrict his carnage to one of the twenty-five sinners he confronts? This suggests that something beyond Ezekiel's fantasy underlies the detail.

The upshot is that Kaufmann has given excellent reason to believe that Ezekiel's report of the polluted Temple is wholly incongruent with other biblical evidence about the state of religion in Jerusalem in the last years before its fall. Archaeological evidence confirms Kaufmann's view and reinforces Ezekiel's isolation.

The hallucinatory context of Ezekiel's report, filled with details that no historian could conceivably accept at face value, does not inspire confidence in its reliability. Neither does the claim, made by the Book of

Ezekiel itself, that Ezekiel was hundreds of miles from Jerusalem when he "saw" the abominations perpetrated in the Temple. If we follow this argument, if we dismiss Ezekiel's report as "pure fantasy," we will find some of the knottiest problems posed by Ezekiel 8–11 easily resolved.

But one obstacle blocks our way. We have so far found no way to make psychologically plausible that a man who had been a Judean priest should have created out of his imagination an utterly false and fantastic picture of the worship in the Jerusalem Temple, that he should have become entirely convinced of its truth, and that he could have conveyed at least some of that conviction to his formerly Judean hearers. A psychological theory that can render all this intelligible will therefore have a powerful claim on our belief.

A psychoanalytic approach to Ezekiel, I will argue, will allow us to meet this challenge.

6. Ezekiel and the Elders: The Chambers of Imagination

I now advance two proposals, which, I believe, will guide us toward understanding the nature of Ezekiel's Temple vision, and its roots in Ezekiel's psyche.

First, the "elders of Judah" (8:1) are not merely part of the framework of the vision of chapters 8–11. They are its audience. They are the objects of its accusations as well. It is they who appear as the twenty-five sun worshipers of 8:16 (called "elders" in 9:6, according to the reading of the Masoretic Text) and as the twenty-five "princes of the people" in 11:1.[19] They appear also as the seventy elders of 8:11; only here their number has been determined, not by the reality of the historical situation, but by a tradition recorded in Numbers 11. (More on this below.) They crop up again and again in the vision, because they are part of its environment.

19. The Masoretic Text has "twenty-five" in both 8:16 and 11:1. The Septuagint reads "twenty" in 8:16, but supports the Masoretic Text in 11:1. I suggest that these numbers reflect the actual number of elders who sat before Ezekiel, which was between twenty and twenty-five. The variations—between the Septuagint's 8:16 and 11:1, between the Masoretic Text's and the Septuagint's 8:16—represent variant approximations to this actual number.

They are, indeed, its main exciting factor. That is why, within the vision, they are indestructible.

Second, the charges made against them are not only fantasy (as Kaufmann says), but are explicitly stated to be fantasy. Only, Ezekiel will not acknowledge the fantasy as his own. He therefore projects it onto the elders, declaring that he is exposing *their* hidden wishes. The grounds for Ezekiel's erroneous conviction are to be elucidated along psychoanalytic lines.

These suppositions will help resolve the central problems of Ezekiel 8–11, as I defined them at the beginning of this chapter. My solutions will emerge from the trend of the argument in this chapter and the next, and will be summarized at the end of Chapter 3. First, however, I must argue for the suppositions themselves.

The situation described in 8:1—"I was in my house, the elders of Judah sitting before me"—recurs twice in the Book of Ezekiel. "Men of the elders of Israel came to me and sat before me" (14:1). "In the seventh year, in the fifth month, on the tenth of the month, men of the elders of Israel came to inquire of Yahweh, and they sat before me" (20:1).

Commentators have pointed out that this situation is stereotypic. Like so much in Ezekiel, it is reminiscent of the prophet stories in 1 and 2 Kings. Specifically, 2 Kings 6:32 represents Elisha as "sitting in his house, the elders sitting with him"; and the language of this passage is very suggestive of Ezekiel's [42]. It does not follow, however, that we are dealing with a purely *literary* stereotype. The situation may have become a staple of prophet narratives precisely because it tended to recur in real life. We have no reason to deny that on certain occasions Jewish elders did sit in Ezekiel's house while they consulted him, or that the Book of Ezekiel describes three such actual occasions.

Now, on the second and third of these occasions, Ezekiel interacts with his visitors in a violently hostile manner.

In 14:3, Yahweh advises his prophet that "these men have lifted up their idols upon their heart, and put the stumbling block of their iniquity before their faces [*he'elu gillulehem 'al libbam umikhshol 'awonam natenu nokhah penehem*]. Am I indeed to let them inquire of me?" Ezekiel must declare to them that anyone "who lifts his idols upon his heart and puts the stumbling block of his iniquity before his face, and then comes to the prophet, I Yahweh have responded to him concerning it [?], according to the multi-

tude of his idols. . . . I will set my face against that person, I will make him
a sign and a subject of proverbs, and I will cut him off from my people"
(14:4, 8).[20] The Israelites must therefore repent of their idols (*gillulekhem*),
turn their faces away from all of their abominations (*to'abotekhem*; 14:6). We
can hardly doubt that Ezekiel indeed delivered this message with appropriate violence.

Notice that Ezekiel does not accuse the elders of actually having worshiped idols, performed iniquitous acts, or committed "abominations."
Rather, they have *imagined* doing these things. They "have lifted their idols
upon their hearts"; that is, admitted them to their thoughts. (The idiom is
most clearly paralleled in Isaiah 65:17, Jeremiah 51:50, and Ezekiel 38:10
[104]. See also note 22 to this chapter.) When Ezekiel tells them to turn
their faces away from their abominations, he is, as Greenberg says, using
"a metaphor for disregarding what is only in the mind" [104]. Yet these
imagined idolatries, whose nature is left entirely vague [297], merit the
most ferocious retribution.

Ezekiel, whatever he may have believed, can hardly have had direct
access to what the elders were thinking. We may suppose, if we wish, that
he constructed his notions of their fantasied "abominations" by some process of inference—however confused and distorted—from what he had
observed of their speech and behavior. But there is another possibility,
which will commend itself to us more and more strongly as our inquiry
proceeds: that their imagined "abominations" were fantasies of his own,
which he projected onto them.

Yet the elders, being human, must occasionally have had thoughts their
consciences disapproved. It is hardly fantastic to suppose that they may
have felt Ezekiel's vague accusations to apply to them, and that they left
his presence feeling guilty and chastened.

Ezekiel's response to the inquiring elders in chapter 20 is no less hostile.
As in chapter 14, Yahweh is indignant that such men have come to inquire
of him (20:3, 31). He blames them for their ancestors' "abominations"
(*to'abot*, in verse 4; this is the word used throughout chapter 8). He demands
to know whether they are defiled in the ways of their ancestors, whether
they go whoring after their ancestors' detestable things (*shiqqusehem*),

20.   Verses 7–8 largely repeat and expand verses 4–5, and both passages are cast in the
style of the Pentateuchal source known as the "Holiness Code" (Leviticus 17:20, for example). The repetitiousness and the use of language akin to that of the Holiness Code are both
characteristic of Ezekiel [43]. The meaning of *bah* in verse 4 is unclear, and the text uncertain
[56,104,297].

whether they continue to offer child sacrifice "to this day" (verses 30–31).[21] "The thoughts that have crossed your minds[22]—that which you say, 'Let us be like the nations, like the families of the lands, serving wood and stone'—will certainly never come to pass" (verse 32).[23]

Here again, Ezekiel claims to know what his visitors are thinking. These alleged thoughts are enough to provoke his accusation that the elders replicate the sins of their forebears—whose hearts and eyes went after abominations (verses 16, 24; cf. Numbers 15:39), who could not bring themselves to cast away the sins they looked after and hankered for (*shiqquṣe 'enehem*, verses 7–8). It again appears, though not so clearly as in chapter 14, that Ezekiel's fury is directed against what the elders have imagined, not what they have done.

In blaming his audience for the sins of the Israelite ancestors, Ezekiel condemns himself together with them. We may read this as an admission that their sins are his. That is to say, the imaginings he condemns in the elders are really his own.

Can we extend these observations, by analogy, to chapters 8–11?

In these chapters, too, people's thoughts come under attack. This is clearest in 11:1–13, where the "princes" Ezekiel denounces are said to be "the men who think iniquity [*hahoshebim 'awen*], and who give bad counsel concerning this city" (11:2).[24] "Bad counsel," it is true, would suggest that the "princes" not only "thought iniquity," but went on to translate their thought into persuasive speech. But 11:5 indicates that they are blamed for their thoughts as well as for their speech. "Thus you have said, house of Israel," Ezekiel declares to them in Yahweh's name, "and I know the

---

21. I read verses 30–31a as a series of four questions, the first beginning with interrogative *he* [170], each of the others with *waw*. This supposition softens, though it certainly does not eliminate, the seemingly implausible charge [113,139] that the Babylonian exiles were practicing child sacrifice. Ezekiel insinuates it with a question (of the are-you-still-beating-your-wife variety), but does not assert it outright. I will suggest (in Chapter 4) that Ezekiel knew perfectly well that the elders were not sacrificing children, yet was driven by his psychopathology to imagine that they *must* be doing so. His insinuating question represents a compromise between his fantasy and his awareness of reality.

22. *Ha'olah 'al ruhakhem*; corresponding to *he'elu . . . 'al libbam* in 14:3.

23. The language used in this passage, *lesharet 'eṣ wa'aben*, is reminiscent of Deuteronomy 4:28, as well as 28:36, 64. (*'Eṣ wa'aben* recurs, in somewhat different contexts, in Deuteronomy 29:16, 2 Kings 19:18 [= Isaiah 37:19]. Jeremiah 2:27 and Habakkuk 2:19 offer more distant parallels.) I note this point in anticipation of the proposal I will make in Chapter 3, that Ezekiel alludes in 8:10 to Deuteronomy 4:17–18.

24. *Ba'ir hazzot*; more commonly translated, "in this city" (e.g., RSV). My reason for translating it as I do will presently become clear. The content of this "bad counsel" (verse 3) is a long-standing crux. We will examine it at the end of this chapter.

thoughts that have crossed your minds [*uma'alot ruḥakhem 'ani yeda'tiha*]."
This boast, of having unmasked the villains' secret musings, would have
little point if these had already been publicly expressed.

We note that the language of this passage echoes that of chapters 14 and
20. *Ma'alot ruḥakhem* corresponds to *ha'olah 'al ruḥakhem* (20:32). The fragmentary denunciation in 11:21, which does not fit very well with its
present context and seems to be connected with 11:1–13, is reminiscent of
20:16.[25]

But I think 8:12 contains a more significant, if less obvious, reference to
evil thoughts. The Hebrew text reads: *hara'ita ben 'adam 'asher ziqne bet
yisra'el 'osim baḥoshekh 'ish beḥadre maśkito*. The Revised Standard Version
(RSV) reflects the nearly universal understanding of this passage: "Son of
man, have you seen what the elders of the house of Israel are doing in the
dark, every man in his room of pictures?"[26]

But, so understood, the text is difficult. Kaufmann, as we have seen,
points out that it appears to contradict the preceding verses, which have
the elders gathered together in a single chamber [163]. To maintain the
conventional understanding, we must suppose that "the vision of the
seventy elders all together seems to have been replaced by another of
each in his private rooms" (Greenberg [104]), or that "the sinful form of
devotion which the prophet saw practiced in an assembly of the seventy
elders took place also in individual houses" (Zimmerli [297]). Cooke,
supposing that the locale must be the Temple, wonders if it is "likely that
each of the seventy elders had a chamber to himself" [56]. Zimmerli
himself, following Carl Heinrich Cornill and Georg Fohrer, considers
deleting the whole passage as a gloss [297]. Clearly, there is a real problem here.

The crux of the problem, and the path to its solution, lie in the word
maśkit.

Outside our passage, the word occurs five times in the Hebrew Bible.[27]

25. Ezekiel 11:21: *we'el leb shiqquṣehem weto'abotehem libbam holekh.* Ezekiel 20:16: *'aḥare
gillulehem libbam holekh.*

26. In a footnote, the RSV translators scrupulously record that the Hebrew has plural
"rooms," as if each elder has not one but several "rooms of pictures." The Septuagint, which
significantly differs from the Masoretic Text in 8:7–12 (see Chapter 3), supports it here,
omitting only the word *baḥoshekh* ("in the dark"), for there is no reason to suppose that *en tō
koitōni tō kryptō autōn* is anything but a guess at the meaning of *beḥadre maśkito.*

27. Other derivatives of the root *śky* [30] are not very helpful, since they are even more
ambiguous than *maśkit.* Job 38:36 uses *sekhwi* in parallelism with *ṭuḥot:* "Who has placed
wisdom in the *ṭuḥot?* Who has given understanding to the *sekhwi?*" If *ṭuḥot* here refers to

Two of these occurrences, Leviticus 26:1 and Numbers 33:52, plainly refer to some sort of idolatrous engravings. Proverbs 25:11, using *maśkiyyot* for a silver frame in which "golden apples" can be set, confirms that the word can mean a skillfully crafted object.

But the other two occurrences suggest another option. In Psalm 73:7, it is not easy to understand *maśkiyyot lebab*—literally, "*maśkiyyot* of the heart"—as anything other than "sinful imaginings" entertained by the wicked, which are followed (in verses 8–9) by arrogant and threatening speech.[28] (By contrast, the psalmist identifies himself in verse 1 with the "pure in heart," and claims in verse 13 that he has purified his heart.) In Proverbs 18:11, "The wealth of a rich man is his strong city, and like a lofty wall *bemaśkito*." The meaning of the last word is not absolutely clear from the context, but the common translation "in his imagination" suits it very well. This is reinforced by the preceding verse, which declares Yahweh's name to be the "strong tower" in which the righteous can find protection. The rich man's wealth, by contrast, is a fortress only in his fantasy.[29] In both of these passages, *maśkit* has a negative connotation.

If we translate Ezekiel 8:12 in accord with this second meaning of *maśkit*, we get "Have you seen, son of man, that which the elders of the house of Israel do in the dark, *each in the chambers of his [wicked] imagination?* [Or, more freely, "each in his own perverted fantasies."] For they say, 'Yahweh cannot see us, Yahweh has forsaken the land.' " In other words, each of the elders—by which we will understand, each of the twenty-odd elders gathered before Ezekiel—is supposed to entertain secret fantasies in which he gathers with his fellows, in an august college of seventy, worshiping monstrosities in an eerie cave.

---

human organs of thought or feeling (as appears from Psalm 51:8, its only other occurrence in the Bible), it is reasonable to suppose that *śekhwi* here is "mind" or "imagination." The context in Job, however, points to some sort of meteorological phenomenon. RSV translates accordingly. In Isaiah 2:16, *śekhiyyot haḥemdah* appear in a list of lofty things that are to be brought low on the day of Yahweh: cedars, mountains, towers, walls, and, in immediate parallelism, "ships of Tarshish." This implies they are some sort of structure. On the other hand, they are followed (verse 17) by *gabhut ha'adam* and *rum 'anashim*, which are best taken as referring to human pride. If *śekhiyyot haḥemdah* are placed in the latter company, we might reasonably take them to be "splendid imaginings"—with a pejorative connotation, as we will see in connection with *maśkit*.

28. In verse 11, these sinners "say, 'How can God know? Is there knowledge with the Most High?' " (*'ekhah yada' 'el weyesh de'ah be'elyon*). The parallel with Ezekiel 8:12—"They say, 'Yahweh cannot see us, Yahweh has forsaken the land' "—is very striking.

29. Pamela Kinlaw points out to me that Proverbs 18:12 confirms this interpretation, declaring that the arrogance of "a man's heart" (*leb 'ish*) precedes catastrophe.

The parenthesis in the preceding sentence, of course, has gotten ahead of the argument. We have seen that, in chapters 14 and 20, Ezekiel accuses the elders who come to consult him of entertaining thoughts of ill-defined abominations. In chapters 8 and 11, he accuses *certain people who figure in his vision*, again, of entertaining wicked thoughts. I have asserted, but have not demonstrated, my belief that the villains of 8:11 and 11:1 are visionary representations of the "elders of Judah" who sit before Ezekiel in 8:1, and that it is these elders who supposedly indulge the "perverted fantasies" of 8:12.[30] My next task must be to demonstrate, first, that this understanding of the vision is plausible and, second, that it is true.

7. Ezekiel and the Elders: Vision and Audience

What exactly happens to Ezekiel when "the hand of the Lord Yahweh" falls upon him (8:1)?

"I saw, and behold, an appearance like that of a man, fiery from the appearance of his loins downward; and, from the appearance of his loins upward, like the color of *ḥashmelah*.[31] He sent forth the likeness of a hand, and grasped me by the hair of my head. The spirit lifted me up between earth and heaven, and brought me to Jerusalem in visions of God" (8:2–3).

Most moderns, no doubt influenced by the Apocryphal "Story of Bel and the Dragon" (which itself presumably reflects exegesis of this passage), have supposed that Ezekiel was carried to Jerusalem by the hair of his head. But the text does not say that [104,253,283]. Rather, the human-like figure holds Ezekiel transfixed. Thus transfixed, he feels the *ruaḥ*—perhaps "wind," perhaps "spirit"—lifting and carrying him to Jerusalem.[32] We are thus assured that, in contrast to 3:14–15 (which in many respects parallels our passage), Ezekiel's body does not follow the exalted wanderings of his spirit.[33] It

30.   These fantasies—to repeat this point—we shall identify as Ezekiel's own.

31.   Following the Masoretic Text, but (1) reading, with the Septuagint, *'ish* for *'esh* as the fifth word of the verse; and (2) deleting, again with the Septuagint, the words *kemar'eh zohar* as a gloss on the cryptic *ke'en haḥashmelah*. (I do not attempt to translate this last word. RSV guesses: "gleaming bronze.")

32.   Keith W. Carley discusses in detail the activities of both the "hand" and the "spirit/ wind" in relation to the prophet, in the Book of Ezekiel and the stories of the preclassical prophets [41]. I will return to this point in Chapter 5.

33.   Ezekiel 3:14–15: "The spirit/wind [*ruaḥ*] lifted me up and seized me, and I went [*wa'elekh*] bitter in the heat of my spirit [*baḥamat ruḥi*], Yahweh's hand being mighty upon me.

remains in place; and, perhaps, remains active in Babylonia even as Ezekiel's spirit is active in its imaginary Jerusalem.

What sort of activity might we expect of Ezekiel's body? Ethnographic
data on trance and related states allow more than one option. A seer may
go into a complete trance and remain unable to describe his experiences
until after the trance has passed. This is, admittedly, what Ezekiel 11:25
would lead us to expect. But this verse would not exclude another sce-
nario, familiar from reports of shamanistic seances, in which the shaman
continues to interact with—and, often, to rebuke—his audience, even
while his spirit wanders through other worlds.

In one such seance, which Knud Rasmussen observed among the
Iglulik, the shaman produces "sounds like those of trickling water, the
rushing of wind, a stormy sea, the snuffling of walrus, the growling of
bear." After the seance is over, the shaman's wife explains that these were
the sounds of the route which the shaman, in the form of the Great Bear,
has been exploring for his audience's benefit. In another episode, again
reported by Rasmussen (from the Copper Inuit), the shaman visibly wrestles with the "Sea Woman" in the presence of his audience, while she
speaks through his mouth and charges the audience with taboo violations.
At the same time, the shaman apparently visualizes himself as being in the
Sea Woman's watery home; for he is able to report that her lamp is once
more turned the right way up.[34]

The Sea Woman's accusations of taboo violations immediately bring us
into Ezekiel's mental world. So does Waldemar Bogoras's report of a seance among the Chukchee, in which a female spirit, speaking through the
mouth of a male shaman, reproaches one of the audience for mistreating
bears. "Afterward she told another listener that she saw that in the last
autumn he had killed a wild reindeer buck" [317]. The shaman thus "sees,"
in his trance, the sins committed by members of his audience. Still in
trance, he rebukes them. This is very like the way I imagine the interaction between Ezekiel and the "elders of Judah."

If ethnographic evidence suggests that a seer may interact with his
surroundings while his spirit wanders in visions, experimental evidence

---

And I came to the exiles at Tel Abib, who dwelt by the river Chebar." Ezekiel correctly fails
to distinguish the "spirit" that carried him from his own. By shifting the source of activity
from the "spirit" to himself (with his use of *wa'elekh*), he shows himself aware that his travel
took place by normal locomotion.

34. Daniel Merkur (who quotes both passages from Rasmussen [369]) called attention to
the last point in a lecture given at Chapel Hill, N.C., on 17 March 1988.

suggests that the surroundings are likely to influence the content of the visions. Leslie H. Farber and Charles Fisher found that the spontaneous dreams of a hypnotized subject "are influenced by his own unconscious needs and the interaction of these with the hypnotist and any other persons included in the hypnotic situation." With a woman present, for example, he may dream "of climbing a staircase; of a sewer pipe running through a tunnel; of driving a car around the left side of a mountain into a tunnel" [330]. The experiments of Robert Rubinstein, Jay Katz, and Richard Newman point in the same direction. "The experimental situation itself . . . emerges as a major determinant" of the contents of dreams experienced under hypnosis or (at the hypnotist's suggestion) the following night [384]. These dreams express, albeit in concealed form (of which more below), "intense feelings about the hypnotist and the hypnotic situation" [378].

If we translate these findings into the biblical setting, we have a fairly clear picture of what might have been expected to happen when the hand of the Lord Yahweh fell on Ezekiel in the presence of the elders of Judah. He went into a trance. He experienced hallucinations that expressed both his prior unconscious concerns and his "intense feelings," conscious and unconscious, toward the elders who sat before him. On the authority of these hallucinations, he conveyed his feelings toward the elders both during the trance and afterward. It is no surprise that these elders should be stimuli and subjects of his visions, as well as their audience.

Certain features of Ezekiel 8–11 become more intelligible if we suppose that this was indeed the case.

To begin with, there is the curious survival of a second-person address in the Masoretic Text of 8:16. This passage describes the climax of the "abominations." Twenty-five men (twenty, according to the Septuagint) stand, their backs to the Temple, their faces to the east: *wehemmah mishtahawitem qedmah lashshamesh* ("and they were _____ eastward toward the sun").

The second Hebrew word in this phrase is unintelligible as it stands. Nearly all translators, from the Septuagint on, treat it as if it were the participle *mishtahawim*, "prostrating themselves." Yet the Hebrew text, impossibly, tacks a second-person plural suffix (*-tem*) onto the participle.

Admittedly, some manuscripts of the Masoretic Text do read *mishtahawim* [56]. But the more difficult reading is certainly ancient, for it is attested unequivocally in a midrash that the Palestinian Talmud attributes to Rabbi Hiyya bar Abba.[35] The text of the midrash is corrupt, but can easily be restored [155]. It explains the peculiar form as a hybrid, combining *mishtaḥawim* ("they were prostrating themselves") with *mashḥitim* ("they were laying waste"). The men were simultaneously "prostrating themselves to the sun and laying waste to the Temple."[36]

The medieval grammarian and Bible commentator David Kimhi (ca. 1160–1235) also saw the word as a hybrid and called attention to other examples of the same phenomenon: 1 Samuel 25:34 (*wtb'ty*) [212,259]; Jeremiah 22:23 (*yšbty . . . mqnnty*) [50,212]; and, most obviously relevant, Ezekiel 9:8 (*wn'š'r*) [50,212].[37] But he proposed a different explanation for it. Following Ibn Ezra, he suggested that it combined the participle *mishtaḥawim* ("they were prostrating themselves") with the second-person plural perfect *hishtaḥawitem* ("you prostrated yourselves"). Ezekiel, he explained, "found those men [in his vision] *prostrating themselves* to the sun; and he said to the men who had come [to consult him]: 'Have you [also] *prostrated yourselves?*' " [51,172,212,259].

Following Kimhi's explanation of the form, William Brownlee has suggested that someone had written *wehishtaḥawitem* in the margin of Ezekiel, as an allusion to Deuteronomy 11:16 and Joshua 23:16. This was then conflated with the text's *mishtaḥawim* [31].[38]

Most modern scholars have preferred simply to emend to *mishtaḥawim*, with the early translations and several Masoretic manuscripts. But it is hard to imagine how, as a simple blunder, *mishtaḥawitem* could have survived. More likely, the earliest scribes knew what the strange suffix meant. By the time its meaning was forgotten, it was too deeply rooted in the textual tradition to disappear entirely.

35. Sukkah 5:5 (55c). There were two scholars named Hiyya bar Abba: one lived at the beginning, one at the end, of the third century A.D.

36. The current text reads *mishtaḥawim* a second time, in place of *mashḥitim*. This makes no sense and does nothing to explain the peculiarity of *mishtaḥawitem*. Rashi and Kimhi (ad loc.) cite the correct text [212]. Their reading is supported by the Targum and by the derivative midrash in *Song Rabbah* 1:6, in which the citation of Leviticus 22:25 ("their corruption [*moshḥatam*] is in them") will make sense only if the midrash presupposes the interpretation *mishtaḥawitem* = *mishtaḥawim* + *mashḥitim*. (So *Mattenot Kehunnah*, ad loc. [208].)

37. Most modern scholars—including the commentators who dismiss *mishtaḥawitem* as a scribal error—acknowledge that *wn'š'r* in Ezekiel 9:8 is a hybrid. They explain it, plausibly, as combining the variants *wa'eshsha'er* and *wenish'ar 'ani*, both of which mean "and I was left [alone]" [50,104,168,297]. (Kimhi himself offers two different explanations of the form, in his grammar and in his commentary. I do not fully understand either of them.)

38. My teacher, the late Isaac Rabinowitz, explained the form as a combination of *mishtaḥawim* with *hishtaḥawayatam* ("their prostration"; cf. 2 Kings 5:18).

Kimhi, I believe, was on the right track. The word is indeed a hybrid, preserving a trace of a second-person variant that goes back to the speech of Ezekiel himself. But "you were prostrating yourselves" is better taken as an accusation than as a question. It is a "slip," in which Ezekiel reveals that the men he sees prostrating themselves to the sun are none other than his audience, the "elders of Judah" who have come to consult him.

I suggest that two versions of Ezekiel's vision of the polluted Temple were once extant. One, more faithfully reproducing the actual occurrences of the seance, preserved the slips and apparent inconsistencies in the words of the ecstatic prophet. The other edited them away. It is not unthinkable that Ezekiel himself may have been this editor. The versions will then represent, not different writers, but the same man in greater or lesser control over the language of his originally unconscious productions.

The Septuagint translators will have had the more elegant and less original of the two versions before them. The scribes whose text ultimately gave rise to the Masoretic Text had both, and conflated them. We will see in the next chapter that other divergences between the Masoretic Text and the Septuagint in Ezekiel 8 can be explained by the assumption that the former reflects the prophet's unconscious more directly than does the latter.

8. Ezekiel and the Elders: Pelatiah and Jaazaniah

This reconstruction of the link between the contents and the audience of Ezekiel's vision yields the key to understanding Pelatiah's death.

The event as reported is, as we have seen, difficult to square with the Babylonian setting of Ezekiel's book. Kaufmann's claim that it never happened outside Ezekiel's imagination is unsatisfying. But a hypothesis offered by Louis Finkelstein will, with appropriate alteration, suit the data.

The trance state described in chapters 8–11, Finkelstein thinks, revived in Ezekiel memories of a childhood visit to the Temple with his father. It was then that Ezekiel saw the idolatrous rites that Jehoiakim, under Babylonian pressure, had introduced into the Temple. "Decades later, as a prophet in Babylonia, he reconstructed the scene, as vividly as though he were passing through it once again. He could identify the very places of these nefarious crimes, he could see the faces of the transgressing priests, he heard once again the voice of God calling for their destruction." Pelatiah was among the idolaters Ezekiel had seen as a child. He was also among the "elders of Judah" who now came to consult him. "In his vision Ezekiel saw Pelatiah once more committing idol worship in the Temple. And as he was telling what he saw, Pelatiah fell down dead" [76].

Against Finkelstein, I would speak of Ezekiel's fantasy of Pelatiah's iniquities in Jerusalem, not his memory of them. (There is, as we have seen, no reason whatever to believe Jehoiakim introduced idolatry into the Temple.) Childhood memories, indeed, are at the root of the vision of chapters 8–11, but only in very distorted form.[39] Apart from this, however, I find Finkelstein's reconstruction persuasive. Ezekiel gave Pelatiah ben Benaiah, with the rest of the elders, a role in his hallucinations of unspeakable deeds perpetrated in the Temple. As we go on, we will uncover some of the grounds for Ezekiel's hostility toward the elders as a group. We will never know why Pelatiah got an extra share of this hostility. But it is clear that Ezekiel did single him out, along with his colleague Jaazaniah ben Azzur (11:1). Ezekiel's rage stirred up powerful and deadly emotions within Pelatiah, as a result of which he collapsed and died.

How could this have happened? Bible readers will recall the story of how Ananias and Sapphira similarly dropped dead in the face of Peter's rebukes (Acts 5:1–11). But a tale of this sort obviously cannot be used to confirm or to explain the death of Pelatiah. Fortunately, more up-to-date evidence is available.[40]

In the late 1960s, George L. Engel (then a physician in Rochester, N.Y.) collected 170 contemporary reports of people collapsing and dying when faced with emotional stress. The cause of death was occasionally known, and often assumed, to be heart failure. Most of these reports came from newspapers. But, in sixteen cases, Engel was able himself to confirm their details [329]. More recently, Bernard Lown[41] and his colleagues have devoted a series of investigations to the phenomenon of "sudden cardiac death," and confirmed on both clinical and experimental grounds that it can be triggered by an emotional stress [322,362,363,365,366,383,407].

Our concern here is not with Lown's formidable efforts to elucidate the physiological workings of the phenomenon, but with his and others' ac-

39. "If his mother had been insulted before his eyes," says Finkelstein of little Ezekiel's experience in the Temple, "Ezekiel could not have been more outraged" [76]. Finkelstein's choice of image is, as we will see, wonderfully perceptive.

40. I am very grateful to my wife, Rose Shalom, M.D., for directing me toward this evidence and helping me to interpret it.

41. Of the Lown Cardiovascular Laboratory, Harvard University School of Public Health, Boston.

counts of the psychological stresses that might trigger it. Engel found that, for men, the single most deadly category of stress is "personal danger or threat of injury, real or symbolic" (27 percent); whereas "loss of status or self-esteem" accounted for 6 percent of his total cases, 9 percent of the males. (Ezekiel threatened Pelatiah with both.) Lown and his colleagues established that interpersonal conflicts, public humiliation [383], and rage [407] can all induce dangerous irregularities in the heart's rhythm. Lown makes the important point that the stress that triggers such irregularities need not in itself be life-threatening. Evoking a painful topic, or bringing a painful memory to consciousness for the first time, may work a deadly effect on the heart [363,365]. In the next chapter, we will look more closely at one of Lown's cases [366], which will suggest just how it was that Ezekiel's word killed Pelatiah.

I am suggesting that Pelatiah's death is the one point, between the beginning of chapter 8 and the end of chapter 11, where Ezekiel's vision touches reality. This reality, however, is not that of Jerusalem, but of Ezekiel's Babylonian seance—which 11:13, like the -tem suffix in 8:16, allows us briefly to glimpse.

Ezekiel's mention of Jaazaniah ben Azzur (11:1) raises another problem, which my reconstruction of the seance will help us resolve. What is this man's relation to Jaazaniah ben Shaphan of 8:11? The two have different fathers, and therefore obviously cannot be the same. It is true that Jaazaniah (ya'azanyahu, "Yahweh gives ear") was hardly a rare name in Judah at the time of the destruction.[42] Yet it seems an odd coincidence that, of the three villains singled out in this one visionary complex, two have the same name.

Zimmerli, following Arnold B. Ehrlich, Johannes Herrmann, and Alfred Bertholet, wants to delete the awkward phrase weya'azanyahu ben shafan 'omed betokham ("Jaazaniah ben Shaphan standing in their midst," 8:11) as a gloss [297]. This is not very helpful, since, as Brownlee points out, it is hard to see what purpose such a gloss would have served [31]. G. A. Cooke's proposal that the two Jaazaniahs are the same after all, Azzur having really been the man's grandfather [57], is also improbable; why

42. The Book of Jeremiah mentions two Jaazaniahs: the son of the Rechabite Jeremiah (35:3; this is of course not the prophet); and the son of the Maacathite (40:8, cf. 2 Kings 25:23), who is probably the same person as the son of Hoshaiah (42:1). (Jeremiah 43:2, strangely, gives "Azariah" as the name of Hoshaiah's son; and the Septuagint has "Azarias" in both 42:1 and 43:2.) Lachish Ostracon I knows yet another Jaazaniah, the son of Tobshillem [14,83,285].

should Ezekiel have introduced this gratuitous confusion? Clearly enough, Cooke was troubled by the coincidence and felt pressed to find some connection between the two names.

Let us imagine that Ezekiel's vision followed patterns akin to those of dreams. Let us further imagine that at least some Freudian beliefs about the understanding of dreams are accurate. We will then suppose that a figure "seen" in a dream or a vision may be a "screen" for the person actually intended, whose importance the dreamer's consciousness is not ready to acknowledge. The insignificant "screen" figure and the significant figure lurking behind it may be linked by some superficial or fortuitous resemblance, such as identity or similarity of name.

A woman of Freud's acquaintance, for example, thought she remembered having dreamt of meeting her old family doctor. Freud was able to show that this recollection was a screen for her actual dream—of meeting her former lover, who shared the doctor's name [344]. Similarly, Newman, Katz, and Rubinstein found that hypnotized subjects dreamed about "relatively neutral procedures carried out by the hypnotist." But these were screens for "intense feelings about the hypnotist and the hypnotic situation," which the subjects had carried over from their past experiences [378].

Freud also proposed that a series of dreams on a given night will often express the same underlying thoughts, and that these thoughts will emerge with increasing clarity as the series progresses [336]. The screens, in other words, will gradually fall away, and that which they disguise will begin to declare itself explicitly. Laboratory experiments on dream sequences[43] suggest that Freud underestimated the complexity of their thematic development, but that what he had to say about the emergence of latent thoughts from their disguise was essentially correct [323,332,379,405].

Two examples will make the point clear. William Dement and Edward Wolpert describe a series of dreams that consistently express the dreamer's rage. At first, its object is a professor. But, as the series unfolds, the professor is replaced by a male acquaintance, then a female nurse, and finally the dreamer's mother. The true object of the dreamer's anger, originally concealed, is thus at last made clear [323]. William Offenkrantz and Allan Rechtschaffen tell of a subject who goes to sleep feeling angry

---

43. Which became possible after the discovery, in the 1950s, that sleepers show rapid eye movements (REMs) when they dream. I owe to Daniel Merkur most of the references cited in this and the next paragraph.

and competitive toward the experimenter. He then dreams of having out-witted an unidentified "rival," with the result that the rival commits sui-cide. In a later dream, however, the object of this murderous rage appears: the experimenter himself, cast in the role of the dreamer's lowly research assistant. At first, in other words, the dreamer prudently disguises his "rival's" identity. (The experimenter, after all, is a powerful figure who might take reprisals.) Only later does he become bold enough openly to subjugate and humiliate his enemy, in his dreams [380].

Applying these observations to Ezekiel 8–11, we are led to the conjec-ture that Ezekiel went into his trance with considerable repressed hatred against one member of his audience, Jaazaniah ben Azzur. Whether this hatred was entirely unconscious—we will later see reason to believe that Ezekiel carried it with him from his childhood, and displaced it onto Jaazaniah and the other elders[44]—or whether he initially forced it out of his awareness for fear of offending a powerful community leader, we cannot know.[45] In either case, Ezekiel will have used "Jaazaniah ben Sha-phan" in an early episode of the vision as a screen for the other, detested, Jaazaniah. Only later, in 11:1, was he ready to express his hostility openly.

This does not, of course, mean that Jaazaniah ben Shaphan did not exist. On the contrary, this hypothesis is best served if we suppose he was a prominent man, well known to Ezekiel and his hearers. There is no reason to doubt the widespread view that his father was Shaphan ben Azaliah, the scribe who conveyed the newly found book of the Torah to King Josiah (2 Kings 22:3–20), and that his brothers included the distin-guished scribe Gemariah (Jeremiah 36:9–12), the ambassador Elasah (29:3), and Jeremiah's powerful patron Ahikam (26:24, cf. 2 Kings 22:12).[46] But we need not wonder at "how far this son had departed from the conduct of Shaphan's family, which remained faithful to Josiah's reform and to Jeremiah" (Zimmerli [297]). Jaazaniah ben Shaphan may have lived and died the staunchest Yahwist in Jerusalem. He owes his villain's role in Ezekiel 8 chiefly to the accident that he had the same name as Ezekiel's bête noire Jaazaniah ben Azzur. He therefore could serve as vehicle for Ezekiel's repressed hostility.

44. "At other times the experimenter would appear as a character in one of the dreams. The subject appeared to utilize the experimental situation as a screen for the projection of transference reactions which were characteristic of his personality" [405].

45. I am grateful to Robert Segal of Louisiana State University for having stressed the importance of this distinction.

46. Who was the father of the future governor Gedaliah (2 Kings 25:22, Jeremiah 40:5).

Two other factors, however, may have influenced Jaazaniah ben Shaphan's appearance in Ezekiel 8. We learn from Jeremiah 29:3 that Elasah ben Shaphan was one of the two men who carried Jeremiah's letter to the exiles. We will presently see that this letter underlies the polemic of Ezekiel 11:1–3. Its bearer, and hence Shaphan's entire family, may thus have been at the forefront of Ezekiel's awareness at the time of his vision.

The second factor relates to Ezekiel's unconscious, and to the use it may have made of the name of Jaazaniah's father. The *shafan* is a small mammal, declared unclean in Leviticus 11:5 and Deuteronomy 14:7, which finds refuge (Psalm 104:18) and a home (Proverbs 30:26) in rocky cliffs. From these references, modern scholars have little difficulty identifying it as the Syrian hyrax [22,201]. A small creature, known for insinuating itself into crevices, it would be an ideal symbolic representation for the penis.[47] In the next chapter, we will see that the hidden chamber of 8:7–12 is (as Broome thought) Ezekiel's representation of the female genitals. It is not astounding that a son of *shafan*, a representation of the male genitals, should appear standing in their midst.

9. "Not Near Is the Building of Houses": The Situation of Ezekiel 11:1–13

Before pursuing this line of thought, I must defend my hypothesis against a potential objection. Is it really possible to regard the sinners of 11:1–13, "who devise iniquity and who give wicked counsel in this city" (11:2, RSV), as exiles in Babylonia?

The phrase "in this city" is hardly an overwhelming objection. As I have already indicated, *ba'ir hazzot* can just as well be translated "concerning this city." Similarly, the accusation in verse 6, that "you have multiplied your corpses in this city and filled its lanes with carcasses," may readily be taken to refer to the effects of the past or present political influence of Pelatiah and the rest in Jerusalem, and not to their current presence in the city. On the other hand, some of the threats delivered against them (verses 9–12) do seem to suppose they are still in Jerusalem. We will need to examine these passages more closely.

---

47. A symbolization of this sort may very well underlie some modern people's fear of mice [331].

But the decisive point lies in verse 3. Ezekiel blames the men for having uttered the slogan: *lo' beqarob benot battim hi' hassir wa'anahnu habbaśar.* The last four words can be translated, easily enough: "It [Jerusalem] is the pot, and we are the meat." In their context, they evidently convey that the speakers feel themselves and Jerusalem to be inseparable [56,104,297].[48] The first four words, literally translated, seem to mean: "Not near is the building of houses." What they signify has long been an enigma.

This much is clear from the responses of the commentators. Cooke tentatively proposes to interpret: "There is not going to be any destruction of the city, no need, therefore, to think of rebuilding the ruins." But, he admits, "This requires a good deal to be supplied in thought." The text, he thinks, must be emended, to supply the "evil plan" supposed in verse 2. He suggests *halo' beqarob nibneh battim: "Shall we not at once build houses? . . .* a determination to ignore what the prophets had threatened" [56].

Zimmerli cites a series of more or less forced interpretations, such as Fohrer's view that the remark expresses the "heartless attitude of the rich who regard it as unnecessary that men should 'soon' build houses for the poor." He confesses: "A definite interpretation of v 3a has so far not been made" [297]. Greenberg (following Fohrer) translates, "No need now to build houses." But he offers an alternative explanation: " 'No time now for building houses'—since all resources must go into the planned rebellion" [104]. Brownlee, following the Septuagint, treats the phrase as a question: "Is the time not near for building houses?" This means, he explains, that Jerusalem's leaders feel the city is now ready to resist a siege, and that "[n]ow is the time to improve upon the internal structures of the city, where the people flocking in from the countryside will be housed" [31].

All of these explanations, assuming as they do that *lo' beqarob benot battim* is spoken by people currently living in Jerusalem, have a strained quality. But, once we allow that the speakers are exiles in Babylonia, a very simple and plausible interpretation becomes available. With this phrase, they mockingly allude to the opening words of a letter sent them by the prophet Jeremiah.

Jeremiah 29 purports to quote a letter that Jeremiah sent from Jerusalem to the exiles of the first deportation. It gives no date for the letter. The events

---

48.   Kimhi paraphrases: "Just as people do not take meat out of a pot until it is cooked, so we will not leave Jerusalem or be exiled from it until our time comes to die; and then we will die in it" [212].

of the preceding chapter, however, are dated to the fourth year of Zedekiah's reign (594/3; 28:1, 17), and it seems a fair inference that Jeremiah wrote his letter not long afterward [25]. We may suppose that it arrived in Babylonia within the year before Ezekiel had his vision of the Temple (September 592, according to 8:1). Its prime addressees are the "elders of the exile" (29:1)[49]—a group that presumably included those "elders of Judah" who sat before Ezekiel.

The letter's message is that the exiles must prepare for a long stay. They will not be coming back to Judea, at least until seventy years have elapsed (29:10, cf. 27:16–22). It opens with an audacious statement of this message: "Build houses and live in them [benu battim weshebu]; plant gardens and eat their produce . . . seek the welfare of the city where I have sent you into exile, and pray to the Lord for its welfare, for in its welfare you will find your welfare" (29:5–7, RSV).

This message shocked at least some of the exiles. One of them, Shemaiah of Nehelam, supposedly wrote to a priest in Jerusalem demanding that he take action against Jeremiah. "For he has sent to us in Babylon, saying, 'Your exile will be long; build houses and live in them [benu battim weshebu], and plant gardens and eat their produce' " (29:28). If we are to trust this information, we can learn that some of the exiles felt themselves so securely tied to Jerusalem that it was madness (verse 26) to doubt they would soon be returning to it, and that the opinions of these men had substantial influence in Jerusalem itself. We learn, also, that they saw the gist of Jeremiah's message in its opening words, which could be used as shorthand for the whole.

Given the evident impact of Jeremiah's letter on the exiles, it is understandable that John Wolf Miller found it "all but unthinkable" (fast undenkbar) that Ezekiel can have failed to be acquainted with it. Yet, to his surprise, he could find no trace of the letter's influence in Ezekiel, apart from an echo of the advice to build and to plant in Ezekiel 28:26 [211].[50] He did not consider 11:3, presumably because he assumed the speakers were located in Jerusalem. More recently, Jeremiah Unterman has noted a series of parallels between Jeremiah 29 and Ezekiel 11, and suggested that Jeremiah 29 may have been a source for Ezekiel 8–11. He juxtaposes the

49. Thus the Septuagint. The version in the Masoretic Text, "the rest of the elders of the exile" (yeter ziqne haggolah), is harder to understand, but does not affect the point made here.

50. The reverse problem, of why Ezekiel is not mentioned in Jeremiah 29 or anywhere else in the Book of Jeremiah [18], does not concern us here.

contrasting statements in Jeremiah 29:5 and Ezekiel 11:3. But, since he assumes that the speakers of 11:3 are in Jerusalem, he cannot give *lo' beqarob benot battim* its natural and obvious meaning [277].

The meaning is this: Ezekiel supposes that, like Shemaiah of Nehelam, Pelatiah and Jaazaniah know Jeremiah's message and reject it. They fit as cozily in Jerusalem, he represents them declaring, as meat in its pot. Surely they will soon go back home! Surely Jeremiah's "housebuilding" is not going to happen any time soon! "Not near is the building of houses."[51]

Ezekiel responds with customary ferocity. Jerusalem's real "meat" is the corpses of those who died in the siege that preceded the first deportation, which Ezekiel now blames on the men who sit before him (verse 6). As for them, God has already brought them out of the city (verse 7, keeping the perfect tense of the Masoretic Text). Yet their sufferings are hardly at an end. "You feared the sword, and the sword I will bring upon you" (verse 8).

Up to this point, Ezekiel's speech has done nothing to contradict my assumption that its audience is in Babylonia. But problems now begin to arise. Verse 9 may go either way. Its three verbs (*wehoṣe'ti . . . wenatatti . . . we'aśiti*) are all perfect with prefixed *we-*. We would normally assume that the prefix is *waw*-consecutive, and that the verbs are to be translated in the future tense: "I will bring you out of its midst; I will give you into the hand of strangers; I will wreak judgments upon you." So understood, the verse would seem to show that its addressees are still in Jerusalem. Yet *we-* + perfect is used in verse 6 (*umille'tem*) to refer to the past. It seems possible to ascribe the same meaning to these verb forms in verse 9 [20,157]. Yahweh will then have already brought the men out of Jerusalem, given them into the hand of strangers, wrought judgments upon them.

The rest of the passage, however, clearly speaks of the future. "[10]You shall fall by the sword; I will judge you on the border of Israel, and you shall know that I am Yahweh. [11]It will not be a pot for you, yet you shall be meat in its midst; on the border of Israel I will judge you. [12]And you shall know that I am Yahweh." How can these threats be reconciled with the hypothesis of a Babylonian setting?

51. Of course, we have no way to know the extent to which Pelatiah and Jaazaniah actually held these views. But Jeremiah 29:24–32 suggests that such opinions were fairly widespread among the exiles. Ezekiel's assumption, that he knows exactly what the people around him are thinking (11:5), may in this case have been basically correct.

Three possible solutions suggest themselves.

First, we may choose to follow Zimmerli, and treat all of verses 9–12 as an insertion [297]. There are reasonably solid grounds for doing so. Ezekiel nowhere else singles out the "border of Israel" as a place for judgment. It is possible to explain this threat with reference to an episode that occurred after the fall of Jerusalem in 587, when the Babylonians blinded Zedekiah and executed the nobility of Judah "at Riblah in the land of Hamath" (2 Kings 25:6–7, 20–21, Jeremiah 39:4–7). Following Ezekiel 6:14 and 47:17, Riblah can be understood as the northern boundary of Israel [107].

If 11:10–11 indeed alludes to the events at Riblah, we may plausibly infer that the passage containing these verses is a prophecy "after the fact." It will have been inserted into the text some time after 587, by a writer who naturally assumed that 11:1–8 was directed against the Jerusalemite nobles who later died at Riblah. Ezekiel 12:13, which can hardly be understood otherwise than as a reference to the blinding of Zedekiah, confirms that such "prophecies" were sometimes added to the text.[52] And, once verses 9–12 are excised, my hypothesis encounters no further problem.[53]

Easy as this resolution is, I am reluctant to follow it. The identification of "the border of Israel" with Riblah is not inevitable. Greenberg suggests other possibilities, admittedly less satisfying [104]; and I will presently offer yet another alternative. Further, one of my aims in this study is to show that a sound approach to Ezekiel and his psychology will allow us to dispense with most of the wonted critical manipulations of his book. I do not want to fall back on such a manipulation the moment I get into a tight spot.

A second possibility is that Ezekiel, having directed his prophecies against Jerusalem throughout the vision, now slides into the fantasy that Jaazaniah and the others are actually part of Jerusalem. He therefore imagines them suffering along with the rest of the city. In 11:1, Ezekiel "sees" them in Jerusalem. In verse 3, he represents them realistically, speaking as

52. The inference that 11:9–12 and 12:13 are insertions is not wholly inevitable, since one might suppose that the surrounding passages as well were written after 587. In the framework of the present argument, though, this is not an option.

53. The variations in the Septuagint text of verses 11–12 are irrelevant to the question. Codex Vaticanus omits all of verses 11–12; most other Septuagint manuscripts omit everything in verse 12 after "you shall know that I am Yahweh." Only the latter is likely to be an early variant. Suppose the end of verse 12 missing from the text, and it is easy to imagine how the rest was accidentally omitted: a scribe's eye jumped from the end of "you shall know that I am Yahweh" in verse 10, to the end of the same phrase in verse 12.

the exiles they are. But, by verse 9, he has come to believe they really belong in the visionary context to which he has assigned them, and predicts their future accordingly.

There is yet a third option, which will involve our interpreting 11:1–13 in the light of chapter 20.

The two passages, as we have already seen, have much in common. In both, Ezekiel is in the presence of "elders." In both, he declares to his audience—assuming my proposition, that the people attacked in 11:1–13 are the "elders" of 8:1—that he knows what they are thinking (11:5, 20:32). The episodes described are separated by about eleven months (8:1, 20:1). There is no reason to deny that the earlier vision may foreshadow some of the ideas expressed in the later one.

With this in mind, let us compare the sequel of 20:32 with that of 11:5. Ezekiel is quite sure that the elders intend to "be like the nations . . . serving wood and stone" (20:32). This, he says, can never be. God will bring the Jews out of their exile by force, as he once did in Egypt. "I will bring you into the desert of the peoples [*midbar ha'ammim*], and there I will enter into judgment with you face to face. As I entered into judgment with your ancestors in the desert of Egypt, so I will enter into judgment with you, says the Lord Yahweh. I will make you pass under the staff . . . and I will purge the rebels and sinners from among you. I will bring them out of the land in which they dwell; but they shall not come upon the soil of Israel" (20:35–38).

Wherever Ezekiel may have envisioned "the desert of the peoples" as having been located, he clearly treats it as an intermediate stage between exile and homeland, as the Sinai desert once had been. There, like their ancestors, the Jews will again be judged. Only those found worthy will be admitted to the land. The rest will presumably die in the desert, like most of those who left Egypt, or, like Moses, at the very border of the land.

Comparison with 20:32–38 will suggest the possibility that *11:10–12 treats not of its subjects' exile, but of their future return.*[54] "You shall fall by the sword" (11:10) will then correspond to 20:38, "I will purge the rebels and sinners from among you." The judgment "on the border of Israel" will become fully meaningful, as the judgment that will determine who is permitted to pass back across that border.

Can Ezekiel have imagined that the corpses of those who will fall in this

54. Verse 9 will then describe the past judgments God has inflicted on the Jews; verses 10–12, their future judgments.

"judgment" will be carried back to Jerusalem, by the survivors? If so, this will make sense of the strange remark in 11:11, that Jerusalem "will not be a pot for you, yet you shall be meat in its midst." The city will not be their protecting "pot"; nothing can protect them. Only their remains, chopped up like meat by the "sword" of verse 10, will eventually lie inside it.[55]

The reader may select whichever of these options he or she prefers. All will allow us to account for 11:9–12, without abandoning the exegetical advantage we gained by understanding the speakers in verse 3 to be the exiled "elders."

Ezekiel 11:1–13 thus confirms the argument developed so far. Ezekiel's prophecy in chapters 8–11 is directed essentially against the elders who sit before him. As in chapter 14, he denounces them not for crimes they have actually committed, but for abominations they have "lifted up upon their hearts" (14:3), "each in the chambers of his imagination" (8:12).

Ezekiel is perhaps occasionally correct when he thinks that "I know the thoughts that have crossed your minds" (11:5). There is no reason to doubt that some of his visitors, like Shemaiah of Nehelam, might have responded to Jeremiah's "Build houses!" with the retort that that wouldn't be any time *soon*. But, when he represents his visitors as worshiping the sun, or burning incense to strange beasts, it is the chambers of his own imagination that are at work. On this point, Kaufmann was right.

But how can this be? Ezekiel's confidence in his own delusions will, on this hypothesis, be baffling. His ability to inspire credence—not to mention sudden cardiac death—in precisely those persons he falsely accuses will be more baffling still.

The only possible explanation is that Ezekiel's accusations, though false, and though consciously known to his hearers to be false, were distorted representations of some psychic reality that all had experienced as irrefutably true.

This may be explicated with regard to the strangest of all the "abominations," which Kaufmann correctly believed to demonstrate the fantastic nature of Ezekiel's charges: the elders' burning incense to horrid creatures in a hidden chamber.

55. Following Rashi [212].

3

A Chamber of Horrors

According to the rules that apply to the interpretation of neurotic symptoms, her conviction
must have been justified; its content may, however, require to be re-interpreted.

—Freud, "A Premonitory Dream Fulfilled"

[344]

1. Ezekiel 8:7–12: Hebrew and Greek

The Masoretic and Septuagint texts of Ezekiel 8:7–12 are so different that
we are obliged to examine them in parallel columns.

Masoretic Text	Septuagint
[7]And he brought me to the opening [*petaḥ*] of the court. And I looked, and behold, one hole [*ḥor*] in the wall.	[7]And he led me in to the entry-spaces [*prothyra*] of the court.
[8]And he said to me, "Son of man, dig in the wall." And I dug in the wall, and behold one opening [*petaḥ*].	[8]And he said to me, "Son of man, dig." And I dug, and behold one door [*thyra*].
[9]And he said to me, "Come and see the wicked abominations that they are doing here."	[9]And he said to me, "Come in, and see the misdeeds that they do here."

¹⁰And I came and saw. And behold, every representation of creeping thing(s) and beast(s), loathsome thing(s), and all the idols of the house of Israel engraved upon the wall all around.

¹⁰And I came in and saw. And behold, vain abominations,

and all the idols of the house of Israel, engraved upon it all around.

¹¹And seventy men of the elders of the house of Israel, Jaazaniah son of Shaphan standing in their midst, standing before them, each one with his censer in his hand, and the (aromatic? thick? smoky?)¹ cloud of incense rising up.

¹¹And [there were] seventy men of the elders of the house of Israel. Jezonias son of Saphan, in their midst, stood before them. And each had his censer in his hand, and the smoke of the incense went up.

¹²And he said to me, "Have you seen, son of man, what the elders of the house of Israel are doing in the darkness, each one in the chambers of his fantasy? For they say, 'Yahweh does not see us; Yahweh has abandoned the land.' "

¹²And he said to me, "Son of man, have you seen the things that the elders of the house of Israel do, each of them in their hidden chamber? For they have said, 'The Lord does not see; the Lord has abandoned the land.' "

Not all of the apparent differences between the two have textual significance. In verse 7, for example, Greek *prothyra* ("entry-spaces") has a different nuance from Hebrew *petaḥ* ("opening"). But it is nonetheless a reasonable translation of the Hebrew word, and is used consistently for it throughout Ezekiel 8–11 (8:8 being the only exception) [202]. "In their hidden chamber" (*en tō koitōni tō kryptō autōn;* verse 12) could easily be a speculative rendering of the difficult *beḥadre maśkito;* which, I have argued in the preceding chapter, should be understood as "in the chambers of his fantasy." It is conceivable that the translator had plural *maśkitam,* "their fantasy," before him. But we need not assume this, and the point is of no importance in any case.

Other divergences, however, can hardly be explained without the as-

1. All of these translations are possible for *'atar,* which occurs only here in the Hebrew Bible [30,104,297].

sumption that the Septuagint translators had before them a Hebrew text different from ours.

Again, not all of the differences are important. It hardly matters for us whether the words "wicked" (*hara'ot*) in verse 9 and "us" (*'otanu*) in verse 12—both missing from the Septuagint—are original or not.[2] But others do affect our understanding of Ezekiel's visionary experience. Thus, the Septuagint has no trace of verse 7b: "And I looked, and behold, one hole in the wall" (*wa'er'eh wehinneh hor 'ehad baqqir*). The Masoretic Text has *baqqir* ("in the wall") twice in verse 8; the Septuagint does not have *baqqir* at all. The wall is missing yet again from the Greek text of verse 10, which renders "upon it" (*ep' autou*, without evident antecedent) in place of "upon the wall" (*'al haqqir*). It is not clear whether the text that the Greek translator had before him read "upon it" (*'alaw*) in place of "upon the wall"; or whether it omitted the phrase entirely, and the translator supplied "upon it" of his own accord.

The problems raised by the Greek text of verse 10a are particularly difficult. "Vain abominations" (*mataia bdelygmata*) stands in place of "every representation of creeping thing(s) and beast(s), loathsome thing(s)" (*kol tabnit remes ubehemah sheqes*). Presumably, "abominations" represents the Masoretic Text's "loathsome thing(s),"[3] and "vain" (*mataia*) is the translator's gloss. It is also possible that *mataia* is an error, within the Greek textual tradition itself, for *panta ta* ("all"; translating Hebrew *kol*, "every").[4] In either case, the words *tabnit remes ubehemah*, and perhaps also *kol*—that is, "(every) representation of creeping thing(s) and beast(s)"— will have been absent from the text that lay before the translator.

In verse 11, the Greek reading is itself uncertain: is the verb "stood" to be read as singular or plural? Our Hebrew text uses "standing" twice, once in the singular and once in the plural: Jaazaniah "stands" among the elders, who "stand" before their images. The translator's source evidently omitted one of these words; but because of the uncertainty of the Greek text, it is not clear which. And, in verse 12, his source apparently did not contain the word *bahoshekh*, "in the darkness."

To sum up, the Hebrew text that lay before the Septuagint translator seems to have been shorter than the current Masoretic Hebrew text by a

2. The Septuagint's omission of *'otanu* accords better with 9:9 (as represented by both the Masoretic Text and the Septuagint) than the Masoretic Text's inclusion of it. This argues neither for nor against the word's originality.

3. *Sheqes*, perhaps vocalized *shiqqus*.

4. So Cornill, cited by Zimmerli [297].

number of words, some of them important. In most of these cases, there is
no obvious way the words might have been omitted by scribal error, and
no reason whatever to think that the translator knew of them but chose to
leave them out. It follows that they must either have been deliberately
added to the text at some point, or deliberately excised from it before it
was translated into Greek.

Most scholars have supposed that the words unique to the Masoretic
Text—that is, the "pluses" of this text—are additions. This view is particularly plausible in verse 10, where *tabnit remeś ubehemah* disturbs the syntax
of the sentence, and is moreover very suggestive of the language of Deuteronomy 4:17–18 (*tabnit kol behemah . . . tabnit kol romeś*). This naturally
promotes the suspicion that *tabnit remeś ubehemah* is a gloss inserted by
someone familiar with Deuteronomy.[5]

Scholars normally suppose glossing in verses 7–8 as well. Emanuel
Tov's comments may be taken as typical. The Masoretic Text's pluses, he
thinks, "disturb the context. There was not yet a hole in the wall when the
prophet came there, since only afterward the hole was created." It is "not
natural" to distinguish between the original "hole" (*ḥor*, verse 7) and the
subsequent "opening" made by Ezekiel's digging (*petaḥ*, verse 8).[6] The
original text is that of the translator's source, according to which "the
prophet is told to dig, and behold a *ptḥ* is created." But, once the text has
been expanded, it appears that "there was a hole from the outset; the
prophet was told to dig and as a result a *ptḥ* was created. No mention is
made in the text of the 'enlarging' of the original hole, although according
to MT the prophet actually enlarges the hole. This tension within MT
betrays the secondary nature of the plus" [274].

The trouble with this explanation is that glosses ought to clarify the text
to which they are attached. The supposed glosses in the Masoretic Text of
Ezekiel 8:7–8 seem only to obscure it, and it is very difficult to explain
why anyone should have added them.[7] Besides, the point made by the

---

5. We will presently see that there is another explanation for the link between the two
passages.

6. Tov adds that "the *size* of the hole is not important; its sole purpose was to allow the
prophet to see through it." I do not know how he accounts for the subsequent command to
"come," which both versions attest in verse 9. It cannot mean "come to the hole," since
Ezekiel was already there. The most plausible understanding is "come in [through the
opening]." (So the Septuagint, and most moderns.)

7. The suggestion of E. Balla (followed by Georg Fohrer), which is perhaps the most
ingenious effort in this direction, nonetheless fails to convince. According to this hypothesis,
the verb which the Greek translator rendered as "dig" in verse 8 was not the Masoretic Text's

supposed "original" seems banal. Ezekiel had to dig—through a wall, presumably, although the Septuagint does not explicitly say so—and, once he had dug, there was an opening. Obviously there would be a hole once Ezekiel had made one. Why does he talk about it at the end of verse 8 (in both versions) as if it were a discovery?

The problem is solved once we recognize that, depending on our perspective, each of the two versions can be seen as the more plausible. As an account of a physical act in the real world, the Septuagint's version is certainly superior. It is indeed strange and awkward for Ezekiel to dig through a wall in which there is a preexistent hole, then to proceed through an opening into a small enclosed chamber.[8] But, considered as part of a dream, the action is perfectly natural and intelligible as the Masoretic Text states it. We need only suppose that its details are symbolic; and that their symbolism, like so much in dreams, is sexual.

Consider the "hole" (*ḥor*). The word is used in the dreamlike erotic sequence in the Song of Songs (5:2–6), where the lover comes knocking at the door of his sleeping lady. Marvin Pope's translation of verse 4—"My love thrust his 'hand' into the hole [*ḥor*], / And my inwards seethed for him"—may somewhat overstate the sexual imagery. But it is very hard to read this passage without supposing that it contains double entendres in which the "hand" is indeed the hand, the "hole" a keyhole in the door, and yet both hint at something far more intimate [227]. (The dripping liquid myrrh of verse 5 obviously suits this understanding.) Assume the same symbolic meaning for the "hole" of Ezekiel 8:7, and it will no longer astonish us that Ezekiel proceeds to "dig" in it.

The root *ḥtr* means not merely to dig, but, in most cases, to dig into some sort of enclosed space: a chamber (Ezekiel 8:8), a house (Exodus 22:1; cf. Jeremiah 2:34, Job 24:16), the protective enclosure of Sheol (Amos 9:2). The only exceptions are Ezekiel 12, which reverses the normal pattern in

---

ḥatar, but *ḥafar*—which can mean "to seek out" as well as "to dig." Hence, in the original text that lay before the translator, God told Ezekiel to "look around" for something, whereupon "I looked around, and behold one door." Thus the expansions in the Masoretic Text rest on the misreading and/or misunderstanding of *ḥafar* as "to dig" [81]. This proposal does nothing to explain why God should have required Ezekiel to hunt for the door, instead of simply leading him to it, as he does throughout chapter 8. We shall presently see other reasons to keep the reading *ḥatar*.

8. The text does not explicitly speak of a chamber, at least before verse 12. But there is no other way to envision a situation in which images are "engraved on the wall all around," and people can stand before them all.

having Ezekiel dig himself *out* of his house (verses 5, 7, 12; see Excursus), and Jonah 1:13, in which sailors caught in a storm try to "dig" their way back to dry land (with their oars, presumably).

Exodus 22:1 certainly uses the noun *maḥteret* for the act of burglary. So, apparently, does Jeremiah 2:34. Yet the context of the latter passage is concerned with sexual behavior. We may suspect that its author has added an erotic nuance to the text from Exodus, upon which he evidently depends [77]; and that "digging" has for him a sexual overtone.

The use of the verb *ḥatar* in Job 24:16 strengthens this suspicion. "He digs into houses in the nighttime; by day they seal themselves up; they do not know light." Most commentators suppose that the subject of these verbs is the "thief" mentioned at the end of verse 14 [70,100,102,123,226, 243,289]. Yet this demands that the text be rearranged; for the intervening verse 15 speaks, not of the thief, but of the adulterer. If we suppose, however, that the author used "digging into houses" (*ḥatar . . . battim*) as an expression for sexual activity, the current sequence will make excellent sense. We will also be able to understand, as Pamela E. Kinlaw[9] has ingeniously proposed, the otherwise puzzling shift from singular "he digs" (*ḥatar*) to plural "they seal" (*ḥittemu*). The subject of the first verb is the adulterer. The subject of the second is his lovers; who "seal themselves" by day—as if they, like the chaste bride of Song 4:12, were a "sealed fountain" (*ma'yan ḥatum*)—yet who are open enough to his clandestine "digging."[10]

Amos 9:2 may perhaps also use the image of "digging" into the female sexual organs in a rather different sense. Jonah 2:3 speaks of the "womb of Sheol"; Job expects to return to his "mother's womb" (1:21), which can hardly be other than Sheol; and the Book of Proverbs, as we shall presently see, links Sheol with the womb and with female sexuality (7:27, 30:16). It is at least thinkable that the Amos passage also envisions Sheol as a womb, which one can dig one's way back into when threatened.

Biblical usage thus strongly suggests that *ḥor* can indicate the female genitals; and that the verb *ḥatar* is particularly appropriate for the act of "digging" in them—and through them, into the enclosure beyond.[11]

9. My research assistant, to whom I owe most of the information in this paragraph.

10. The idea will then be precisely parallel to that expressed in Herbert Kretzmer's lyrics for the musical *Les Misérables:* "You play a virgin in the light / But need no urgin' in the night!" [411]. Or, as an ancient Mesopotamian writer put it (see section 3): "By night there is not a good housewife, / By night a married woman creates no difficulty" [182].

11. If it is permitted to invoke modern Hebrew usage, I have heard Israeli men use *ḥafar bah* ("digging in her") to refer to intercourse. The verb is *ḥafar* rather than *ḥatar*, but the sexual use of "digging" is the same.

Broome had excellent reason to suppose this to be the underlying meaning of Ezekiel 8:7–12 [29].

Surely Ezekiel was not consciously aware of this, any more than we are normally conscious of the meanings of our dreams. His "vision," like ours, came to him as a symbolic picture. He understood it, as we normally do, according to its surface meaning, and went on to insist that this surface meaning was objective reality. Only the cracks in this surface—what Tov calls the "tension within MT" [274]—betray the unconscious significance beneath.

The version preserved in the Septuagint is best understood as an effort to smooth this surface. It reshapes verses 7–8 to accord with the standards of daylight reality. It suppresses the most obvious clues to the passage's underlying sexual meaning: the erotically charged word ḥor, and the detail that the ḥor was already present before Ezekiel started digging in it. It omits the word "wall" (qir) throughout, perhaps for similar reasons: the word might evoke associations with the thoughts underlying 23:14, in which the phrase "engraved upon the wall" (8:10) recurs, this time in a blatantly sexual context.[12] The same motives, as we will see, probably account for this version's abbreviation of 8:10.

The creation of this shorter version resembles the process of "secondary revision" of dreams, as Freud described it. The original dream is incoherent, therefore unacceptable to waking consciousness. Consciousness reshapes it, rationalizes it, and in the process distorts and further conceals its original meaning [337,343]. The distinction between the "revised" and "unrevised" dream is akin to, though not quite the same as, the distinction between a dream as written down on awakening, and the same dream as remembered two or three hours later.

If we take this analogy seriously, it raises the possibility that both the Masoretic *and* the Septuagint versions of the Temple vision may be the authentic words of Ezekiel.

We may imagine that the Masoretic Text preserves elements of an immediate, raw, and partly incoherent account of the images that flooded in upon Ezekiel's consciousness during his trance.[13] This material may reflect, as I suggested in Chapter 2, his utterances to the elders while in trance, perhaps written down by someone in his audience. Some time after he returned to normal consciousness, Ezekiel reviewed this material,

12. *Meḥuqqeh 'al ḥaqqir.* We will examine Ezekiel 23 more closely in Chapter 4.

13. Daniel I. Block has offered a parallel explanation of the grammatical and stylistic irregularities of Ezekiel 1 [21].

revising it in accord with what his conscious logic told him he must have seen. In the process, he suppressed features of his vision that pointed to concerns too disturbing to be consciously acknowledged. It was this revised version that eventually fell into the hands of the Greek translator.

This proposal accords with, extends, and is to a great extent inspired by Moshe Greenberg's important discussion of the Hebrew and Greek texts of Ezekiel 2:1–3:11. Greenberg argues that both versions may be authentic, in the sense that both go back to the time (within a generation or two of the prophet himself) when Ezekiel's messages were first collected. Unless there is obvious textual corruption in one or the other, divergence between them is no reason to "correct" one in accord with the other [117].

I find Greenberg's arguments entirely persuasive. They invite speculation—which Greenberg himself undertakes only very hesitantly—on how the two versions of the same oracles might have come into existence. I now suggest that a psychoanalytic perspective will allow us to discharge this task, for at least one portion of the text,[14] by tracing the two versions back to conflicting forces within the man whom both correctly claim as their author.

I am in almost complete agreement, too, with a comment Daniel Merkur makes about the *merkabah* vision:

> Most modern scholars impeach whatever does not conform to their expectations that God, and therefore the "original" content of Ezekiel's vision, must be logical and coherent. The result is a consensus effort to rewrite the extant text—a practice already commenced in the Septuagint translation of the Bible—by omitting the very features that are of the keenest interest to psychoanalytic research. [371]

I disagree with Merkur only in that I would not credit the Septuagint's "rewriting" to the translator, who may be presumed to have faithfully rendered the Hebrew text that lay before him. It was Ezekiel himself who had the best reason to omit from his vision "the very features that are of the keenest interest to psychoanalytic research." These were the features that, had he contemplated them, might have taught him things about himself he could not bear to learn.

14. Others, I hope, will be encouraged to test how well my hypothesis applies to the divergences of Septuagint and Masoretic Text throughout the Book of Ezekiel.

In his need not to know himself, as in so much else, Ezekiel shows himself to have been our true brother.

2. The Dread of the Chamber: Cross-Cultural Evidence

Ezekiel, then, unconsciously imagines himself penetrating the female genitals into the chamber within. What he sees there fills him with loathing and rage. Why?

Broome, whom I have followed to this point, supposes that Ezekiel has come to see himself as female. "The digging, the little door, and the small room are symbolic of the act of coitus, but the experience is abominable to Ezekiel now that his 'feeling that he is a woman' makes it so" [29].

Broome's explanation may be right, as applied to some of the deeper levels of Ezekiel's psyche. In what follows, we will see traces in Ezekiel of a homosexual fascination, which may accord with his "feeling that he is a woman." Yet there is also a simpler explanation, which well fits the more overt aspects of Ezekiel's personality, for why 8:7–12 represents the inside of the female body as a locus of horror and corruption.

Male dread of the female, of female sexuality, and of the female sexual organs is, if not universal, known from many different cultures and many different periods. Psychoanalytic writers have variously explained the roots of this terror, which seems irrational to the point of incomprehensibility [308,324,351,353,358]. But that it exists, and that it has done incalculable injury to human happiness, seems beyond question.

Writers of Freudian inclination who have explored the topic normally agree that the dread is somehow rooted in the male child's relation to his mother. They offer three main explanations for it, which, although distinct, tend to overlap, and can easily coexist. The first of these supposes that the small child, particularly the male, must struggle to distinguish himself from his mother, and thus comes to see her as an engulfing threat to his individual existence [350]. The second presumes that the infant at the breast wants to gobble up his mother. He projects this desire onto her, and therefore fantasizes her as a monster who wants to gobble *him* up. We will see in Chapter 4 that this theme, of the child's being eaten up, was important for Ezekiel.

A third option, which Philip Slater has argued in detail for ancient Greece [395], brings societal factors into the explanation. In cultures where mothers are given all or most of the responsibility for bringing up children, and where they are at the same time socially restricted and sexually frustrated, they take out their anger on their little sons and make sexual demands on them. The little boys thus grow up with an image of woman as an immensely powerful, malevolent, and sexually rapacious being. This image leads them, as adults, to maintain the traditional restrictions on women, and thus to keep the vicious cycle turning.

Jungians, no less than Freudians, recognize the reality of this dread, and the need to account for it. But they approach the problem from a different perspective. Erich Neumann has gathered and analyzed a wealth of pictorial materials and artifacts from all over the world relating to the "Terrible Mother." He denies that the fear of her can be rooted in actual mother-child relationships, or that it afflicts men alone. Men and women alike, Neumann claims, share an archetypal perception of consciousness as male, the engulfing and retarding unconscious as female. It follows that the "evil" female must be fought off if the precious consciousness is to come into its own. This contest properly belongs in the realm of the archetypes. But men and women who are unaware of this naturally tend to project it onto each other; and the result is sexual fear and hostility [375].[15]

In what follows, I will proceed on the assumption that some combination of Freudian approaches will best explain the phenomenon as a whole, and will be our most useful tool in elucidating the Book of Ezekiel. I do not insist on this point. What is crucial for us now is not what causes the dread of the female, but how this dread manifests itself in male psychology—and how these manifestations will help us make sense of Ezekiel 8.

The male, says Neumann, tends to conceive the feminine "as avid womb," which "attracts the male and kills the phallus within itself in order to achieve satisfaction and fecundation" [377]. This perception may express itself in the belief that folklorists refer to as *vagina dentata:* the notion that the female genitals contain teeth, or some other implements hard and sharp enough to mutilate horribly anything inserted in them. Wolfgang Lederer calls this belief "incredibly prevalent," citing examples from Native American myths and from India [328,359]. It has been known in the

---

15. Robert Segal called my attention to the importance of Neumann's work for this study.

more advanced technological societies as well. "In China, they used to tell in the Army, the women put razor blades in their cunts in case the Japanese tried rape; Rabbit's scrotum shrivels at the thought" (John Updike [418]).

A variant of the *vagina dentata* motif is the belief that the female sex organs contain some noxious creatures, or indeed swarms of them. This notion crops up in cultures widely scattered, where the possibility of direct influence is remote or altogether excluded. Verrier Elwin quotes stories of women with snakes in their vagina, who cut off the penises of their lovers—from the folklore of India, and also from the fourteenth-century *"Voiage"* of Sir John Maundeville [328]. ("Of old tyme, men hadden ben dede for deflourynge of Maydenes that hadden Serpentes in hire Bodyes, that stongen men upon hire Zerdes, that thei dyeden anon.") A nineteenth-century representation of Kali shows her waist belted with a cobra, whose head emerges from before her genitals; a Peruvian jar depicts a Gorgon-like goddess as "a belly with snakes" [376]. In a legend of the Mehinaku Indians of Brazil, "Spirit Woman" warns the sun, who has just propositioned her: "My vagina is very dangerous and frightening. Inside there is Stinging Ant . . . snakes . . . Scorpion. . . . There are many of these between my labia too. I am really dangerous and frightening" [349]. A Korean story tells of a "widow into whose vagina a mouse accidentally runs, later biting the penis of her lover"; an American variant has an eel in place of the mouse; a British story, intended to be funny, has a cheap prostitute's vagina infested with maggots [360].

Such are the creatures some men have imagined to reside in the sexual organs of real, or at least life-sized, females. When the female is mythically gigantic, or when her organs are symbolically represented by caverns or chambers, the creatures inside her can be imagined as larger and more menacing. H. R. Hays calls attention to Milton's description (*Paradise Lost*, book 2) of Sin as a female monster who guards the gates of Hell. She "seem'd Woman to the waste, and fair, / But ended foul in many a scaly foud / Voluminous and vast, a Serpent arm'd / With mortal sting." She is surrounded by hideous "Hell Hounds," who, "when they list, would creep, / . . . into her woomb, / And kennel there. . . ." [352,414].

Among the images, from men's dreams, that Karen Horney takes to represent the dreaded vagina is that of "a cellar with uncanny, blood-stained plants and animals" [353]. What manner of uncanny animals these might be is indicated by an episode from the 1940 fantasy film, *The Thief of Baghdad*.

In this sequence, an enormous djinni carries one of the heroes, a young thief named Abu, to the far-away "Temple of the Dawn." There Abu is to climb to the forehead of a gigantic image of the "Goddess of Light" and steal the "All-Seeing Eye" from her forehead. The djinni pushes Abu through the doors of the temple (he is too big to get more than his arm through them) and blows him to the base of the statue. Abu enters the hollow statue and "begins his climb to the forehead, ascending a huge web. Far below awaits an octopus pit; above, the giant spider of the web. Abu sees skeletons entombed in the grip of the web and then spots the spider. Warding off the monstrous arachnid with his sword, Abu cuts the strand of web holding the spider, and it falls into the octopus pit." Only then can Abu climb out to the goddess's face through one of her eyes, climb up to her forehead, and take from it the All-Seeing Eye [416,419].

Jacques Schnier, who calls attention to this sequence,[16] reasonably suggests that "Scylla and Charybdis, the spider and the octopus, are manifestations of the same unconscious fear of the mother" [387]. This fear is transferred to the female body, which the film represents by the goddess's temple as well as by her image. Abu, who seems to function as an extension of the djinni's arm, will then stand for the penis, which serves here as surrogate for the entire man. Like Ezekiel, who also is brought into a temple, he enters into the hollow within the woman. And, like Ezekiel, he finds dreadful creatures awaiting him.

A considerably grimmer version of the *Thief of Baghdad* fantasy, which leaves no doubt about its sexual symbolism, occurs in a 1973 issue of *House of Mystery* comics. The story is called "The Exterminator." An attractive widow, one "Mrs. Latrodectus," entices the title character to her mansion with the promise of their "celebrat[ing] together." Drawn on by her "haunting melodious voice," he plunges into a dark room in the mansion, crying out "I'm coming!" There he finds himself caught in a giant spider web, and (as the story ends) looks up to see a huge spider with a woman's head descending on him. "You should have known that **Latrodectus** is the scientific name for the black widow spider—and that the female black widow **always devours her mate!**" [307].

All of these creatures—from scorpions and stinging ants to "Hell Hounds" and giant spiders—seem to me cognate to the "creeping things

---

16. Without, unfortunately, naming the film from which it comes. My research assistant, Dexter Hall, identified the film for me and located the literature describing it by dint of tireless and creative detective work.

and beasts, loathsome things" that Ezekiel's hallucination locates in the chamber on the other side of the hole.

3. The Dread of the Chamber: Ancient Near Eastern Evidence

I anticipate two objections to this hypothesis.

The first is methodological. Not everyone will be comfortable with my using *The Thief of Baghdad* or *House of Mystery* comics to interpret the Book of Ezekiel. The material I have assembled is eclectic, and derives from a variety of disparate cultures, all of them separated from Ezekiel by more than two thousand years. My case would be more convincing if I could produce evidence for horrific sexual fantasies of this sort from the Bible itself, or at least from the literature of the ancient Near East.

The second is textual. The argument of the preceding section rests heavily on Ezekiel's having seen "representations of creeping things and beasts" (*tabnit remes ubehemah*) in his hidden chamber. Yet, as we have seen, the text that lay before the Greek translator apparently omitted these words. The sentence reads more easily without them; and their resemblance to Deuteronomy 4:17–18 suggests the possibility that they are a gloss based on that passage. Can they be retained for Ezekiel? And, if not, what will be the effect on my argument?

We must reserve discussion of the second issue for section 6, and focus our attention on the first.

It is possible to respond to the first objection in general terms. Even if I am not able to produce the evidence my critics demand, this failure is hardly damning. The images of sexuality we have examined, after all, are not ones that most people dwell on with any great pleasure. They are crude and frightening. Contemplating them, one is led toward thoughts that few care consciously to entertain. It is natural that they will often be banished from a society's higher cultural expressions. In our culture, they will tend to appear in comic books parents would prefer their children not read. In societies that do not produce comic books, they will circulate in oral lore that only anthropologists care to preserve. Only where such material is available in large quantities will we be able to uncover traces of these hidden terrors.

If no such traces had survived in the Bible, or in other writings from the ancient Near East, we would have no reason for astonishment.

Yet we do in fact have evidence from both biblical and extrabiblical writings of an irrational dread of female sexuality—sometimes expressed, in images similar to those we have already examined, as revulsion against the female genitals.

My colleague, Jack M. Sasson, has called my attention to W. G. Lambert's translation of a series of very peculiar Akkadian poems, which survive in fragments of cuneiform tablets from both Assyria and Babylonia [182]. Lambert dates the texts to the first millennium B.C. He notes that a few of the fragments were found in the library of Ashurbanipal (king of Assyria, 669–627) at Nineveh. It is reasonable to suppose that the poems were still being read within the half-century or so before Ezekiel had his Temple vision, even if they may have been composed a few hundred years earlier.

"The main actors" in the texts, says Lambert, "are named occasionally as Marduk, his consort Zarpānītum, and Ištar of Babylon, his 'girlfriend' (*tappattu*) or 'concubine' (*k/qinītu*). More often names are not given, though changes in person and gender of grammatical elements give hints but not explicit information." He adds: "Imagery of the boldest kind is commonplace, and the eroticism is the most explicit for ancient Mesopotamia" (page 99).

"Erotic," however, hardly seems the right word for lines such as these:

[Genitals of] my girl-friend, the district of Babylon is seeking a rag,
[To] wipe your vulva, to wipe your vagina,
[Now] let him/her say to the women of Babylon, "The women will not give her a rag
To wipe her vulva, to wipe her vagina."

[Into] your genitals in which you trust, like your precious stone before you,
Set your [. .] before you, sniff the smell of the cattle
Like something not mended by the tailor, like something not soaked by the laundrymen.

Into your genitals in which you trust I will make a dog enter and will tie shut the door;
I will make a dog enter and will tie shut the door; I will make a ḫaḫḫuru-bird enter and it will nest.

Whenever I leave or enter
I will give orders to my (fem.) ḫabḫuru-birds,
"Please, my dear ḫabḫuru-bird,
Do not approach the mushrooms."
Ditto. The smell of the armpits.

(Page 123)

There was apparently more of this sort, which has not survived. A "ritual tablet," consisting largely of incipits, quotes the opening lines of these poems, plus two others: "Genitals of my girl-friend, why do you constantly do so?" and "Genitals with two fingers(?), why do you constantly provoke quarrels?" (page 105).

One very fragmentary text begins pleasantly enough, but goes on to develop the repellent theme of animals in the female genitals:

In your vulva is honey(?) [. . .]
In its recesses . [. . .]
My seeder plough . . . [. . .]
That which is not pleasant of [your] vulva [. . .]
The sailor of [your] vulva [. . .]
The cook of [your] vulva [. . .]
The basket-maker of [your] vulva [. . .]
The lizard of [your] vulva [. . .]
The gecko of [your] vulva [. . .]
The cat of [your] vulva [. . .]
The mouse of your vulva [. . .]

(Page 113)

The point of these ditties seems to have been abuse of Ishtar, the most unabashedly sexual deity in the Babylonian pantheon [150,179,282,291].[17] The poet, or one of his characters, makes the point explicitly: "In my hostility to Ištar of Babylon, / For shade or open air I have covered my side" (page 109).[18] They were evidently intended for recitation in the goddess's presence, in "the street of Eturkalamma" where she had her temple (page 98). One line, entirely fragmentary and isolated, contains the words "as in the month Tammuz, the .th day" (page 103). Without a

17. Who, as the Sumerian goddess Inanna, glories in "her wondrous vulva" [292].
18. I cannot guess what the second part of this sentence is supposed to mean.

context, we have no way of knowing what to make of this reference. But it is at least possible that it alludes to the yearly rites of lamentation for the god Tammuz [122,234], who, as we will see, figured in some first-millennium traditions as a notorious victim of Ishtar's charm. His rites are well known from Ezekiel's hallucination of the polluted Temple (8:14), in which context we will presently consider them.

The writer's "hostility to Ištar of Babylon" must be taken as a vehicle for his hostility to the sexuality this goddess represents. Human women, he indicates in the same passage, are just as bad. "By night there is not a good housewife, / By night a married woman creates no difficulty" (page 109). Writing perhaps within Ezekiel's lifetime, he chooses to express his aversion with the image of the female genitals as a cavity housing noxious creatures.

This image was hardly his innovation. Pictorial representations of it survive from a vastly more ancient time. L. Legrain has published three seal-impressions from the predynastic period at Ur—perhaps the end of the fourth millennium b.c.—that depict a naked woman, her legs spread wide, her genitals very clearly marked [185]. In the first two seals, she is flanked by a pair of scorpions. In the third, she has a lizard on her left and, on her right, a scorpion whose tail is a snake. Other seals show a scorpion beside two copulating lovers [186] or (in a specimen from Tell Asmar, published by Henri Frankfort [85]) under their bed.[19]

We cannot, of course, be sure what the artists had in mind. It is at least thinkable that, as Frankfort and E. Douglas Van Buren have supposed, they intended the seals to represent the sacred marriage, and the scorpion to symbolize the fertility goddess Išḫara [84,278]. Yet Van Buren herself finds it "strange" that the scorpion, according to her reading of the iconographic evidence, "far from being regarded as dangerous to mankind, was considered to be a propitious symbol of fertility and prosperity" [278].

The data we have considered so far suggest an alternative interpretation. The seals express a perception of sex as a dangerous activity, and the woman's genitals as the locus of the danger. Her legs, invitingly spread, are gateway to a realm of lizards, snakes, scorpions. As the Mehinaku

19. Neumann reproduces two of Legrain's seals depicting the naked woman [374]. Pierre Amiet reproduces one of these, plus the two seals that connect the scorpion with copulation [10]. Pope uses Amiet's three seals, with two others, as illustrations for Song 5:1: "Eat, friends, drink, / Be drunk with love!" [228]. The upshot is that three of Pope's five depictions of the delights of love Mesopotamian style link sex with scorpions.

"Spirit Woman" put it, thousands of years later: "My vagina is very dangerous and frightening. Inside there is Stinging ant . . . snakes . . . Scorpion. . . . I am really dangerous and frightening" [349].

4. The Dread of the Chamber:
The "Strange Woman"

In the Bible, as we have seen, the "hole" (*hor*) can be an entry to erotic
pleasure when the lover thrusts his "hand" into it (Song 5:4, following
Pope). But, as in Ezekiel 8:7, it can lead to less pleasant things as well.
Isaiah's famous idyll envisions a harmonious world where an infant can
"play by a snake's hole [*hur paten*]," while an older child can "stretch out
his hand upon a viper's den" (Isaiah 11:8). In this imperfect world of ours,
the passage implies, a "hole" is not a particularly safe place to put your
hand.

Small wonder that the rabbis, who knew that a *hor* might be the work of
reptiles (Mishnah, Ohalot 3:7), were surprised to find the divine lover of
the Song of Songs putting his hand to such a place. "Is it not characteristic
of a *hor* to be a breeding place for reptiles [*megaddel sherasim*]?" (*Song of Songs
Rabbah* 5:4, cited by Pope [229]).[20]

The biblical usages of *hor*, however, can carry us only so far in our
search for evidence that the horror of the female I have attributed to
Ezekiel was a feature of ancient Israelite as well as modern American
culture. We have a more promising field in the Book of Proverbs.

Claudia V. Camp has demonstrated that Proverbs is filled with feminine
imagery, most of it highly positive [37]. The first nine chapters of the book
represent "Wisdom" as a gracious lady, nurturing (9:5) and life-giving
(3:16–18)—albeit with a certain tendency to vindictiveness if spurned
(1:24–31). Its last chapter introduces her human counterpart, in the robust
person of the "virtuous woman" (31:10–31). In between, we are told that
"a virtuous woman is a crown to her husband" (12:4), that "a woman's
wisdom builds up her home" (14:1), and that "he who finds a wife has
found goodness" (18:22).

20. A somewhat larger *hor* might serve, as in Nahum 2:13, as a lions' den—again, a
dwelling for dangerous animals.

Yet Proverbs also knows a death-bringing female, whom it calls the "strange woman" (*zarah*), or the "alien woman" (*nokhriyyah*). Scholars have debated whether these terms point to her being an adulteress (which she certainly is) and therefore socially marginal, or whether they designate her as a Gentile [204]. Camp (following Aletti [5,38]) has observed that the language Proverbs uses for her tends to parallel that which it applies to her benevolent counterpart. This suggests that the two are at bottom the same. The "strange woman" represents an aspect of the feminine the authors of Proverbs found disturbing, and which they therefore split off from those traits they were willing to attribute to "Wisdom" or to the "virtuous woman." Her "strangeness" and "alienness" then signify that this aspect is something "other" than what the authors can accept in a woman.[21]

The most striking trait of the "strange woman" is her uninhibited sexuality. It is true that the "good" women of Proverbs are not entirely lacking in sex appeal, as 5:19 shows. But, in this respect, the unacceptable female far outshines her approved sister. Contrast "Wisdom's" stately invitation to her public banquet (9:1–12), with the lush seductiveness of the "strange woman" who wanders in the twilight:

> She seizes him and kisses him,
> And with impudent face she says to him:
> ". . . I have come out to meet you,
> To seek you eagerly, and I have found you.
> I have decked my couch with coverings,
> Colored spreads of Egyptian linen;
> I have perfumed my bed with myrrh,
> Aloes and cinnamon.
> Come, let us take our fill of love till morning;
> Let us delight ourselves with love.
> For my husband is not at home . . ."
>
> (7:13–19, RSV)

And so, like the "exterminator" seduced by Mrs. Latrodectus,

> he follows her,
> As an ox goes to the slaughter,

21. The masculine *zar* is used in 14:10 and 27:2 to mean simply "another person," without any indication that he is a Gentile or socially marginal.

Or as a stag is caught fast
Till an arrow pierces its entrails;
As a bird rushes to the snare;
He does not know that it will cost him his life.

And now, O sons, listen to me,
And be attentive to the words of my mouth.
Let not your heart turn aside to her ways,
Do not stray into her paths;
For many a victim has she laid low;
Yea, all her slain are a mighty host.
Her house is the way to Sheol,
Going down to the chambers of death.

(7:22–27, RSV)

Bound up with the "strange woman's" sexuality is her mysterious deadliness. The author evokes her deadliness through a string of frightening images, but does not try to define it. In his various descriptions of the seductress, he comes back to this point again and again, but nowhere with any explanation. The lady's victim, whom she lures into her house, "does not know that ghosts [refa'im] are there, that her guests are in the depths of Sheol" (9:18). "Her house sinks down to death, and her paths to the ghosts [refa'im]. Those who come to her do not return, nor do they attain the paths of life" (2:18). "Her end is bitter as wormwood, sharp as a double-edged sword. Her feet go down to death; her steps support Sheol" (5:5).[22]

What exactly is the woman's threat? Adultery was, of course, a dangerous practice in ancient Israel. The author himself emphasizes that a jealous husband may well be unwilling to accept compensation, and turn to violence instead (6:32–35). But this explanation does not do justice to the ghostly terrors evoked in the passages, or to their insistence that the woman herself is the locus of danger and destruction. The ominous language points to a realm of thought beyond the rational. It is no wonder that William McKane (among others) finds himself looking for allusions to the underworld gods of Canaanite mythology [203]. But the relevance of

---

22. *She'ol ṣe'adeha yitmokhu*. RSV translates, for reasons that are not very clear, "her steps follow the path to Sheol," remarking in a footnote that the Hebrew has "*lay hold of*" (which is a thinkable translation of *yitmokhu*). The text is certainly difficult. I will presently suggest a way in which the woman's "steps" could be said to "support Sheol."

these mythological references to the author's purpose remains unclear; the fatal role of the woman remains unexplained.

The "strange woman's" resemblance to Mrs. Latrodectus points us toward a more effective solution. We have already seen that the *vagina dentata* and its attendant horrors have been part of the male imagination in a wide variety of cultures, the "advanced" no less than the primitive. Let us now suppose that they left their mark on the fantasies of some, at least, of the men of ancient Israel. It is in this complex of delusions—where the woman's sexuality is obscurely but dreadfully dangerous, her genitalia a place of death and destruction—that we will find the deadly power of Proverbs' "strange woman."

In a certain (very primitive) manner of speaking, that which enters the woman indeed perishes, or at least loses its strength. This is perhaps why her house is the dwelling of "ghosts," *refa'im*. The Hebrew word can be derived from the root meaning "sink down, relax, decline, withdraw, abate" [30]. It is therefore easy to imagine an unconscious association of the *refa'im* with the detumescing penis. Proverbs elsewhere warns, through the mouth of a "good" woman (the mother of King Lemuel), against "giving your strength to women, your thighs to those who destroy kings" (31:3).[23] What this warning expresses in the language of conscious discourse, 7:22–27 and its parallels convey in the far more effective fantasy-images of the unconscious.

The "strange woman's" Sheol, into which her victims disappear forever, will then have been inside her body. It is perhaps in this sense that 5:5 speaks of her "steps" as "supporting" Sheol. This interpretation gains powerful support from 30:15–16, which explicitly compares the "womb" and its appetites to Sheol.

> There are three things that are never satisfied,
> Four that never say "Enough":
> Sheol; the barrenness [?] of the womb;
> The earth, which never gets enough water;
> And the fire, which never says "Enough."

It is conceivable that *'oṣer raḥem* should not be translated (as it almost invariably is), "the barren womb," but rather "that which closes off the womb"; that is, the genitalia.[24] The issue of fertility versus barrenness,

---

23. Reading, with McKane [203], *yerekhekha lemoḥot melakhin*.
24. The root *ṣr* means "restrain, shut up, hinder, retain" [30].

which is generally of little interest to the Book of Proverbs [39], will then
be entirely irrelevant to this passage. But even if we keep the traditional
interpretation, the point remains that the womb and Sheol are both insatiable. It is only a step from here to identifying the two, and transferring the
deadliness of Sheol to the woman's body.[25]

Can we interpret along these lines the first five words of verse 15
(omitted from the preceding quotation): la'aluqah shte banot hab hab? The
meaning of this sentence, and its relation to what follows, are very unclear.
Its key word, 'aluqah, occurs nowhere else in the Bible. Most scholars take
the word to mean "leech," on the basis of Syriac and Arabic cognates. The
normal translation thus runs something like, "The leech has two daughters: give, give" [30,203,275].

This is, of course, something less than lucid. J. J. Glueck consequently
proposes a sweeping reinterpretation, based on another set of cognates, of
both 'aluqah and hab hab. If the sentence is read together with the rest of
verses 15–16, he points out, we get a numerical progression from two to
three to four. He suggests treating the entire passage as a unit, which
begins either "As for (erotic) passion, two maidens of burning (desire) . . ." or "Two girls are (addicted) to passion (excitement), fire, (and
three are insatiable and four never say 'enough')" [99].[26] But Glueck's
lexical proposals have not inspired much confidence; and McKane points
out that the two-three-four sequence he suggests has no parallel. McKane
therefore prefers to interpret the 'aluqah passage in isolation. But he is
unable to do so convincingly. ("Verse 15a is based on observation of nature, and the two grasping daughters are the suckers of the leech . . . a
parable of grasping greed in human society" [203].)

It is possible to accept the conventional translations of 'aluqah and hab
hab, and still to conclude that Glueck (and the Septuagint before him) were
on the right track. The content of the sentence seems well to accord with
what follows, even if we agree with McKane that it cannot formally have
been part of the same unit. The reference to "daughters" hints that, like
verse 16, the passage expresses some disparagement of females. It can
easily be interpreted in the light of the widespread fantasy that dangerous
creatures of some sort infest the female sex organs. Here, perhaps,

25. It is surely significant that four of the nine occurrences of "Sheol" in the Book of
Proverbs are in the passages we have discussed so far; while a fifth (1:12) can be linked to
these passages by way of the comparison of the "alien woman" to a robber in Proverbs 23:28.

26. The Septuagint seems to have understood hab hab in some such way. It translates
(literally) "with love beloved" (agapēsei agapōmenai), as if both words were from 'ahab, "to love"
[133].

women's genitals are themselves the leech, endlessly demanding their victim's "blood."

One more passage from Proverbs demands our attention. Proverbs 23:27–
28 compares the promiscuous "alien woman" to a "deep pit . . . narrow
well [shuḥah 'amuqqah . . . be'er ṣarah]." She waits in ambush "like a robber." She is thus compared to the robbers of 1:10–19, who promise to
swallow people up "alive, like Sheol."

Now, Proverbs 5:15 uses the "well" as a positive sexual image, urging
the young man to be faithful to his wife. "Drink water from your own
cistern, flowing waters from your own well [be'er]." The eroticism of Song
4:12–5:1 is considerably more convincing, but the point is the same [39].
The woman is there "a well [be'er] of living water, flowing from Lebanon,"
which nourishes a garden of delicacies and spices. She invites her lover to
come into "his" garden and eat as he pleases.

Proverbs 23:27–28 perverts this image. The woman's sexuality is now
seen as violent and unrestrained. It is, in a word, "alien." Her "well" is a
source of danger rather than nourishment—"a well of narrow diameter in
which one experiences intolerable confinement without even a firm founda-
tion for the feet. Apart from outside help and ropes there is no hope of
escape (cf. Jer. 38.7f)" (McKane [203]). This "well," and the "Sheol" of
7:22–27 and its parallels, are at bottom the same.

5. The Dread of the Chamber: The "Fountain of Blood"

If the "well" of Proverbs 5:15 can turn "alien" and terrifying, so perhaps
can the "fountain" (maqor [39]) of 5:18. If so, it must be avoided.

I suspect that there is a link between this pattern of thought and the
ruling of Leviticus 20:18: "If a man lies with a menstruating woman, and
uncovers her genitals, he has laid her fountain bare and she has uncovered
the fountain of her blood [meqor dameha]. The two of them shall be cut off
from their people."

Menstrual taboos are found, in one form or another, in a very wide
range of cultures, biblical and modern Judaism included. The problem of
what motivates them is exceedingly complex, and I cannot here go into it

in any depth. But, because some psychoanalytic anthropologists link it precisely with that complex of male sexual terrors that is our subject [320,398], and because it is particularly relevant to Ezekiel, I cannot leave it unremarked.[27]

The menstrual restrictions of ancient Israel were not, by anthropologists' standards, exceptionally severe. On William Stephens' scale of 1 to 5, they would rate at most a 3 [399]. They may have come into existence fairly late, and it is not clear how long it took for them to become widespread. In Genesis 31:33–35, Rachel steals her father's household gods, sits on them, and pretends she cannot get up because she is having her period. My research assistant Dexter Hall has pointed out to me that Laban shows no revulsion at her condition. It does not prevent him from searching her tent or, the next day, kissing her (31:55). Laban, of course, is not an Israelite. Yet it is hard to imagine the storyteller speaking so casually of menstruation if he expected his audience to feel any horror at it.

In 2 Samuel 11:4, David lies with Bathsheba when she is "purified from her uncleanness" (*mitqaddeshet mittum'atah*), which presumably refers to menstruation. John Van Seters's work with the "Court History" of David has cast serious doubt on the conventional view that it is a more or less contemporary document [281], and we cannot be sure that it is even pre-Exilic. As far as the antiquity of the taboo goes, therefore, this passage adds nothing to what we could gather from Ezekiel.

The Priestly Code of the Pentateuch takes for granted that the menstruating woman is ritually impure, and lays down detailed rules defining in what ways her impurity is contagious (Leviticus 15:19–24). But it sets forth parallel rules for a man with a genital discharge (15:1–15), and does not suggest that there is anything particularly reprehensible about either impurity unless it somehow comes into contact with the sanctuary (verse 31). It is very striking that P does not prohibit sex with a menstruating woman. A man who makes love to her shares her impurity and contagion, but does not seem to be punished (verse 24). Leviticus 12 (also P) compares the impurity of the child-bearing woman to that of the menstruating woman. She, too, has a "fountain of blood" (*meqor dameha*, 12:7), from which she must be purified.

27. I am grateful to Robert Daniels of the Anthopology Department at the University of North Carolina, for taking the time to discuss with me some of the issues treated in this section.

Only two biblical sources treat sex with a menstruating woman, not merely as a way of incurring ritual uncleanness, but as a serious religious offense standing apart from other issues of impurity. One is the Holiness Code (H) of Leviticus 17–26—normally assumed to be older than P—which prohibits "approaching a woman impure in her menstruation, to uncover her genitals" (18:19), and prescribes punishment for both man and woman (20:18, quoted above). The other is the Book of Ezekiel.

Thus, Ezekiel 22:10 accuses the Jerusalemites of having "raped women who were unclean because of menstruation," among other sexual atrocities. Their crime is aggravated by rape, but is not limited to it; for, in 18:6, the very act of "approaching a menstruating woman" is a sin comparable to idolatry and adultery. In two other passages, Ezekiel expresses the emotional stance that underlies these judgments. "They shall throw their silver into the street, and treat their gold as if it were *niddah*. . . . His lovely ornament . . . I have made *niddah* for them" (7:19–20).[28] "When the Israelites lived on their land, they polluted it with their ways and with their wicked deeds. For me, their ways were like the impurity of the *niddah*" (36:17). The word *niddah* is normally—not invariably, to be sure— used specifically for menstrual uncleanness.[29] "Severe loathing," writes Zimmerli, "in which what had previously seemed good becomes abhorrent and despised, finds a strong expression in this word" [301].

The first chapter of Lamentations similarly portrays menstruation as something shameful, disgusting, to be avoided. Jerusalem, represented as a noble lady fallen on bad times, had sinned. "She therefore became a *niddah*. All who had honored her despised her, because they had seen her genitals. She groaned, and turned her back" (1:8). The city "became a *niddah*" among its enemies (1:17).

The author of Lamentations 1 was surely Ezekiel's contemporary. The Holiness Code contains parallels to the Book of Ezekiel so striking that most scholars have supposed some direct link between the two sources [43,171]. Taken together, this evidence argues that the Jewish revulsion

28. Ezekiel 7:20 is difficult both textually and exegetically. I discuss it in detail in Chapter 4, section 4.

29. This meaning is clear in Leviticus 12:2, 5, 15:19–33 (six times), 18:19, Ezekiel 18:6, 22:10; likely in Lamentations 1:8, 17; possible in Zechariah 13:1. On the other hand, Leviticus 20:21 uses *niddah* for sex with one's sister-in-law, and Numbers 19 uses the phrase "*niddah*-water" (*me niddah*) for the water used to cleanse people from corpse-impurity (verses 9, 13, 20, 21). Second Chronicles 29:5 and Ezra 9:11 extend the word to "unclean" religious objects and practices. The meaning of menstruation predominates in the rabbinic use of *niddah*.

against menstrual blood was particularly strong in the early sixth century, especially in the priestly circles with which Ezekiel was connected.[30] It was they who turned this revulsion into a religious prohibition. Later on, its force perhaps waned. Later priestly writers, as evidenced by Leviticus 15, seem to have viewed menstruation fairly calmly, as one source of impurity among many.

Why did Ezekiel, and some at least of his contemporaries, find menstrual sex so repellent? Many scholars have approached the problem, reasonably, by linking this prohibition with others stated or implied in the priestly documents. Walter Kornfeld, for example, connects it with H's prohibition of eating blood (Leviticus 17:10–14). Both are directed against usurpation of Yahweh's right to blood, which is the source of life [178]. Howard Eilberg-Schwartz, disregarding the apparent difference between H's and P's attitudes toward menstruation, tries to find a place for the prohibition within the system of P's purity regulations. Menstrual blood, he suggests, is to be avoided because it simultaneously symbolizes death over against life, the female over against the male, and the involuntary over against the controllable [326].

All of these suggestions have some plausibility, and all may represent a part of the truth. Given, however, that menstrual taboos are found in societies the world over, it is at least worth asking whether there may not be some element of motivation common to all of them. Other motives, specific to the individual cultures, may of course also be present.

In 1962, the anthropologist William N. Stephens proposed one such universal motive. Psychoanalytic theory, he argued, will predict that certain cultural phenomena can be used as indicators of a strong Oedipus complex in a given society; and ethnographic data show that the expected correlations do in fact occur. Menstrual taboos are among these indicators [398].

In societies where women are kept from having sex for long periods after they give birth, they are apt to behave seductively toward their children. As a result, young boys "become sexually attracted to their mothers. This

---

30. Isaiah 30:22 seems to say that the people of Jerusalem will treat the silver and gold platings of their idols "like a menstruous woman" (the word here is *dawab*, used for a menstruating woman in Leviticus 15:33 and 20:18, and perhaps also Lamentations 1:13). Most scholars agree that 30:18–26 is not the genuine work of Isaiah [72,159]. We may suspect it is an Exilic composition, perhaps influenced by Ezekiel 7:19, which verse 22 closely resembles [104].

generates lasting fears and avoidances" (pages 48, 182). One such fear is the fear of castration; one such avoidance is the avoidance of sex with menstruating women. The link between the two is that "the sight or thought of a person who bleeds from the genitals . . . is frightening to a person who has intense castration anxiety. It is a reminder of genital injury" (page 93).

Surveying seventy-one primitive societies for which pertinent data were available, Stephens found high correlations between menstrual taboos and indications of sexual anxiety (punishment for masturbation, prohibition of premarital sex, folktales describing punishment for sex, and the like). These taboos could be correlated, too, with the long postpartum sex taboo—which Stephens identified as the root of the entire complex. He pointed out that most of the societies that have menstrual taboos perceive the menstruating woman as dangerous specifically to men. Seldom do they remark on her threat to other women, children, or to herself. This would suit the assumption that menstrual taboos are in some way linked with fear of castration, that they are intended to protect males from some hazard inherent in the woman's bleeding genitals.

If anthropologists had found Stephens's argument persuasive, his work would powerfully support the thesis I have advanced here. Most, however, seem to have been unconvinced. Karen Erickson Paige and Jeffery M. Paige find flaws in Stephens's methodology [381]. Thomas Buckley and Alma Gottlieb endorse the Paiges' criticisms, and consequently judge Stephens's correlations "statistically weak and more suggestive than conclusive." They add objections of their own. The whole notion of an Oedipus complex existing outside Western societies is open to question; so is the fundamental premise of Stephens's argument, that men impose menstrual restrictions on women for their own (supposed) benefit. They urge us to give up looking for some global explanation which will explain the menstrual taboo in all societies. Rather, each society's taboo should be explained from within that culture itself [320]. In explaining the Holiness Code's ban on menstrual sex, Buckley and Gottlieb would surely sympathize with the approaches of Kornfeld and Eilberg-Schwartz, against that of Stephens.

Where specialists differ, an outsider can hardly feel comfortable expressing a judgment. Surely we will not be justified in taking Stephens's conclusions for granted and using them as proof that Ezekiel's aversion to things menstrual must be rooted in his experiences with a seductive mother. (Which, as will emerge, I think is likely to have been the case.)

Yet I cannot escape the impression that Stephens's case is far more powerful than his critics will allow. The Paiges' objections seem to turn on two cardinal points. First, Stephens's data do not support the more ambitious structure of correlations proposed by his teacher, the neo-Freudian anthropologist John W. M. Whiting. Second, his sample of societies represents some parts of the world more extensively than others. Yet the Paiges do not make clear why this geographical imbalance—to which Stephens himself calls attention (page 68)—is supposed to be significant. They do not suggest that Stephens chose to report only on those societies that would support his argument, instead of (as he claims) taking into account all societies for which information was available. They show no reason to think that a geographically more balanced sample would have yielded different results. They do not argue for diffusion of practices from one society to another. And, as to their first point, surely it is enough if Stephens's evidence will support his own thesis? Surely he cannot be blamed for failure to prove his teacher's thesis as well?

Melford Spiro has, in my view, effectively met Buckley and Gottlieb's skepticism about whether the Oedipus complex exists in primitive societies [397]. Their point, that we should not simply assume that menstrual taboos are imposed by men on women, and not by women on themselves, is well taken. (They do not remark that Stephens had anticipated that objection and tried to respond to it.) But the evidence they put forward for the contrary position—a paper by Denise L. Lawrence showing that rural Portuguese women make strategic use of menstrual taboos in their competition with their neighbors [357]—seems hardly to prove the point. People can manipulate, for their own advantage, restrictions imposed on them by others.

If we are prepared to grant some truth to Stephens's argument, it has several implications for our study of Ezekiel. Ezekiel's "severe loathing" (Zimmerli) for the *niddah*, and especially for the idea of sex with the *niddah*, will be one more piece of evidence for the sexual psychopathology that I attribute to him. It will be clear, however, that his psychopathology was not entirely unique. He shared it, in some measure, with at least some of his contemporaries or near-contemporaries—the authors of Lamentations 1 and of the Holiness Code.

We may perhaps include the author of Proverbs among these near-contemporaries. The book is practically impossible to date. "Virtually all commentators put [its] date in the post-exilic period, although few offer concrete evidence for doing so, such evidence being difficult to come by" [47]. It is hardly fantastic to suppose that, at least in substance, it may be slightly earlier. Its terrifying seductress, luring men into her "Sheol," will then be a part of the common cultural pathology that reinforced Ezekiel's private pathology. Its image of the female genitals as an insatiable leech (if I have correctly understood 30:15) will be part of the background of Ezekiel's and H's abhorrence of menstruation. That is the time of month a woman's "fountain" turns to blood; when it reveals itself as the blood-glutted parasite that destroys the penis (= man) by sucking out its life.

Ezekiel's obsessive horror of blood, which emerges particularly clearly in chapter 16 (see Chapter 4), is one indication among many that his sickness was exceptionally severe. But we cannot entirely dissociate it from a broader sickness of his culture. Considered in this way, there is indeed a measure of justice in Carl Gordon Howie's plea (see Chapter 1) that Ezekiel's "strange words and ideas may not have been important deviations from 'the norm' established for that time" [143].

It is therefore very likely that some at least of the "elders of Judah" who sat before Ezekiel shared many of his unconscious yearnings and terrors.

This, as we will see, will help explain why they responded to his hallucinations as if they were reality.

6. Ezekiel 8:10, Deuteronomy 4:17–18

What, now, of the textual problem of Ezekiel 8:10? How are we to explain the omission of the "representations of creeping things and beasts" (*tabnit remeś ubehemah*) from the Septuagint text, and these words' apparent link with Deuteronomy 4:17–18?

By itself, the existence of the shorter version creates no difficulty. If we accept that the longer text of verses 7–8 more faithfully reflects Ezekiel's unconscious sexual fantasies, nothing prevents us from saying that the longer text of verse 10 is the more accurate and original representation of his revulsion at these fantasies. The shorter text of both passages will then have resulted from the partial censoring of these elements.

It is true, however, that verse 10 will read more smoothly if the words *tabnit remeś ubehemah* are left out. The resemblance to Deuteronomy 4:17–18 (*tabnit kol behemah . . . tabnit kol romeś*) also demands some explanation. It does not seem to be coincidental; and it is hardly likely that the

Deuteronomic writer has borrowed his phraseology from Ezekiel 8:10. Ezekiel himself, as well as any glossator, may have alluded to earlier Israelite literature [119]. He, as well as a glossator, may have allowed the allusion to disrupt his syntax.[31] This assumption is particularly plausible in that, as we will see, Ezekiel 8 elsewhere shows traces of the influence of Deuteronomy 4 [108]. Yet it involves us in some difficulty; for most recent scholars do not regard Deuteronomy 4:1–40 as prior to Ezekiel.

Since the original appearance of Martin Noth's *Überlieferungsgeschichtliche Studien* (1943), most have agreed that this passage belongs to a fairly late stage of the process by which the original Deuteronomic law code was incorporated into the Deuteronomistic history—roughly, the biblical books from Deuteronomy through 2 Kings—and that it is not earlier than the Exile [195,198,218,221,223,239]. If we accept this view, we must either deny that the resemblance of Ezekiel 8:10's *tabnit remeś ubehemah* to Deuteronomy 4:17–18 is significant, or else concede that these words are a gloss.

The concession will not devastate my hypothesis. The word *sheqeṣ*, which follows the supposed gloss, evidently *did* appear in the text used by the Greek translator. Since *sheqeṣ* ("loathsome things") is used everywhere else in the Bible to refer to ritually unclean animals,[32] the shorter text still implies that Ezekiel saw repellent creatures of some sort. But there is no question that its image of those creatures is far less vivid than that of the Masoretic Text.

We must ask, therefore, whether the Exilic dating of Deuteronomy 4:1–40 is in fact beyond challenge.

When we examine the argument for this dating, we find that it rests on two main pillars. The first is the prophecy of exile and restoration in 4:25–31, which can be understood as intended for an audience that knew exile and hoped for restoration. The second is the position of 4:1–40 within the hypothetical structures that scholars, from Noth onward, have erected to explain how the Deuteronomistic history came into existence, and what its relation was to the law code of Deuteronomy 12–26.

Noth's starting point was the peculiar fact that the Deuteronomic code seems to have two introductions: chapters 1–4 and 5–11. Only the second introduction, he suggested, actually belonged to the code. Chapters

31. As does James M. McPherson, in his history of the Civil War: "These defenders of the South doth protest too much" [413].

32. Eight occurrences in Leviticus 11, plus Leviticus 7:21 and Isaiah 66:17.

1–3, which consist of a historical narration set in the mouth of Moses, are to be understood as an introduction to the entire Deuteronomistic history, extending to the end of 2 Kings. Since the Deuteronomistic history ends with King Jehoiachin's release from prison in 561 B.C. (2 Kings 25:27–30), chapters 1–3 cannot be earlier than this date. Deuteronomy 4:1–40, an appendix to chapters 1–3, will have been later still [218,221].

A.D.H. Mayes modified Noth's view in the light of Frank Moore Cross's theory that there were two editions of the Deuteronomistic history, of which the first was pre-Exilic and carried its narrative only as far as Josiah's reform. Deuteronomy 1–3, Mayes argues, was the introduction to this original Deuteronomistic history. Deuteronomy 4:1–40 is the work of the "second deuteronomist," who expanded and extended the earlier text some time after 561. Other parts of Deuteronomy—sections of chapters 6–8, 10–11, 26–29, and 32—are the work of the same writer, whose Exilic date is confirmed by the resemblances between his ideas and expressions and those of Jeremiah, Ezekiel, and the Second Isaiah [196].

It would be impossible here to enter into, or even adequately to summarize, the complex and ramified debate that has raged among biblical scholars over how many Deuteronomistic authors and redactors contributed to the shaping of Deuteronomy–2 Kings. The most recent study of the problem, by Mark A. O'Brien [223], includes a helpful account of the earlier proposals. O'Brien's own views are broadly similar to those of Cross and Mayes. The original Deuteronomistic history was written during Josiah's lifetime; the nucleus of Deuteronomy 1–3 served as its introduction; it was subjected to a series of Exilic and early post-Exilic redactions, the last of which was responsible for Deuteronomy 4:1–40 (along with chapters 29–30). The view that Deuteronomy 4:1–40 is a later addition to the Deuteronomistic history is "generally accepted" and requires no defense (pages 60–61).

To argue along these lines for an Exilic or post-Exilic date for 4:1–40, however, requires that we accept three premises: first, that Deuteronomy 1–3 cannot reasonably be understood as an introduction to the Deuteronomic code (as opposed to the Deuteronomistic history); second, that the "history" in question must be the complete history as we have it, down to Jehoiachin's release; third, that chapter 4 either is part of or presupposes chapters 1–3. Discard any one of these premises, and the date of chapter 4 is again an open question.

Each of them is in fact debatable. Structural analogies between Deuteronomy and ancient Near Eastern vassal treaties, whatever their full significance may turn out to be, suggest at least that a historical prologue to a law code might be very much in place [200,287]. Mayes, as we have seen, undermines the second premise by identifying Deuteronomy 1–3 as the introduction to the pre-Exilic edition of the Deuteronomistic history, and then arguing for the Exilic date of chapter 4 on other grounds. As to the third point, the beginning of chapter 4 shows that it cannot in its present form have stood alone; it must have served as the continuation of something. But we cannot be sure that Deuteronomy 1–3 was its original context.

It seems that, whatever solution we choose to give to the problem of how the Deuteronomistic history took shape, we can bring it into accord with the supposition that Deuteronomy 4:1–40 was among the pre-Exilic materials that its author (or one of its redactors) drew upon.

What of the supposed internal evidence for the passage's lateness? The most obvious is its prophecy of exile (4:25–31). This can, of course, be explained as a *post eventum* prediction of the Babylonian Exile. But this is not the only, or even the most plausible, option.

Deuteronomy several times threatens national destruction if the Israelites disobey its commands (6:15, 7:4, 8:19–20, 11:17, 30:17–18). Four passages—28:36–37, 63–64, and 29:27–28, in addition to 4:25–31—specify exile as part of the destruction. Yet all of these threats are vague and general, devoid of anything that would require knowledge of the actual events of the Exile [161,164]. The one detail they insist on, that the Jews will serve gods of wood and stone in the land of their exile, cannot be verified from other sources. (I will discuss Ezekiel 20:32 shortly.) The context of 29:27–28 represents exile as preceded by God's turning the land of Israel into a sulphurous waste, as he once did to Sodom and Gomorrah. This suggests that the exile in question is not the historical Babylonian Exile, but the climax of a visionary nightmare of retribution.

It is not, after all, very hard to imagine that pre-Exilic Judeans, contemplating the dreadful end of the Northern Kingdom, should have conceived the possibility that the same might happen to them. Nor is it difficult to think that the reforming preachers whose creations were deposited in the Book of Deuteronomy should have included this threat in their armory of intimidation.

Mayes's parallels between Deuteronomy 4 and Second Isaiah [196] are very general, and may easily be explained by supposing that Second Isaiah was inspired by the rhetoric of the older passage.[33] Parallels with Jeremiah or Ezekiel are open to the same explanation. Their implication will then be the reverse of the dominant view; namely, that the Deuteronomic passages in question are pre-Exilic.

Two such parallels, not discussed by Mayes, are particularly interesting. Jeremiah Unterman—one of the few recent scholars to dispute the Exilic dating of Deuteronomy 4—points out that the language of 4:29 parallels that of Jeremiah 29:13 very closely.[34] Yet the teaching of Jeremiah 29:10–14 is sufficiently distinct from that of Deuteronomy 4:29–31 to rule out the likelihood that both were written by the same Exilic Deuteronomist. "The conclusion must be that Jer. 29.10–14 is the product of someone who knew Deuteronomy but was not so influenced by it that he could be termed a 'deuteronomist' " [276].

The passage in question is part of Jeremiah's letter to the exiles (29:4–23). We saw in Chapter 2 that this document, which probably arrived in Babylonia within the year before the vision described in Ezekiel 8–11, was in the background of Ezekiel's harangue against Pelatiah and his colleagues (11:1–12). If Unterman is right, Jeremiah used Deuteronomy 4 as a traditional source, whose words, woven in with his own, would add weight to his message. It will then follow that Jeremiah expected his audience in exile to be familiar with that source.

Ezekiel, addressing much the same audience, perhaps draws on the

33.   Deuteronomy 4:16–19 provides a taxonomy of the elements of creation that might come to be worshiped; and this taxonomy, as Michael Fishbane observes, reads very much like a reversal of the order of creation in Genesis 1:14–27. Fishbane infers that the Deuteronomic passage is "an explicit aggadic interpretation of Gen. 1," which "reuses the very language and sequence of its prototype to indicate the typical instances of prohibited idolatry" [78]. His conclusion is possible, but unnecessary. There are differences as well as similarities between the language of the two passages. (Genesis 1 refers to birds as '*of;* Deuteronomy 4 calls them *ṣippor.* Deuteronomy 4 speaks of the sun and the moon as *hashshemesh* and *hayyareaḥ;* Genesis 1, *hamma'or haggadol* and *hamma'or haqqaṭon.*) Deuteronomy 4's sequence of animals (beasts–birds–creeping things–fish) does not precisely reverse that of Genesis 1, which has fish and birds created on the fifth day, beasts and creeping things on the sixth. Rather, it corresponds closely to the sequence used in Hosea 2:20, 1 Kings 5:13, Genesis 9:2. The first of these passages, provided we do not deny its attribution to Hosea, dates from long before the Exile; the second may perhaps derive its essential content, if not its precise formulation, from the early days of the Israelite monarchy (so Albrecht Alt [9]); the third is from P. Surely we are dealing with a traditional Israelite system for classifying the animal kingdom, which remained more or less consistent for centuries. The author of Deuteronomy 4 incorporated that system into his warning against idolatry; the author of Genesis 1 may have incorporated it, independently, into his narrative of creation.

34.   Deuteronomy: "From there you shall seek Yahweh your God, and you shall find [him], when you seek him out with all your heart and all your soul." Jeremiah: "You shall seek me and you shall find [me], when you seek me out with all your heart."

same source. In 20:32, as we have seen, he claims to know the private thoughts of the "elders of Israel" who have come to consult him (20:1). Their alleged intention is to "become like the families of the lands, serving wood and stone." Shemaiah of Nehelam's reaction to Jeremiah's letter (Jeremiah 29:24–28), and Ezekiel's furious counterresponse (11:1–12), suggest that the accusation of 20:32 is fantastically wrong. The opponents of Jeremiah and Ezekiel were so sure they were about to come home to Jerusalem that they could hardly countenance the idea of building houses and planting gardens in Babylonia, far less worshiping wood and stone. Where, then, did Ezekiel get his conviction that his "sinful" contemporaries were plotting to turn *en masse* to some crude idolatry? I suggest that he found it prophesied in the "Mosaic" teachings that are now part of the Book of Deuteronomy. "There [in exile], you shall serve gods that are the work of human hands, wood and stone" (4:28; similarly, 28:36, 64).[35]

If Ezekiel could allude (in 20:32) to Deuteronomy 4:28, we have no reason to deny that he might have alluded (in 8:10) to Deuteronomy 4:17–18. On the contrary, there is reason to affirm that he did just that. For, considered as a gloss, the allusion in 8:10 is banal. Considered as Ezekiel's own, it is a self-revelation, pointing toward what underlies the hallucinatory horrors of 8:7–12.

Let us look at the context in Deuteronomy 4. Moses warns the Israelites to remember well that "you did not see any image [*temunah*] on the day that Yahweh spoke to you at Horeb from the midst of the fire" (verse 15), lest they make some kind of graven image (verses 16–18), or worship the heavenly bodies (verse 19). The possible varieties of graven image are first mentioned in general terms: "a graven representation of any image" (*pesel temunat kol samel*).[36] They are then enumerated in a series of five phrases, each of which begins with *tabnit:*

tabnit zakhar 'o neqebah	a representation of male or female;

35. The expression "wood and stone" (*'eṣ wa'eben*) occurs elsewhere only in Deuteronomy 29:16, 2 Kings 19:18 (= Isaiah 37:19), where it speaks of Gentiles' worshiping their false gods. Jeremiah 2:27 and Habakkuk 2:19 use "wood" and "stone" in synonymous parallelism, both passages in reference to idolatry.

36. The word *semel* ("image") recurs in Ezekiel 8:3, 5, which I will discuss. It is found elsewhere only in 2 Chronicles 33:7, 15, which is perhaps dependent on Ezekiel 8 [108]. Ezekiel's sharing this rare word with Deuteronomy 4 confirms my view that he was familiar with that passage.

tabnit kol behemah 'asher ba'areṣ	a representation of any beast that is on earth;
tabnit kol ṣippor kanaf 'asher ta'uf bashshamayim	a representation of any winged bird that flies in the heaven;
tabnit kol romeś ba'adamah	a representation of anything that creeps on the ground;
tabnit kol dagah 'asher bammayim mittaḥat la'areṣ	a representation of any fish that is in the water under the earth.

With his *tabnit remeś ubehemah*, Ezekiel alludes to this series. He thus alludes, silently, to its first and most general member. The horror of the hidden chamber is the horror of things male and female, and of what may happen when they come together.

As Ezekiel sat in trance in the presence of the elders of Judah, his unconscious mind hit upon the allusion to Deuteronomy 4:17–18 as a way of revealing the secret that his visual images still veiled.[37]

Later, thinking over his experience and how he had described it, he dimly perceived that the allusion revealed more than he could allow himself to know. He excised it.

Thus was created the shorter text of Ezekiel 8:10, which eventually came to be translated into Greek.

7. Again, the Elders

To this loathsome room Ezekiel has come. He is not the first.

The elders' presence in the sealed chamber, so hard to explain if Ezekiel

---

37. Freud's *Interpretation of Dreams* gives example after example of the subtlety with which our unconscious uses all manner of allusion to express yet conceal the thoughts behind our dreams. In the dreams of well-read people, literary allusions may often discharge this function. Thus, the dream of one of Freud's male patients was linked to its underlying sexual wishes and infantile reminiscences via allusions to Daudet's *Sappho*, Uhland's *Wanderlieder*, and Goethe's *Faust*. A female patient expressed powerful wishes for a better sex life with her husband, by dreaming of beetles crushed and suffocating; allusions to *The Magic Flute*, *Tannhäuser*, Eliot's *Adam Bede*, Daudet's *Le Nabab*, and Kleist's *Käthchen von Heilbronn* provided some of the links between her hidden wish and its disguised representation [335]. There is no implausibility in supposing that Ezekiel's unconscious made similar use of a passage from the contemporary Torah literature, as a link between latent thought and manifest image.

8 is taken as a description of events in the physical world, becomes perfectly natural once we suppose it is a hallucination determined by Ezekiel's unconscious concerns. In view of Ezekiel 16 and 23, which we shall examine in the next chapter, we need not be surprised to find Ezekiel's horror of the female organs combined with rage that others—first and foremost, the phallic "son of the hyrax"[38]—have entered them before him.

They are seventy. This number is hardly determined by the actual number of elders who sat before Ezekiel; we have seen reason to believe that there were between twenty and twenty-five of them. It presumably reflects the Pentateuchal story of how Yahweh extended the gift of his spirit, from Moses alone to "seventy men of the elders of Israel" (Numbers 11:16–17, 24–30).[39] Critics normally assign this story to the JE source; which would, according at least to the conventional dating of the Pentateuchal sources, make it earlier than Ezekiel [222].

The parallels between the Pentateuchal passage and ours go beyond the number seventy. Here, the elders are inside a chamber in the Temple precincts. In Numbers 11, they are at the "tent of meeting," the sanctuary at which Yahweh reveals himself in the desert to his wandering people. According to 11:24–25, Moses "caused the elders to stand around the tent"—on the inside, presumably[40]—whereupon "Yahweh descended in the cloud." *Sebibot ha'ohel* ("around the tent") is perhaps reflected in Ezekiel's *sabib sabib* ("all around," 8:10); *wayya'amed* ("he caused to stand"), in the doubled use of the same root in 8:11. The suspicion remains, however, that Ezekiel's peculiar repetition of "standing . . . standing" (*'omed . . . 'omedim*)—which, like so much else of interest in this passage, is omitted in the Septuagint's text—points in another direction as well, toward an emphasis on being sexually erect.

In one respect, Ezekiel reverses the Pentateuchal tradition. In Numbers 11:25, a cloud (*'anan*) descends. Ezekiel 8:11 also knows a cloud, this time ascending. Ezekiel would surely have conceived the cloud of the desert tradition as phallic in shape; for Exodus 33:7–11 and Numbers 12:4–13, which belong to the same cluster of materials as Numbers 11 [222], speak of a "pillar of cloud" descending to the entrance of the tent of meeting. The Bible does not tell us what Ezekiel's "rising cloud of incense" might have looked like. But the rabbinic perceptions of the incense-cloud of

---

38. Jaazaniah ben Shaphan; see Chapter 2.

39. Compare Numbers 11:16, *shib'im 'ish mizziqne yisra'el* (cf. verse 24), with Ezekiel 8:11, *shib'im 'ish mizziqne bet yisra'el*. Cf. also Ezekiel 14:1 and 20:1, *'anashim mizziqne yisra'el*.

40. Suggested by the parallel Numbers 12:4–5.

Second Temple times, if we are willing to admit them as evidence, suggest we are to envision it also as a pillar.[41]

With his phallus-cloud, Yahweh once penetrated the space proper to him. The elders now use a similar phallus-cloud, in the opposite direction, to penetrate a space forbidden to them. The instrument and its use are the same in both cases. This will serve as our first indication that the elders, and the God in whose name they are condemned, had for Ezekiel the same unconscious meaning.

Ezekiel's "elders," it cannot be stressed too often, were actual persons, whose behavior had presumably offended Ezekiel in some way. We cannot be sure just what they did that was wrong. Like Shemaiah of Nehelam, they seem to have reacted with contempt and outrage to Jeremiah's advice to prepare for a long exile (see Chapter 2). They would thus have challenged Ezekiel's belief that the Temple was irrevocably doomed. Given the importance of this belief for his psychic structure (see Chapter 4), this alone would have been enough to bring down his fury upon them.[42] We cannot disregard, moreover, Ezekiel's hints that his fellow exiles sometimes treated him badly (2:6, 3:25). Some of the elders, perhaps Pelatiah ben Benaiah and Jaazaniah ben Azzur, may have taken part.

Yet surely the real Pelatiah and the real Jaazaniah did not evoke Ezekiel's hatred, so much as certain fantasy figures with whom he identified them. We will examine these figures more closely in Chapter 4. I will there suggest that the promiscuous women, whom chapters 16 and 23 describe in pornographic detail, reflect the same psychic prototype as the corrupted Temple of chapter 8. The elders who dominate Ezekiel's hallucinations in chapters 8–11, and who call forth his denunciations in chapters 14 and 20, play a role in his fantasy world very similar to that of the wicked women's lovers.

We will then see that Ezekiel's attitude toward his powerful male figures

41. The incense smoke, according to the Tosefta, "would rise up like a column [*metammeret*] until it reached the ceiling. Then it would spread out in all directions, and descend" (T. Kippurim 2:6; Lieberman [188] cites parallel texts). A baraita quoted in the Babylonian Talmud, Yoma 53a, puts it a little differently: ". . . it would rise up like a stick until it reached the ceiling, then slowly come down along the walls." Cf. Palestinian Talmud, Yoma 5:2 (42c top).

42. The event, of course, justified Ezekiel's belief: the Temple *was* destroyed. This does not contradict my view that the belief was rooted in Ezekiel's psychopathology, and not in any rational political considerations. A person may hold a correct belief on entirely irrational grounds.

is far more ambivalent—or, at least, the ambivalence is far more obvious—than is the case with his women. His dominant feeling toward them is hatred, which we may suppose to be compounded of envy, rage, and fear. The lovers of Ezekiel's fantasy women are accomplices in their cruelty; the dread Ezekiel feels for the female can consequently be extended to the male. And, as his loathing of the forbidden chamber surely conceals a measure of frustrated longing, so his fury at those who are its regular visitors surely contains a wish to be in their place.[43]

Yet we will also see that Ezekiel is capable of identifying with these men, so that his "fury and jealousy" (16:38) becomes theirs. And the fascination he evidently feels for their gigantic sexual organs (23:20)—or for the phallic incense-cloud that penetrates the chamber—perhaps encompasses not only envy but attraction. It is possible to detect homosexual elements in Ezekiel's hallucinations, which hint dimly at memories or fantasies of sexual humiliation at the hands of some powerful male.

Ezekiel displaces these memories or fantasies, heavily freighted with both desire and resentment, onto Israel's elders. He also displaces them, with the rest of the package of envy, rage, and fear, onto Israel's God.

With this assumption, as we will see, some of the stranger and more repellent features of Ezekiel's theology will find their resolution.

8. The Other Abominations: The "Image of Jealousy"

To recapitulate: I have argued that Ezekiel 8:7–12 describes an act of sexual intercourse, represented in symbolic language and freighted with a heavy load of male sexual dread. I have shown that the language of the passage, especially the words *ḥor* and *ḥatar*, is well suited to this interpretation. I have shown also that the sexual dread of which I speak has every claim to be regarded as a universal phenomenon. It occurs in cultures separated by centuries and by oceans. We find it, in different forms, in ancient Mesopotamia and Israel. It may be considered likely *prima facie* that Ezekiel was at least touched by it.

The burden of Chapter 4 will be to turn this supposition into a demonstrated fact. We will find that same fear and loathing of female sexuality,

43. Pointed out to me by Robert Segal.

presented in heavy symbolic disguise in 8:7–12, to be expressed all but openly in chapters 16 and 23. We will find it, further, underlying Ezekiel's self-reported behavior at the death of his wife (24:15–27). It did not merely "touch" Ezekiel; at times, it all but dominated him.

One task remains for us, however, before we leave Ezekiel 8–11.

The chamber of 8:7–12 is indeed the centerpiece of Ezekiel's hallucinatory "abominations." The attention Ezekiel devotes to it—as much as to all the others put together[44]—by itself attests its central importance. But it is not alone. We must ask whether the rest of the "abominations" can be understood along the same lines.

In this and the next two sections, I will attempt such an understanding. My interpretations of the rest of chapter 8 are more speculative, less securely grounded in the text, than that of verses 7–12. Not all of them would commend themselves to me, if I were to take them in isolation. (I am thinking particularly of my understanding of the underlying meaning of 8:16's accusation of sun worship.) But I do not take them in isolation. My argument, no less than Broome's, is cumulative. The question is not, Does my interpretation of each individual point have the decisive advantage over all other interpretations?—although, in the case of the "weeping for Tammuz," I think it does. It is, rather: Can these points, taken together, be plausibly and coherently understood as a symbolic representation of a psychosexual nightmare? The answer to that question, I will argue, is yes.

Formally, chapter 8 is divided into four episodes. Each begins with the claim that God "brought" Ezekiel from one place to another (verses 3, 7, 14, 16). Then come descriptions of the "image of jealousy" (3–5), the sealed chamber (7–12), the women weeping for Tammuz (14), the sun worshipers (16). A comment of God's follows each account. It is slightly different each time, but is normally along the lines of: "Have you seen this? You shall see even greater abominations" (verses 6, 13, 15, 17–18).

The last of God's comments is the most elaborate. Naturally enough, it does not end with the promise that Ezekiel will see yet worse. Yet, like its predecessors, it does seem to point to something beyond what Ezekiel has already seen. "Have you seen this, son of man? Is it a trivial matter for the

---

44. Ninety-three words in the Masoretic Text; compared to forty-seven for the "image of jealousy" (verses 3–5, beginning with *wattabe' 'oti yerushalaymah*), seventeen for the "women weeping for Tammuz" (verse 14), twenty-eight for the men worshiping the sun (verse 16).

house of Judah to perform the abominations they have done here, that they have filled the land with violence? They have enraged me yet more— they send the branch to their nose" (verse 17). The Hebrew idiom for "enraged me yet more," *wayyashubu lehakh'iseni*, echoes the earlier promise that Ezekiel will see yet more, or greater, abominations (*tashub tir'eh*, verses 6, 13, 15). This may encourage us, as it has encouraged some commentators, to see in the "branch to the nose" a fifth, climactic abomination, the nature of which has so far resisted elucidation [246].

We can glimpse the first of the "abominations" only very dimly. The "spirit" brings Ezekiel to Jerusalem, "to the opening of the inner gate that faces northward, where was the seat of the image of jealousy that provokes jealousy [*semel haqqin'ah hammaqneh*]. There was the glory of the God of Israel, according to the vision I had seen in the plain. He said to me, 'Son of man, raise your eyes northward.' So I raised my eyes northward; and, north of the altar gate, was this image of jealousy in the entrance [*semel haqqin'ah hazzeh babbi'ah*]" (verses 3–5).

What precisely is a *semel?* In Phoenician inscriptions, "*sml* denotes a statue of a divine or human being" [108] which, curiously, changes its gender to accord with the sex of the person dedicating it [270]. Outside Ezekiel 8, the word occurs only three times in the Bible. Second Chronicles 33:7 has wicked King Manasseh place "the graven representation of the image" (*pesel hassemel*) in the Temple. Later, repentant, he removes it (verse 15). Finally, the warning against idolatry in Deuteronomy 4:16–18 (discussed earlier) opens its list of graven images with "a graven representation of any image" (*pesel temunat kol samel*).

Second Chronicles 33:7 is an obvious paraphrase of 2 Kings 21:7, which, however, speaks of *pesel ha'asherah*, "the graven representation of the asherah." It follows that the Chronicler identified the "asherah" of Kings with something he called the *semel*. It is not easy to understand his point unless we assume that he was following some historical tradition that designated Manasseh's asherah as the *semel;* or that, as Greenberg thinks, he was trying to provide an interpretation for Ezekiel 8:3–5 [108]. The second option, of course, does not necessarily exclude the first.

The Chronicler's equation, even if correct, is less helpful than we might hope. The meaning of Hebrew *'asherah* is itself far from clear. Ugaritic texts, to be sure, leave no doubt that Asherah was a Canaanite goddess of sex, fertility, and war, consort of the supreme god El [190]. But the Hebrew word, as used in the Bible and in the strange graffiti from Kuntillet

'Ajrud, seems normally to refer not to the goddess but to some sort of cult object perhaps connected with her [191,224,266].[45] Even if Ezekiel's *semel* was an asherah, this by itself will not tell us what he conceived it as looking like, or what it meant to him.

But Deuteronomy 4:16–18, taken in conjunction with the Chronicler's evidence, will put us on the right track. In 8:10, as we have seen, Ezekiel alludes to the sequence of five "representations" (*tabnit*) condemned in Deuteronomy 4:16b–18. In 8:3–5, he points toward the prelude to that series (Deuteronomy 4:16a). Between the two allusions, in Deuteronomy's sequence, lies the "representation of male or female":

Ezekiel 8	Deuteronomy 4
[3]. . . the image [*semel*] of jealousy that provokes jealousy . . . [5]this image [*semel*] of jealousy in the entrance. . . . [6]Son of man, do you see what they are doing? Great abominations . . .	[16a]. . . lest you act corruptly, and make for yourselves a graven depiction of any image [*samel*]—
	[16b]a representation [*tabnit*] of male or female;
[9]Come and see the wicked abominations . . . [10]every representation of creeping thing(s) and beasts [*kol tabnit remeś ubehemah*] . . .	[17]a representation [*tabnit*] of any beast [*behemah*] . . . [18]. . . a representation of anything that creeps [*romeś*] . . .

Ezekiel's first and second "abominations" thus serve to bracket the root—itself unspoken, because unconscious—of the horror he feels at both.[46]

In Deuteronomy 4:23–24, Moses repeats his warning against making "a graven representation of anything whatever," on the ground that "Yahweh your God is a consuming fire, a jealous God ['*el qanna*]." This will confirm the commentators' assumption that, in Ezekiel 8:3–5, the "jealousy" that

---

45. Saul M. Olyan, however, thinks that 2 Kings 21:7 is one of those "few cases" in which "it seems as if the asherah were a wooden likeness of the goddess" [225].

46. Or shall we suppose that Ezekiel's digging through the hole (which falls between verses 6 and 9) itself corresponds to Deuteronomy's "representation of male or female"?

the *semel* arouses is Yahweh's. As in Ezekiel 16:38, 42, 23:25, his "jealousy" here amounts to vindictiveness born of sexual frustration.[47] The fourth-century rabbis who expounded 8:5 understood this clearly. Rabbi Aha thus explains the word *bi'ah* (normally translated "entrance," but occurring nowhere else in the Bible) as derived from Greek *bia*, "violence." "Violence! violence! The visitor is ejecting the master of the house! Rabbi Berechiah said: It is written, *The bed is too short to stretch out on* [Isaiah 28:9] . . . a bed cannot hold a woman, her husband, and her lover at the same time."[48]

The rabbis took the "image of jealousy" to be the lover who has usurped God's bed and ejected him from his own house. In the light of Ezekiel 16:38, 42, 23:25, we may incline toward the older interpretation attested by the Chronicler. Whatever its obscurities in detail, the Chronicler's equation of *semel* with *'asherah* certainly links Ezekiel's "image" with the rampantly sexual female who so tormented his fantasies.[49]

It is even thinkable that the *semel*, as imagined by Ezekiel, managed to combine male and female and to represent their coupling. *Bi'ah*, found in the Bible only here, is regularly used in rabbinic Hebrew for sexual intercourse [154]. This meaning is well attested for the root *bw'*, in the Bible as well [30]. Apply it in Ezekiel 8:5, and the passage will describe "this image of jealousy *in the act of coitus.*" The "jealousy" is that of the excluded male—ostensibly Yahweh, in reality Ezekiel.

A dim childhood memory of Manasseh's asherah may perhaps have contributed to this part of Ezekiel's hallucination. The Chronicler's identification of Ezekiel's *semel* with Manasseh's idol will then turn out to have been essentially correct; although we have no way of knowing how much of Ezekiel's image of the *semel* was memory, and how much was erotic symbolization created by his own unconscious. Zimmerli's objections—Manasseh's asherah is not likely to have been restored after Josiah's reform; Ezekiel locates it in the wrong place within the Temple complex [297]—are, on my hypothesis, entirely irrelevant.

In the light of our earlier observations on the shorter text of the Septua-

47. The noun *qin'ah* ("jealousy") occurs eight times in Ezekiel, outside chapter 8: at 5:13, 16:38, 42, 23:25, 35:11, 36:5, 6, 38:19. In all but one of these cases (35:11), the "jealousy" is Yahweh's; in three of the eight, it is clearly sexual. The verb *qinne'*, "to be jealous," is used of Yahweh in 39:25, of the trees of Eden in 31:9; in neither passage does sex seem to be involved.

48. *Leviticus Rabbah* 17:7 [194]; *Lamentations Rabbah*, Proem 22 [34]; adapted in *Deuteronomy Rabbah* 2:20.

49. We shall look more closely at these fantasies in Chapter 4.

gint, it will come as no surprise that this text leaves out the concluding phrase of 8:5 (". . . was this image of jealousy in the entrance/act of coitus"), even though the sentence is obviously incomplete without it. It is hard to imagine a scribal error that would account for the omission. More likely, someone—probably Ezekiel himself—deliberately suppressed material he found too revealing. A similar hypothesis will account for the shorter text of 8:3, which seems to have omitted the word "jealousy" (*haqqin'ah*) after "image." It will also explain the odd Masoretic spelling of the following *hammaqneh*, which has the effect of linking the verb with the root *qnh* ("to acquire"), rather than *qn'* ("to be jealous") [169,269].[50]

9. The Other Abominations: Lamentation for Tammuz

After showing Ezekiel the hidden chamber, God promises him that he will see yet "greater abominations." And so: "He brought me to the entrance of the gate of Yahweh's house, that faces northward; and there the women were sitting, lamenting Tammuz" (8:14).[51]

Most interpretations of this passage have proceeded on the assumption that Ezekiel was a passive witness to something that actually went on in the Temple. My hypothesis, by contrast, requires him to have unconsciously created the episode, on the basis of his antecedent perceptions of the Mesopotamian god Tammuz and his cult. To understand 8:14, therefore, we must try to picture for ourselves what Ezekiel might have known about Tammuz, and what meaning this knowledge might have had for him.

Tammuz, and women's ritual laments for him, were ancient in Mesopotamia by Ezekiel's time. The roots of the cult are tangled and complex. The prototype of Tammuz, the Sumerian Dumuzi, was perhaps originally a historical person, a king of the first dynasty of Uruk [6,122,180].[52] But he was also perceived as a vegetation god or numen of some sort. If Thorkild

50. This spelling seems to have been in the shorter text as well; for the Septuagint translates *bē stēlē tou ktōmenou*, "the pillar of the one who acquires" (*semel hammaqneh*, presumably). Perhaps it originated in this "censored" text, and from there contaminated the text that gave rise to the Masoretic.

51. Or, more literally, "*the* Tammuz."

52. In the first half of the third millennium B.C.

Jacobsen is right, he was associated at various times with the sap in trees and plants, the date palm, grain and beer, and milk [148].

Whether as god or as human, he appears in Sumerian texts as lover and husband of the goddess Inanna, whom the Assyrians and the Babylonians were later to know as Ishtar. Their courtship is among the steamiest in ancient literature. ("Then plow my vulva, man of my heart! Plow my vulva!")[53] Yet, beloved as he is, he is doomed to a violent and mysterious death; after which he will be mourned by Inanna, by his sister, by his mother, by women in general. And, in at least some versions of the story, it is precisely the lusty Inanna who destroys him.

"For Tammuz, the lover of thy youth," the *Epic of Gilgamesh* has its hero tell Ishtar, "thou hast ordained wailing year after year" (Tablet 6, lines 46–47 [255]). The ritual lamentations for Dumuzi-Tammuz, then, were well known in Assyria and Babylonia in the late second millennium, the period to which the standard Akkadian text of the *Epic* is normally dated [151,263]. "The hemerologies," says O. R. Gurney, "state that the lamentations and 'binding' of Tammuz were celebrated in the month Tammuz (Du'uzu); the weeping took place on the second day and on the 9th, 16th and 17th there were processions of torches. On the last three days of the month there was a ceremony called *taklimtu* in which the effigy of the dead god was laid out for burial" [122]. These annual wailings, according to the Muslim writer Ibn al-Nadim, survived in Harran down to the tenth century A.D. [238]. There is no reason whatever to doubt that they were being practiced in Babylonia when Ezekiel and his fellow exiles arrived.

The situation in Palestine was very different. Although Dumuzi-Tammuz had his counterparts in the Levant—the best-known being the god whom the Greeks called Adonis [145,236]—he himself seems to have been unknown in Phoenicia or Palestine at least until the Christian Era.[54] The god whom Ezekiel saw bewailed at the Jerusalem Temple will then have been (according to Flemming Hvidberg) a native Palestinian god to whom Ezekiel gave a name drawn from his Babylonian surroundings, perhaps in order to impress his fellow exiles with the idolatrous character of the cult. "If he really was the Babylonian Tammuz, the weeping for him

53. So Wolkstein and Kramer [180,293]. Jacobsen, however, gives a considerably tamer translation: "The man of my heart! The ploughman is the man of my heart!" [149].

54. A Christian apology attributed to the second-century bishop Melito of Sardis, preserved in Syriac translation, links "Tamuz" with the Phoenician city of Byblos [58,237]. According to Hvidberg, there is evidence Tammuz was worshiped in Syria early in the Christian era [146].

in Jerusalem undoubtedly was an isolated phenomenon limited in time"
[146,147]. We may add that it took place in the wrong month. Tammuz
was the fourth month of the Babylonian and Jewish year, but Ezekiel had
his vision in the sixth (8:1) [108].

These considerations will confirm our premise that the proper context
for Ezekiel's third "abomination" is not the reality of the Jerusalem cult,
but the Babylonian myth of Tammuz, and what this story meant for
Ezekiel himself.

Let us begin with the account of Dumuzi's death, in a Sumerian text
modern scholars call "The Descent of Inanna" [149,181,294]. The goddess
descends, for reasons never explained, to the netherworld. There she is
made prisoner by her dark "sister" Ereshkigal. She is liberated by a trick,
but given the condition that she must find a substitute to take her place.
She thus rises from the netherworld accompanied by a troop of demons,
waiting for her to name their victim. They meet her maid and two of her
sons, all of them mourning in sackcloth. Inanna forbids the demons to
touch them. But, when they reach Uruk, there is Dumuzi, "dressed in
noble garments . . . sitting on a lofty throne" (Samuel Noah Kramer).

> She looked at him, it was a look of death,
> spoke to them, it was a word of wrath
> cried out to them, it was the cry of "guilty!"
> "Take this one along!"
> Holy Inanna gave the shepherd Dumuzi into their hands.
>
> (Jacobsen)

Our main text breaks off shortly after this passage, and the sequel is not
very clear. It appears that Dumuzi escaped several times from the demons,
but was recaptured each time, and eventually carried down to the netherworld. There he would have remained forever, if his sister Geshtinanna
had not volunteered to take his place six months of each year. And so
Inanna offered her icy verdict, on him who had once been the "man of my
heart":

> "You half a year, your sister half a year:
> while you are walking around (alive), she will lie prostrate,
> while your sister is walking around (alive), you will lie prostrate."
>
> (Jacobsen)

We have other Sumerian stories of Dumuzi's death, which do not seem to implicate Inanna. It is not clear whether we are to treat them as contradicting the version given in "The Descent of Inanna" (Jacobsen, Bendt Alster [7,149]), or whether we are to harmonize all the accounts into a single elaborate narrative (Kramer [181]). Other Sumerian texts, at any rate, reflect the "Descent of Inanna" version. In one passage, Dumuzi protests to the sun-god Utu: "I took your sister to wife. / She descended to the Nether World. / Because she descended to the Nether World, / she gave me as a substitute to the Nether World" [8]. Kramer [181] quotes a dirge in which Inanna herself appears remorseful:

"My beloved, my man of the heart,
You, I have brought about an evil fate for you, my brother of
    fairest face,
My brother, I have brought about an evil fate for you, my brother
    of fairest face.

"Your right hand you placed on my vulva,
Your left, stroked my head,
You have touched your lips to mine,
You have pressed your lips to my head,
That is why you have been decreed an evil fate,
Thus is treated the 'dragon' of the women, my brother of fairest
    face."

The point could hardly be made more clearly. It was Inanna's sensuality that destroyed Dumuzi.

This version of Dumuzi's death must have survived in Babylonia down to the late second millennium, when Inanna had become Ishtar and Dumuzi Tammuz. Without it, there is no way to account for the allusion in Tablet 6 of the *Epic of Gilgamesh*, which plainly blames Ishtar for Tammuz's fate [255].

The context of the allusion is worth describing. Ishtar has set her eyes on the handsome Gilgamesh, and proposes that he become her lover and her husband. Gilgamesh angrily rebuffs her:

[Thou art but a brazier which goes out] in the cold;
A back door [which does not keep out] blast and windstorm;
A palace which crushes the valiant [. . .];

A *turban* whose cover [. . .];
Pitch which [soils] its bearers;
A waterskin which *cuts* its bearer;
Limestone which [*springs*] the stone rampart;
A siege engine which des[troys] the enemy land;
A shoe which pinches [the foot] of its owner!
Which lover didst thou love forever?
Which of thy shepherds pleased [thee for all time]?
Come, and I will *na*[*me* for thee] thy lovers . . .

And so he does. First comes "Tammuz, the lover of thy youth," for
whom Ishtar has ordained annual wailings. She loved a bird and broke his
wing; a lion, and dug pits for him; a stallion, and gave him over to beatings
and drinking foul water; a shepherd, and turned him into a wolf; her
father's gardener (the first to reject her), and turned him into a mole. "If
thou shouldst love me, thou wouldst [treat me] like them."

Ishtar storms up to heaven, to her father Anu. She demands vengeance
on Gilgamesh, who "has recounted my stinking deeds, / My stench and
my foulness." Neither she nor Anu denies the truth of Gilgamesh's accusations. The Babylonian audiences of the epic would surely have taken their
accuracy for granted [90]. The epic's enduring popularity—there were
several copies in Ashurbanipal's library, and copies continued to be made
down to the second or first century B.C. [263]—would have guaranteed
that these audiences never forgot the awful deadliness of Ishtar's seduction.

An Akkadian version of the descent of Ishtar, which evidently circu-
lated in Assyria in the first half of the first millennium, links her adventure
with the ritual laments for Tammuz [232,254]. Unlike its Sumerian ances-
tor, this text never clarifies the nature of the link. But, taken together with
the *Epic of Gilgamesh*,[55] it leaves no doubt that the memory of Ishtar's
callous sacrifice of her lover survived well into the first millennium.

As in the Sumerian story, Ishtar descends to the netherworld for unclear
reasons, is trapped there, and is released by a trick. The poet describes
how Ishtar emerges from the netherworld's seven gates. He then abruptly
concludes his narrative by speaking of Tammuz, who so far has not been
mentioned:

55. Tigay has remarked on the close ties between the Akkadian *Descent of Ishtar* and the
Epic of Gilgamesh [262]. Both texts use the same epithet for Tammuz: ḫāmiru ṣuḫretiki /
ṣuḫretiša, "lover of your / her youth" [97,98].

". . . As for Tammuz, the lover of her youth,
Wash him with pure water, anoint him with sweet oil;
Clothe him with a red garment, let him *play* on a flute of lapis.
Let courtesans *turn* [*his*] mood."
[When] Belili was string[ing] her jewelry,
[And her] lap was filled with "eye-stones,"
On hearing the sound of her brother, Belili struck the jewelry on
[. . .]
So that the "eye-stones" filled [. . .] . . .
"My only brother, bring no harm to me!
On the day when Tammuz comes up to me,
When with him the lapis flute (and) the carnelian ring come up to
me,
When with him the wailing men and the wailing women come up
to me,
May the dead rise and smell the incense."

                                        (E. A. Speiser [254])

The meaning of these lines is hardly less obscure than is their connection with their context. The first four lines are best understood as describing the funeral rites for Tammuz. Gurney's view, that the last line speaks of his return from the dead, is at least plausible [122]. Immediately before this passage, one of the two surviving copies of the text has Ereshkigal (or one of her subordinates) deliver the instruction: "If she [Ishtar] does not give thee her ransom price, bring her back."[56] In the light of the Sumerian story of Inanna's descent, we cannot doubt that Ishtar goes on to "give" Tammuz as her "ransom price"; that is, she abandons him to the netherworld. What follows will then describe the ritual consequences of this abandonment.

I do not imagine for a moment that Ezekiel had read the *Epic of Gilgamesh*, or any version of the "Descent of Ishtar."[57] But it is hardly fantastic to suppose that, in his six years in Babylonia, he had noticed the local women's passionate summertime lamentations for their dead god; and that he had picked up enough of the vernacular to ask what those wailings were about.

56. The other copy contains a similar passage a few lines earlier.
57. The contrast between my suggestions, and those made by Stephen Garfinkel (see Chapter 1 [92,94]), will thus be apparent.

The evidence we have considered allows us to guess at the reply he would have gotten. He would have been told a story that depicted the female as powerful, seductive, treacherous, and cruel. Consciously, he may well have dismissed the story as heathen falsehood. But, unconsciously, it could not have failed to appeal to his own sexual antipathies.

This feature of Ezekiel's hallucination, then, will have functioned for him on several levels. Most obviously, the weeping women are demonstrating, in their husband's own house, their passion for a lover they have preferred over him. They are thus embodiments of the faithless wives of chapters 16 and 23.

Dexter Hall has suggested to me that the peculiar character of the "lover" may well have heightened Ezekiel's fury. If Jacobsen is right, Tammuz was an utterly passive creature, devoid of any virtue or ethical value. His only power lay in the "quiet, doting, sensuously contemplative love" he was able to evoke in women [148]. He thus contrasts devastatingly with Ezekiel's Yahweh—an active, forceful, monumentally unlovable being, driven largely by frustrated rage that he cannot get the affectionate loyalty he thinks he deserves. To the extent that Ezekiel identified with his God, the sight of Babylonian women lamenting Tammuz must have activated his thwarted longings. He displaced the rage he felt onto the Jerusalem Temple.

Yet at the deepest level, I believe, Ezekiel identified himself with the Tammuz of the Babylonian myth: seduced, once loved, then cruelly abandoned. The weeping women, Ishtar's embodiments, hypocritically mourn their victim, in the precincts of a structure that has itself become for Ezekiel an emblem of the treacherous and dangerous female.[58]

We need no longer worry about a Babylonian god's being worshiped in Palestine under a Babylonian name (Hvidberg), in the wrong month of the year (Greenberg). We have no reason to think that Tammuz was ever lamented in the Jerusalem Temple, in any month, under any name. Ezekiel "saw" his rites in the Temple, not because they had any real existence there, but because this scene could function for him as a symbol that brilliantly coalesced different (and partly contradictory) aspects of his fear, rage, and yearning. All, or nearly all, of these underlying feelings were unconscious. That was what gave the symbol representing them its immense power of conviction.

58. If Ezekiel identified himself with Tammuz, he is likely to have given Yahweh a villain's role in his private myth. We shall see that this manifests itself in various ways in the Book of Ezekiel; most strikingly, in the singular brutality of Ezekiel's God.

We will see in Chapter 4 that the offense for which Inanna condemns Dumuzi to the netherworld—his failure properly to mourn for her—has an eerie reflex in Ezekiel's own behavior at the death of his wife.

Tzvi Abusch's recent discussion of "Ishtar's Proposal and Gilgamesh's Refusal" [2] lends powerful support to my hypothesis.

Gilgamesh's sharp rejection, Abusch argues, can only be understood if Ishtar's proposal has a double meaning. On the surface, she is offering marriage. But, in reality, what she holds out to Gilgamesh is death, and lordship over the netherworld. Her links with her chthonic "sister," Ereshkigal, are far stronger than appear at first sight. She, too, is a goddess of death. In this way, Abusch suggests, her otherwise mysterious decision to visit the netherworld is to be explained.[59] The abusive epithets Gilgamesh hurls at Ishtar all have overtones of the tomb. In other words—here I extend Abusch's argument—Gilgamesh is straining to avoid the deadly sexual trap that once swallowed up the less wary Tammuz.

Abusch proposes at one point that the author of *Gilgamesh* assumes an equation of vagina, house, and tomb, Ishtar being all three. This reminds us that some of Gilgamesh's insults—notably, that Ishtar is a "shoe which pinches [the foot] of its owner"—are at least as suggestive of the *vagina dentata* as they are of the grave. Like Lambert's texts, the sixth tablet of *Gilgamesh* is engaged upon abuse of Ishtar's genitals. Its language is less foully obscene. But the images it evokes are vastly more horrific.

> For many a victim has she laid low;
> Yea, all her slain are a mighty host.
> Her house is the way to Sheol,
> Going down to the chambers of death.[60]

Is it any wonder that a man inclined to this sort of sexual dread would have found the myth of Ishtar and Tammuz irresistibly compelling? That, once heard, it would lodge itself in his mind? Or that an allusion to it would find a place within his hallucination of a feminine structure corrupted beyond hope of redemption?[61]

59. Diane Wolkstein makes a similar point [296].
60. Proverbs 7:26–27. Abusch observes the parallel.
61. Ishtar, says Gilgamesh, is a "palace which crushes the valiant [. . .]" (Table 6, line 35). The Akkadian word translated "palace," *ekallu* [3], is cognate to the Hebrew *hekhal*, used for the Jerusalem Temple in Ezekiel 8:16 (and often in the Bible).

10. The Other Abominations:
The Buttocks and the Branch

Ezekiel 8:16 seems to break this pattern of displaced sexuality. The "abomination" there described seems to be sun worship pure and simple. "He brought me to the inner court of Yahweh's house. At the entrance to Yahweh's Temple, between the vestibule and the altar, were about twenty-five men. Their backs were toward Yahweh's Temple, their faces toward the east; and they were prostrating themselves eastward toward the sun."[62] Here, at least, there seems no hint of sex.

Yet a midrash on this verse, quoted three times in the Babylonian Talmud (Yoma 77a, Sukkah 53b, Qiddushin 72b), suggests that rabbinic expositors saw something more beneath the surface. "Do not the words *their faces toward the east* already communicate, by implication, that their backs were toward the Temple of the Lord? What, then, is conveyed by [the explicit statement that] *their backs were toward the Temple of the Lord?* That they were exposing themselves and squirting excrement in God's direction."[63] *Song Rabbah* 1:6 offers a slightly different version: "They were prostrating themselves to idolatry, while they exposed themselves to the Temple."

How seriously are we to take this midrash? We must acknowledge that the scatological obscenity of pagan cults was a rabbinic *topos*, which served at times as subject for a gross sort of humor.[64] Here the midrash perhaps reads this stereotype into a biblical text innocent of it. It will then provide entry to the mind of no one but its own author.

Yet Ezekiel's remark, that *their backs were toward Yahweh's Temple ('aḥorehem 'el hekhal YHWH)*, is indeed unnecessary, as the midrash observes. It is at least thinkable that it communicates something that does not appear on first reading.

---

62. So in the Masoretic Text; ignoring for the moment the hybrid *mishtaḥawitem*, which I discussed in Chapter 2. The Septuagint has "twenty" in place of "twenty-five" (see Chapter 2, note 19). It omits the second *qedmah* ("eastward"), while retaining the first. (The translation of this first *qedmah* with *apenanti* is unusual, but has its parallels in the Greek Ezekiel and elsewhere in the Septuagint—Genesis 3:24, Jonah 4:5, Ezekiel 10:19 and 11:23—and does not point to a different Hebrew original.) It is conceivable that the second *qedmah* was omitted from the Septuagint's *Vorlage*, in order to soften the implication (which would later occur to the rabbis) that the position of the worshipers' "backs" had a significance of its own.

63. Reading *kelappe ma'lah* (literally, "upward"), with Qiddushin 72b. The reading of the parallels, *kelappe maṭṭah* ("downward"), is a euphemism.

64. Babylonian Talmud, Sanhedrin 64a. Gary Rendsburg gives other references [234].

Exactly what part of the body is indicated by *their backs?* The word *'aḥorim* (plural, "back parts") is used only four other times in the Hebrew Bible, nowhere else with reference to human beings. It can mean the "rear" of the Tabernacle (Exodus 26:12); or the "hind parts," turned away from the viewer, of the sculpted oxen who carry the "sea" in Solomon's Temple (1 Kings 7:25 = 2 Chronicles 4:4). It is that part of Yahweh's body he is willing to show Moses: ". . . you shall see my back parts, but my face shall not be seen" (Exodus 33:23). We cannot be sure just what "back parts" he intends. But, taken together with Ezekiel 8:16, this passage suggests it is all right for Yahweh to show people his "back parts," but not the other way round.

In a society that stresses the concealment of the body, the thrusting out of the buttocks in the act of prostration is likely to be perceived as sexually provocative. Such, at any rate, is often the case among Muslims [318], who, perhaps as a consequence, have tended to be "uneasy with regard to the admission of women to public services in the mosque" [348]. Ezekiel's apparent linking of the sun worshipers' "back parts" with their act of prostration implies that it was precisely their buttocks that he had in mind.

Their offense, so understood, is more complex than appears at first sight. Not only do they adore the sun; they use this adoration as an excuse for making a gesture to God that is at once contemptuous and provocative. I suggest that it was the gesture, and not its ostensible purpose, that aroused Ezekiel's fury. It had this effect because it had unconsciously aroused him sexually.

I argued in Chapter 2 that the sun worshipers, like the "elders" of 8:11–12, are hallucinatory representations of the community leaders who have come to consult Ezekiel. The language of 8:16 now hints—very faintly and ambiguously, to be sure—that his fascination with their imagined sexual behavior contained something more than the revulsion, perhaps mixed with envy, that is expressed in 8:11–12. There was an element of homosexual attraction as well.

This supposition is confirmed in the very next verse.

Ezekiel's concluding accusation, that the Jews "send the branch to their nose" (*hinnam sholeḥim 'et hazzemorah 'el 'appam*), has generated extensive discussion among modern scholars. The controversy entails three basic questions. First, what is the meaning of *zemorah* in this verse? Second, are we to credit a widespread rabbinic tradition that the original reading of 8:17 was not *'appam* but *'appi*, "my nose"; and that the text was deliberately

changed out of respect for the Divinity [199]? Third, is the accusation a
general statement summarizing the Jews' evil behavior (Gordis [103])? Is it
some additional wickedness, worse than any that has gone before (Cooke,
Greenberg, Nahum Sarna [56,104,246])? Or is it, perhaps, linked specifically to the accusation of sun worship (H.W.F. Saggs [244])?

Zemorah occurs in four other passages of the Bible. In all of them, it
seems to mean "branch" or "shoot" (especially of the vine) [245]. The
obscurity of Ezekiel 8:17, however, has led some scholars to look for a
different meaning here. Thus, Nahum Sarna proposes to link *zemorah* with
Ugaritic *ḏmr*, "band of toughs." Ezekiel's charge—"they send forth bands
of toughs to execute their anger," or the like—will then accord with his
immediately preceding accusation, that "they have filled the land with
violence." This interpretation, unfortunately, requires a very strained exegesis of *'el 'appam* [246].

Two traditional Jewish interpretations have made their way into the
modern discussions [103,104,147,199,244,297]. One, attested in midrashic texts going back to the fifth century, and apparently reflected in the
Targum, understands Ezekiel's *zemorah* as slang (or perhaps a euphemism)
for the penis.[65] The other, put forward by medieval grammarians and
commentators,[66] takes it to be a fart, which the sinners of Judah impu-
dently send up to God's nose.

This second interpretation, which works best if we suppose the reading
"my nose," was perhaps suggested (as Rashi seems to imply) by the Talmud's excretory exegesis of Ezekiel 8:16. Moderns who favor it must take it
less than literally. "This abominable insult to Yahweh, which is the exact
opposite of the 'sweet-smelling savor' expected on the altar of the place of
his presence, represents the unsurpassable height of blasphemy, over which
Yahweh's wrath must break out" (Zimmerli [303]). They are obliged, however, to recognize (as Zimmerli does) that it has no etymological basis.[67]

The *zemorah* = phallus theory fares, in this respect, considerably better.

---

65. *Pesiqta de-Rab Kahana, Zakhor* no. 11 (ed. Mandelbaum [192]; the translation of
Braude and Kapstein [23] is speculative but plausible); *Tanḥuma, Teṣe'* no. 10; Buber's
Tanḥuma, Teṣe' no. 14 [35]; *Pesiqta Rabbati* 7:3 [89]; *Numbers Rabbah* 13:3. The details of the
midrashic texts are often obscure, but their phallic interpretation of *zemorah* seems clear [193].
Targum translates *zemorah* with *baḥata*, "shame"; which surely does not mean "stench" (as
Zimmerli thinks), but sexual organs [193].

66. Carmel McCarthy cites Menahem ben Saruq, Ibn Janah ("Abulwalid"), Rashi, and
Kimhi [199].

67. Unless one wants to count Rashi's suggestion [212] that it derives from the "tune"
(root *zmr*) whistled by the expelled gas.

The shape of the "branch" will naturally encourage its use as slang for the penis. Surely the rabbis were familiar with such a usage, which may well have survived from biblical times, and based their exegesis of Ezekiel 8:17 upon it.

Robert Gordis claims, without supporting argument, that "the Rabbis did not know the meaning of *zemorah* in Ezekiel, and were interpreting it homiletically" [103]. This would be a very odd sort of homiletics. Indeed, pre-Freudian interpreters could hardly have done much with an interpretation of Ezekiel 8:17 based on *zemorah* = phallus. What could it mean for people to "send" a phallus to God's nose or to their own? It is far more likely that the rabbis knew that *zemorah* could be used colloquially for the penis, perceived that this usage had something to do with the strange accusation in Ezekiel 8:17, but were unable clearly to define its relevance. This is perhaps why the midrashim in question are so confusing; and why the medieval Jewish commentators (even the conservative Rashi), for whom the living tradition of spoken Hebrew was a remote memory, turned their backs on the midrashic understanding and struck out on their own.

In the context of a psychoanalytic treatment of Ezekiel's Temple vision, however, the understanding of *zemorah* as phallus is entirely plausible. Indeed, it is hardly escapable. Once we accept "my nose" as the original reading in 8:17 (despite Carmel McCarthy's strictures [199]), the picture it yields is entirely clear. Ezekiel is accusing his hearers of thrusting their penises at God's mouth, for fellatio.

The point of the accusation will become clear once we recognize that it is a reversal of the hallucination Ezekiel describes in 2:8–3:3, as this is understood by Broome and Arlow [29,310]. There, God offers his "scroll" to Ezekiel and demands, repetitively and insistently, that Ezekiel eat it. "But you, son of man, hear what I say to you; be not rebellious like that rebellious house; open your mouth, and eat what I give you. . . . Eat what you find; eat this scroll. . . . Feed your belly and fill your insides with this scroll."

God's insistence points to some reluctance on Ezekiel's part. It is of course true that a person confronted with a scroll and told to eat it will tend to flinch. But we must remember that the situation described in 2:8–3:3 is entirely a product of Ezekiel's mind. We must not ask why Ezekiel should have refused to eat the scroll—as if the scroll had really been there for him to eat—but why he should have hallucinated both the demand that he eat the scroll and his reluctance to do so. The most plausible answer is that Broome and Arlow are right in seeing the scroll as a representation of a penis.[68] Underlying the hallucination is a fantasy or memory of having been compelled to perform fellatio on some adult male.[69]

In his fantasies, Ezekiel got revenge. Had the big man forced Ezekiel to eat his "scroll"? Well, Ezekiel would thrust his "branch" under the man's nose and force him to swallow that! But, once Ezekiel's imagination had turned the big man into Yahweh himself, his revenge fantasy was too dangerous to be allowed. He must project it onto other people, and then denounce them furiously for having permitted such an "abomination" to cross their minds. In this denunciation, he identifies himself with the being against whom his vengeful rage was once directed.

In a similar way, Ezekiel's image of the sun worshipers' offering God their buttocks may be a projection of what he was once compelled to do, and of a forbidden pleasure that he derived from it.

In our current Hebrew text, 'appam ("their nose") stands in place of what I have supposed to be the original 'appi ("my nose"). The rabbis explained this as a "correction of the scribes." It is at least thinkable, however, that it was a correction of Ezekiel himself. Not content with projecting his fantasy onto his villains, he disguised it still further by "correcting" its language. The reading 'appam will then be a manifestation of the same process of censorship that turned "you were prostrating yourselves" in 8:16 (hishtahawitem) into "they were prostrating themselves," and that yielded the shortened text of the Temple vision used by the Greek translators.[70]

On this hypothesis, it is hardly possible—and perhaps hardly neces-

68. We must then suppose that the opening of the scroll and the revelation of its unpleasant contents (2:10), which conveys Ezekiel's distaste for the act he is obliged to perform, does not affect its shape at the moment of ingestion.

69. Was it a fantasy, or was it a memory? Classical Freudian theory tends to discount recollections of childhood sexual abuse by supposing that the child has projected his or her erotic fantasies onto the adults who were originally the objects of these fantasies. ("I want to have sex with him" is remembered as "he wanted to—and indeed did—have sex with me.") Some recent psychoanalytic thinkers, notably Alice Miller, have passionately protested this view; the child's memory of sexual exploitation, they say, is all too authentic [367,372]. It would be presumptuous for me to take sides in this debate. Yet Miller's opinion seems well to accord with what we now know of how appallingly common it is for adults to use children for sexual gratification [321]. In Chapter 4, I will proceed on the assumption that Ezekiel's unconscious memories of his childhood suffering were essentially true. We will see that this hypothesis does much to account for the intensity of his rage.

70. McCarthy points out that the ancient versions presuppose the reading 'appam, and uses this (mistakenly, in my opinion) as an argument for its originality [199].

sary—to choose among the several views on how the "branch to the nose" relates to the four abominations Ezekiel was shown. Gordis is right: it does indeed summarize all that has gone before, in that it distills the sexual rage of chapter 8 into one stunning act of revenge upon the father-god. Saggs is right, in that its homosexual orientation connects it most closely with the "sun worship" of 8:16.

Yet there is also truth in the view held by Cooke, Greenberg, and Sarna. The "branch to the nose" is a culminating atrocity, vastly worse than anything that has gone before. For it points to what was perhaps the most carefully guarded secret of Ezekiel's unconscious: his repressed loathing and contempt for his God.[71]

11. Why Pelatiah Died

The sexual agonies of Ezekiel's unconscious, then, included a mixture of rage, envy, dread, loathing, homosexual and heterosexual desire—all combined with the guilt they aroused. He projected these feelings onto the "elders of Judah" who had come to him, to hear the word of Yahweh. It is they who penetrate the horrid chamber of his hallucination, with their phallic incense-cloud and with themselves (8:7–12). They offer Yahweh first their buttocks, then their penises (8:16–17). They boast, using an image whose sexual content will only now be evident, that they are the "flesh"[72] filling Jerusalem's "pot" (11:3).

In reality, we may suppose, these monsters of polymorphous sexuality were sober community leaders, whose view of the world was in many ways similar to Ezekiel's own. We may guess that they shared, at least to some degree, his sexual inclinations and aversions. Ezekiel was surely unique in the severity of his sickness, and in the power of the images he found to express it. But his sickness must have been rooted in a more general cultural pathology, which the elders could not entirely have escaped. We have seen that the author of the Holiness Code felt much as Ezekiel did about menstruation. We can hardly imagine that Ezekiel's other irrational sexual revulsions afflicted no one but him.

In a sense, Ezekiel was right when he claimed to know what the elders

71. I will develop this point in Chapter 4.
72. *Baśar;* used for the male genitals in Ezekiel 16:26, 23:20 (cf. 44:7, 9).

did "in the chambers of their imagination." He did know these "chambers," insofar as they were haunted by desires, resentments, and fears akin to his own. It follows that his hallucination, which gave these feelings visual representation, is likely to have evoked some echo in the elders' unconscious.

This leads to the solution of a problem that has long troubled us. Ezekiel's charges of Temple "abominations" were, as Yehezkel Kaufmann has shown, baseless and fantastic. The elders must have known they were baseless and fantastic. Why, then, did they not reject Ezekiel as a liar or a lunatic? Why did they continue at least to entertain the possibility that "a prophet was among them" (33:33)?

We may now answer: Ezekiel's conviction, derived from an internal reality that could not be denied, overwhelmed his rational knowledge of external reality. In a similar way, the images he found to express his conviction called forth assent from men whose internal reality was in crucial ways like his own. His inner demons, laid out before the elders, evoked kindred demons in themselves.

These demons, emerging, took the life of Pelatiah ben Benaiah.

In 1976, Bernard Lown and his colleagues reported a case of cardiac arrest in a thirty-nine-year-old man [366]. The man had been in excellent physical condition. He was athletic, did not smoke, had normal blood pressure and no circulatory problems. Yet one afternoon he collapsed in his home, turning a bluish color, with muscle spasms and heavy breathing.[73] "His wife, a registered nurse, immediately initiated cardiopulmonary resuscitation. On arrival at a community hospital, he was found to be in ventricular fibrillation." Right before the heart attack, he had been roughhousing with his two teenaged daughters; and a neighbor had rung the doorbell.

The man spent twenty days in his community hospital, and was then transferred to the Peter Bent Brigham Hospital in Boston. During his sixth night in Brigham, he suffered a second heart attack. "He was restless and expressed vague premonitions. He fell asleep readily at 10:30 and appeared to sleep peacefully when ventricular fibrillation was noted on the monitor oscilloscope at 4:00 A.M."

It is not clear from the report how long the man stayed at Brigham. But

---

73. In the original language of the report: ". . . he collapsed, and turned cyanotic, with the development of clonic activity and agonal respirations."

he did recover. His doctors put him on a regimen of drugs and meditation. As of 1988, he was still in good health [364].

Psychiatric interviews provided Lown and the others with clues to what had caused his original collapse:

> During the interviews, he seemed hyperalert and defensive, although he had a languid, folksy manner. There was an undercurrent of hostility and competition. He was loquacious and resisted interruptions. He repeatedly denied having depressive or angry thoughts. In spite of his recent cardiac arrest, he dismissed all fears.
>
> Control of aggression was a pervasive theme in his daily life. He grew up in a tough mining town, was intensely competitive with his only brother, overcame great obstacles in achieving higher education, and devoted fierce energy to every project and enterprise, and yet he was deeply religious, dedicating his life to the promotion of brotherhood and a career of service. He frequently found himself surging with anger, which he allayed by vigorous solitary exercise. He avoided violent television programs. Violence frequently appeared in his dreams; this symptom he disowned as not part of his true self.
>
> His strong moral prohibitions against aggression were matched by his restraints regarding sexuality. He insisted that he had no sexual thoughts about women other than his wife, although his work involved close contact with many women in his community.
>
> In the six months before his illness, he suffered his first career setback, when the faltering economy frustrated plans for expansion. His wife was depressed over the recent death of her father and was unresponsive to his psychologic needs and his two daughters were increasingly active outside the family. With these changes he grew angrier.
>
> The rough-housing with his daughters, just before the episode of ventricular fibrillation, provoked both aggressive and erotic impulses in him. The girls had matured physically. On this occasion there was much sexually provocative rough-housing, which was interrupted by the ring of the doorbell announcing the arrival of a neighbor. It was when one daughter answered the bell that he slumped to the floor. His last words were, "I'm sorry." [366]

What caused the second attack? A subsequent polygraph study of the man's sleeping behavior pointed to a connection between irregular heartbeats and REM (rapid eye movement) sleep—that is, the kind of sleep that regularly accompanies dreaming. "At the same time the patient recalled dreams with emotionally charged content." Though there is no way to be sure, it is reasonable to suppose that the heart attack also occurred during a disturbing dream.

In other studies, Lown found that people can experience irregular heart rhythms (cardiac arrhythmias) during conversations that evoke painful memories or emotions. Yet: "There is a singularity in the effectiveness of anamnestic recall of aversive events. Once shared with an outsider, these experiences cease to provoke arrhythmias" [364]. "The anamnesis of emotionally charged material that provokes arrhythmia is unlikely to do so on repetition" [365]. This suggests that it is the initial entry of repressed material into consciousness that poses a danger to the heart.[74] On this basis, we may conjecture that Lown's patient had a dream that, like the earlier incident in his home, threatened to allow forbidden impulses into his consciousness. He could not bear it. For a second time, his heart nearly gave way.[75]

Naturally, we cannot know how closely Pelatiah ben Benaiah resembled Lown's patient. We might imagine an elder of ancient Judah to have been "deeply religious, dedicating his life . . . to a career of service," well habituated to "restraints regarding sexuality." Lown's patient had suffered a career setback six months before his attack. Six years before his death, Pelatiah had seen his world fall apart. His frustration and rage must have been incomparably greater.

But, if we cannot easily compare the two men, we can compare their crises. In 1975 or thereabouts, an athletic thirty-nine-year-old experienced the sudden emergence of repressed desire and rage. This was followed by a signal (the doorbell) which he surely interpreted to mean that someone was coming to condemn him for his unspeakable impulses. ("I'm sorry.") He collapsed and nearly died. In 592 B.C., an "elder"—perhaps no older

74. We may perhaps see in this a clinical confirmation of one of the basic assumptions of analytic psychotherapy: that repressed feelings and memories, once admitted to consciousness, lose their power to harm.

75. Lown calls attention to the mysterious deaths that, since 1977, have afflicted Laotian immigrants to the United States. At least eighty healthy men in their thirties have gone to sleep and never woken up. "In the rare case in which the terminal event was monitored, the mechanism was ventricular fibrillation" [365]. Here too, perhaps, dreams were vehicles for the emergence of unconscious materials which the dreamers could not endure?

than Lown's patient, but surely less robust physically—became a vicarious participant in an overwhelmingly powerful hallucination that called forth his repressed sexual yearning and dread. He then heard himself condemned, with all of Ezekiel's savage ruthlessness, in the name of the most terrifying Judge he could imagine. Is it any wonder his heart failed him?

And is it any wonder that Ezekiel, who knew that Pelatiah's secret "sins" were also his own, thereupon himself collapsed—in fear, in grief, in remorse? "When I prophesied, Pelatiah the son of Benaiah died. And I fell on my face, and I cried in a loud voice: 'Oh, Lord Yahweh! Are you making an utter end of the remnant of Israel?' " (11:13).

12. Conclusion

At the beginning of Chapter 2, I defined as follows the crucial questions raised by Ezekiel's Temple vision:

1. To what extent are chapters 8–11 a unity? If they contain secondary material, how are we to distinguish the layers of this material, and how are we to locate the original nucleus?
2. To what extent does this section of the book—or, depending on how one answers the preceding question, the original nucleus of this section—reflect actual events taking place in Jerusalem, in the last decade of the existence of the kingdom of Judah?
3. Precisely what are the "abominations" these chapters describe?
4. What was the nature of Ezekiel's experience, and what was his role in the events he describes? Most obviously, if he was physically in Babylonia, how did he know what was going on in the Jerusalem Temple? How could he have brought about Pelatiah's death in Jerusalem?

On the basis of the arguments I have offered in this and the preceding chapter, I now propose the following answers:

I cannot assert that everything in chapters 8–11 was spoken by Ezekiel, or spoken by him on the same occasion. I stand by my judgment that 10:9–17 is an insertion by some later author [124]. 11:14–21, though Ezekiel's, hardly seems to belong in its present context. But, to a far greater extent than most commentators have supposed, the vision is a unity. It represents, by and large accurately, the hallucinations that Ezekiel experienced on a single occasion, while in a state of trance.

The vision's claims about its setting are to be believed. Ezekiel, as the text says, had his vision in Babylonia; and more of the vision reflects its Babylonian surroundings than has previously been recognized. Where Ezekiel describes events that happened around him at the time of his trance experience (Pelatiah's death), he reports them more or less as they happened. Where he describes events in Jerusalem, his relation to them is that of a dreamer to his dream. His account of the Temple abominations deserves credence, certainly, but only as a reflection of what was going on inside himself.

Certain details, to be sure, reflect external realities of one sort or another. The ritual lamentations for Tammuz were real enough. We have seen reason to believe that Ezekiel had encountered them in Babylonia, and that he had some familiarity with the underlying myths. All of this he transferred, in his vision, to the Jerusalem Temple. There is no reason to doubt the truth of the political accusation Ezekiel launches against Pelatiah, Jaazaniah, and the rest: that they, like Shemaiah of Nehelam, regarded Jeremiah's advice to "build houses" as a poor joke (11:2–3). But, on the whole, we must accept Kaufmann's judgment that Ezekiel's picture of the defiled Temple is "pure fantasy"—without going on to infer that it is therefore negligible.

For, if we wish to understand Ezekiel as a human being, this fantasy is of the greatest importance. Ezekiel's "abominations" are his own aversions, fears, and desires. All are, at bottom, sexual. Some may reflect events of his early life. They are our guides to the psychopathology of an extraordinary and influential man and, indirectly, to the psychopathology of a society that bore him and that ultimately canonized him.

4

Will You Judge Them, Son of Man?

> There's hell, there's darkness, there is the sul-
> phurous pit; burning, scalding, stench, con-
> sumption. Fie, fie, fie! pah, pah! Give me an
> ounce of civet; good apothecary, sweeten my
> imagination!
>
> —*King Lear*, Act IV, scene vi

My analysis of Ezekiel 8:7–12, and of the vision in which this passage is embedded, points clearly to Ezekiel as a man possessed by fear and loathing of women and their sexuality, and by rage and envy that other men might partake of that sexuality.

My analysis also suggests, rather more obscurely, an ambivalent attitude toward powerful males. Combined in this attitude were love, admiration, homosexual attraction, envy, contempt, hatred, and longing for revenge. In general, Ezekiel turned the positive elements of this constellation toward Yahweh, the negative elements toward the community elders. We have already seen hints, however—and we shall pursue those hints in this chapter—that his real feelings toward both were considerably more mixed than he would have consciously allowed.

We must now test my analysis, by asking whether the portrait it has revealed accords with what we can learn about Ezekiel from the rest of his book.

1. Ezekiel's Wicked Women

Two passages of Ezekiel's book set forth his feelings on female sexuality a great deal more explicitly than most readers could wish.

Chapters 16 and 23 represent Jerusalem and Samaria as Yahweh's promiscuous wives.[1] They flaunt their infidelities before their baffled and frustrated husband, but they are dreadfully punished in the end. Their lovers seem to correspond sometimes to pagan gods, sometimes to foreign peoples.

Ezekiel did not innovate either theme. It was Hosea who gave classic expression to the image of idolatrous Israel as an unfaithful wife (chapters 1–3). Isaiah knew this image, though he did not try to elaborate it (1:21). Jeremiah took it up and developed it in ways that anticipate Ezekiel (2:2, 20–25, 3:1–25)—perhaps, as I have suggested in Chapter 2, confusing the real sexual liberties of his contemporaries with their imagined yearnings for alien gods. Similarly, as Greenberg points out, both Hosea (8:9) and Jeremiah (22:20, 22, 30:14) represent the Israelites' foreign alliances as erotic adventures [112,304]. But Hosea and Jeremiah, even at their most severe, manage some measure of tenderness for their errant ladies (Hosea 2:16–17, 21–22, 3:1; Jeremiah 2:2, 3:12–13). In Ezekiel, the prevailing emotion is pornographic fury.

The ancient rabbis were hardly inclined to criticize their Scriptures. Yet they found the obscenity and cruelty of Ezekiel 16 hard to stomach. The Mishnah, Megillah 4:10, attributes to Rabbi Eliezer (ca. A.D. 100) the ruling that this chapter must not be read publicly in the synagogue. One unfortunate, we are told, began to read from it in Rabbi Eliezer's presence: *Son of man, proclaim to Jerusalem her abominations* (16:2). "Why don't you go out," Eliezer said to him, "and proclaim the abominations of your mother?"[2]

With this comment, we will soon see, Rabbi Eliezer penetrates to Ezekiel's unconscious purpose.

In Ezekiel 16, Jerusalem is represented as an abandoned infant who grows up to be a famous beauty. Yahweh marries her and lavishes gifts upon her. Yet, ungrateful, she betrays him with innumerable lovers.

---

1. Julie Galambush's *Jerusalem in the Book of Ezekiel: The City as Yahweh's Wife* [91], which appeared too recently for me to take account of it in my discussion, arrives independently at several of the conclusions drawn in this chapter.

2. Tosefta, Megillah 3(4):34 [188]. Parallels in Palestinian Talmud, Megillah 4:12 (75c); Babylonian Talmud, Megillah 25b [131].

In chapter 23, Yahweh takes two wives: "daughters of one mother . . . Oholah, the elder, and Oholibah, her sister." The two women correspond, we are told, to Samaria and Jerusalem; that is, to the Northern and Southern Kingdoms (verses 2–4). They, too, are wildly promiscuous.

The outcome is much the same in both passages. At Yahweh's instigation, the women's lovers turn against them and destroy them. The difference lies mainly in the degree of gruesomeness with which their ends are described.

Modern commentators speak of these stories as historical allegories. There is a certain justice in this designation, given that Ezekiel is very definite that he intends his "women" to represent cities or nations. But, at least on first reading, their relation to the traditional account of Israelite history, as it had crystallized by Ezekiel's time, seems very tenuous.

Chapter 16 begins with a claim about Jerusalem's origins—"your father was an Amorite, your mother a Hittite" (verse 3)—found nowhere else in the Bible. It contains no recognizable version of the patriarchal, Exodus, or conquest traditions. It says nothing of the united kingdom or of its division. Ezekiel is not even clear whether by "Jerusalem" he means the city, or all Israel. Verses 4–43 make the most sense on the latter hypothesis; yet, in verses 44–58, Jerusalem is "sister" to Samaria as well as to Sodom. It is true that Ezekiel's accusations of idolatry and child sacrifice reflect, in exaggerated and overgeneralized form, the historical books' charges of apostasy. It is also true that most of his allusions to Egyptians, Assyrians and Chaldeans (verses 26–29), and Philistines and Edomites[3] (verses 27, 57) can be brought into some relation with Israel's and Judah's political alliances and animosities. This is about the extent of the "history" in Ezekiel 16.

Modern scholars have tried, with greater or lesser plausibility, to fill in some of the gaps. Zimmerli has gathered a few indications that Hittites did play some role in Jerusalem's earliest history. Deuteronomy 32:10, and perhaps also Hosea 9:10, seem to hint at a tradition that Yahweh found Israel abandoned in the wilderness. The seemingly inappropriate reference to the Philistines in 16:27 may be rooted in events following the collapse of an anti-Assyrian rebellion in 701 B.C. [104,304]. Greenberg, following rabbinic exegesis, understands the infant's abandonment in 16:4–7 to represent Israel's slavery in Egypt. He has perhaps detected a few other places where traditional Israelite history has influenced the

3.   Or perhaps Arameans, depending on whether or not one emends the *benot 'aram* of the Masoretic Text to *benot 'edom*.

supposedly allegorical text [104].[4] But, even if all this is granted, the fit between historical tradition and Ezekiel's "historical allegory" remains very weak. A person who had read only Ezekiel 16 could not possibly reconstruct anything of the Deuteronomistic history.

Chapter 23 handles Israel's early history with equal freedom. It thus represents Oholah and Oholibah ("Samaria" and "Jerusalem") as distinct ("sisters") even in Egypt, where they begin their notorious sexual careers (verse 3). It does, however, correspond somewhat more closely to the political events surrounding the end of the kingdoms of Israel and Judah. After marrying Yahweh and bearing (his?) children, Oholah takes up with Assyrians, while continuing to sleep with her old Egyptian flames. The Assyrians, presumably jealous, kill her (verses 4–10). Oholibah, also Yahweh's wife, has affairs with both Assyrians and Babylonians. But she cannot overcome her nostalgia for the Egyptians and their gigantic sexual organs (verses 11–21). She will suffer, Ezekiel goes on to threaten, hideous retribution at her lovers' hands.

Once we understand that sexual liaisons are used to represent political associations (of whatever kind), the allegory of chapter 23 is at least intelligible. The judgments it expresses remain, as Yehezkel Kaufmann says, "bizarre." The "whoring" Ezekiel denounces could, with far greater truth, be described as rape. "In fact, of course, Samaria's 'lust' after Assyria was the result of subjugation by an iron fist. . . . During Ezekiel's time, there was only one man in Jerusalem who 'doted upon' the Chaldeans— Jeremiah. After Jehoiakim became a Babylonian vassal, the 'doting' went on three years; thereafter Judah continuously plotted rebellion. Zedekiah spent all his days planning revolt; when he revolted, who denounced him for treachery toward his 'lover'? Ezekiel!" [163].

We must conclude that the details of Ezekiel's "allegories," although not entirely alien to the history they purport to represent, are in no way controlled by that history. His stories of the wicked women have their sense and coherence on the level of the narratives themselves. It is at this level that we must seek to understand them.

This realization prompted Hermann Gunkel to identify the "foundling" story of chapter 16 as a fairy tale, which Ezekiel reworked and pressed into service as an allegory. The story, Gunkel writes, "defies interpretation in

---

4. The "oath" and "covenant" of verses 8 and 59, Greenberg thinks, reflect God's promises to the patriarchs, and his covenant with the Israelites in the desert. The "high places" of verse 16 are the cultic *bamot*. The details of the destruction of the woman and of her houses (verses 39–41) are based on what Ezekiel expected to happen to Jerusalem.

connection with the destiny of Jerusalem. Here one can palpably feel how Ezekiel has adopted material derived from elsewhere. . . . All this is evidently fairy-tale material with strong oriental coloration" [121]. In a similar way, Johannes Hempel and Georg Fohrer (cited by Zimmerli) have detected behind chapter 23 a myth of Yahweh and his two goddess-consorts.

Zimmerli is very cool toward all of these suggestions. Yet he himself recognizes that in both chapters "the gap between the metaphor and the fact portrayed can easily disappear, and the reality referred to may arise directly out of the metaphor" [304]. He recognizes that in 23:36–49 Oholah and Oholibah do not function as symbolic representations of two nations, but as themselves: "sinful, adulterous, and murderous women, who are to serve as a warning example so that other women in the future may not do likewise" [297]. But he draws from this the mistaken conclusion that 23:36–49 is a late addition to the text and a misinterpretation of its original intent. The opposite is the truth. It is in this passage that Ezekiel's true intent, which he elsewhere tries to mask with historical allegory, forces its way to the light.

Similarly, we may affirm the realization that prompted Gunkel's "fairy tale" hypothesis, while rejecting the hypothesis itself. Greenberg is surely right when he objects that the fairy tale reconstructed by Gunkel does not in fact fit the appropriate fairy-tale pattern [112]. Gunkel was right to say that Ezekiel 16 is a story that must be understood in its own right, without allegorical referent. But he was wrong to infer that it must therefore have been "material derived from elsewhere." Its "material" was Ezekiel's own, in the most intimate sense, created of his intense private pain. He interpreted and justified his pain by projecting his experience outward, onto the history of Israel.

The disguise of a "historical allegory" is thus a secondary development. We must discard it if we are to understand Ezekiel 16 and 23 at their deepest levels. But the disguise served its purpose. Had Ezekiel not distanced himself in this way from his inner experience, it is unlikely that he could have brought himself to speak about it at all.

2. The Women and Their Lovers

The power of Ezekiel's experience is reflected in the erotic intensity—perverted into obscenity—with which he describes his wicked women.

Chapter 16 describes the lubricity of Yahweh's wicked wife with a bitter vividness that has no parallel anywhere in the Bible. She takes the gold and silver jewelry Yahweh has given her, constructs phallic images (*ṣalme zakhar*), and masturbates with them (verse 17). She spreads her legs on every street corner for all passers-by (verse 25). She carries her lust to her "neighbors the Egyptians, the ones with the big organs" (verse 26). She is insatiable (verses 28–29). Her juice positively drips from her (verse 36, following Greenberg [104]). She is strikingly beautiful, sexually aggressive, and—still more alarming—economically independent (*shallaṭet*, verse 30 [120]). Men therefore cannot control her, as they can ordinary harlots, through her need for money. On the contrary, she is able to pay her lovers (verses 31–34). Yahweh, helpless to dominate her, can only solace himself by punishing her. His rage is practically orgasmic: "I will exhaust [*wahaniḥoti*] my fury upon you, and my jealousy[5] will turn away from you; and I will be at ease, angry no more" (verse 42).

Chapter 23 is not quite as graphic, but it comes close. Ezekiel describes Oholah and Oholibah's youthful sex play in some detail. "There [in Egypt] their breasts were squeezed; there they pressed [?][6] their virgin nipples" (verse 3; cf. 8, 21). Their lovers' enormous genitals—"their organs were asses' organs, their issue was horses' issue" (verse 20)—continue to fascinate him.

Who are the lovers? Ezekiel uses the image in two distinct, and contradictory, ways. At times, he follows the familiar tradition of Hosea and Jeremiah, which represents Israel's flirtations with alien cults as "whoring" after other gods (Hosea 1:2). The lovers accordingly stand for pagan gods, or idols. But, at other times, Ezekiel describes the lovers as Egyptians, or Assyrians, or Babylonians. The women's promiscuity then represents Israel's and Judah's political involvements with foreign states.

Zimmerli observes, correctly, that the cultic symbolism predominates in chapter 16, the political in chapter 23. In a move characteristic of his critical method, he then jumps to the conclusion that chapter 16 must have originally contained *nothing but* cultic symbolism, chapter 23 *nothing but*

5. *Qin'ati;* recall *semel haqqin'ah* ("the image of jealousy") in 8:3, 5.
6. *'Iśśu.* The Pi'el of *'śh* occurs nowhere outside this chapter, and it is not clear just what Ezekiel intends by it. If I am right in supposing that 23:25, 29 allude back to verses 3, 8, 21 (below), the verb will presumably designate an action that can be performed in a hostile as well as a loving manner.

political symbolism. All evidence to the contrary must be treated as secondary accretions, to be excised from both passages.

Left unmutilated, chapters 16 and 23 show clearly that the two interpretations of the lovers, contradictory as they are, existed side by side in Ezekiel's mind. In 16:36, "Jerusalem" fornicates with *gillulim*, a favorite word of Ezekiel's for idols. Her masturbating with phallic images of silver and gold (verse 17) is surely a graphic representation of the same idea. She uses "high places" (*bamot;* that is, shrines) for bedrooms (verse 16). In an obvious allusion to child sacrifice, she slaughters her children for her lovers to eat (verses 20–21, 36). But, in the middle of all this, Ezekiel has "Jerusalem" whore with Egyptians, Assyrians, Babylonians (verses 26–29).

In chapter 23, the dominant interpretation of the two sisters' promiscuity is political. Yet, in fornicating with the nations, Oholah and Oholibah also become polluted with their *gillulim* (verses 7, 30). Indeed, "they have committed adultery with their *gillulim*. They have even given them their sons, whom they bore to me, for them to eat. This also they did to me: they polluted my sanctuary on that day, and profaned my Sabbaths. When they slaughtered their sons for their *gillulim*—on that day they entered my sanctuary to profane it. That is what they did in my own house" (verses 37–39). Ezekiel plainly refers back to the cultic "abominations" of his Temple vision, which he links with child sacrifice. The connection is peculiar, and will require further elucidation.

It is arbitrary to force consistency on these passages by slashing them to pieces. We do better to take their inconsistency as a given and seek to discover how it can be made psychologically intelligible.

I propose that Ezekiel's contradictory representations of the lovers derive from his desperate efforts to rationalize, and thus make acceptable to his consciousness, a primitive experience that would otherwise have been too painful for him to recall, much less express. I will assume, for the moment, that this experience was essentially the familiar Oedipal conflict of father with male child, over the love of the mother. We will need presently to consider why Ezekiel found this conflict so painful and intractable, and why it continued for so long to dominate his mental life.

Accordingly, the child Ezekiel will have discovered that the woman who was his first and best love preferred to sleep with another male. His rival's genitalia, compared with his own, will have seemed like those of a horse or of an ass, capable of the perpetual erection of a phallic statue. His mother's

preference for this rival will have appeared a stunning and outrageous betrayal, which he could explain only as a mark of her heedless promiscuity.

The adult Ezekiel's experience of captivity, we may imagine, revived
and sharpened the child's pain. Led off to exile—no doubt "naked and
barefoot, with uncovered buttocks" (Isaiah 20:4), thirsty, exhausted, and
sick—Ezekiel could not have failed to contrast his own impotent misery
and shame with the power and splendor of his captors. The sexual humiliation of the child became fused with the physical humiliation of the adult.

Ezekiel thus conflated the triumphant villains of both episodes. In his
fantasy, the woman he desires cannot suppress her yen for "the men clad in
blue, officials and rulers, all of them splendid young men; cavalrymen,
mounted on horses" (23:6).[7] She sees "men engraved on the wall, images of
the Chaldeans ['anshe mehuqqeh 'al haqqir salme kasdim], limned in scarlet;
sashes around their waists, flowing headgear on their heads, the very image
of officers, all of them. . . . She was smitten with love at the very sight of
them, and sent messengers to them to Chaldea. And so the Babylonians
came to make love to her, and polluted her with their lust" (23:14–17).

Through this conflation, Ezekiel found one way to project his inner
experience onto the common history of Yahweh and Israel, and thereby find
outlet for an otherwise unendurable memory. Following hints provided by
Hosea and Jeremiah, he represented his sense of sexual betrayal as if it were
Yahweh's response to the foreign entanglements of the Israelite kingdoms.
But Hosea and Jeremiah offered him a different solution as well, which he
also seized upon. Once again, he projected his experience of betrayal outward. This time, it was Israel's abandoning Yahweh for other gods.

Neither historicization, in truth, was very plausible. Israel and Judah
hardly "lusted" for the embrace of the Assyrians and Babylonians, and
Judah's apostasies were far too sporadic to give color to Ezekiel's charge of
continual "whoring" (Kaufmann). But, as far as the unconscious is concerned, two unconvincing rationalizations are better than one, even when
they happen to contradict each other. We may say of Ezekiel's identifica-
tions of the "lovers" much the same as what Freud said about one of his
own dreams. It "reminded one vividly of the defence put forward by the
man who was charged by one of his neighbours with having given him
back a borrowed kettle in a damaged condition. The defendant asserted

7. In this perspective, the distinction between Oholah and Oholibah, Assyrians and
Babylonians, is unimportant. Notice how the horse does double duty, as an image for the
military (23:6, 12, 23) and the sexual power of the lovers (23:20).

first, that he had given it back undamaged; secondly, that the kettle had a hole in it when he borrowed it; and thirdly, that he had never borrowed a kettle from his neighbour at all. So much the better: if only a single one of these three lines of defence were to be accepted as valid, the man would have to be acquitted" [334,339].

Both of Ezekiel's rationalizations are neatly condensed in 23:14. Oholibah falls in love with *ṣalme kasdim*, "images of the Chaldeans." The reference to Chaldeans shows clearly that her lovers are foreigners. But the word *ṣalme* suggests that they are idols as well. The Bible uses *ṣelem* commonly, though admittedly not exclusively, for the kind of "image" that is worshiped (Numbers 33:52, 2 Kings 11:18 [= 2 Chronicles 23:17], Amos 5:26). In 7:20 Ezekiel calls Judah's idols *ṣalme to'abotam*, "the images of their abominations." In 16:17 he uses the same word for "Jerusalem's" phallic images, *ṣalme zakhar*, which presumably correspond to the *ṣalme kasdim* of 23:14.[8]

Ezekiel equates these "images" with "men engraved on the wall" (*'anshe meḥuqqeh 'al haqqir*). The language obviously recalls 8:10, where "every representation of creeping things and beasts, loathsome things, and all the idols of the house of Israel" are "engraved upon the wall all around" (*meḥuqqeh 'al haqqir sabib sabib*). *Qua* idols, the "images" are identified with the deadly monstrosities that haunt the loathed yet desired chamber. *Qua* Chaldeans, they are the envied men who have penetrated that chamber, polluting it with their lust.

3. The Women's Names

The names "Oholah" and "Oholibah" seem to point toward this chamber.

The traditional interpretation of these names (which, according to Zimmerli, goes back to Jerome) renders them as "her tent" and "my tent is in her," respectively. If we suppose that "tent" can mean "sanctuary" (like the Pentateuch's "tent of meeting"), we will naturally see these names as referring to the historical situation Ezekiel claims to represent. "My tent" will be the Temple Yahweh has established for himself in Jerusalem, "her

---

8. Ezekiel uses *ṣelem* only in these three passages (always as a plural construct). Other biblical occurrences are in P's creation story, in which it is the "image" of God in which humans are created (Genesis 1:26–27, 9:6) or the "image" of Adam in which Seth is begotten (5:3); 1 Samuel's story of the Ark in the land of the Philistines, in which it refers to representations of tumors or of mice (6:5, 11); and the obscure Psalm 39:7 and 73:20.

tent" a condensed representation of the renegade sanctuaries of the North-ern Kingdom.

The name "Hephzibah" ("my desire is in her")—given to a woman in 2 Kings 21:1, to Jerusalem in Isaiah 62:4—obviously supports this interpreta-tion of "Oholibah." Yet Zimmerli is not convinced. He objects that, unlike "Hephzibah," neither "Oholah" nor "Oholibah" has in its last letter the Masoretic marking (the dot called *mappiq*) that indicates a feminine pro-noun. Ezekiel, moreover, does not use the word "tent" (*'ohel*) to mean "sanctuary," or anything else. (Ezekiel 41:1, which uses *'ohel* in connection with the future Temple, is "a textual error.")

Zimmerli's alternative is remarkably weak. "The names of the two women must simply, in Ezekiel, echo and set forth the slightly archaizing sound of Bedouin names, indicating that the two girls with the similar sounding names (Ewald points here to the two sons of Ali, Hasan and Husein) did not belong in Egypt and were not born there." He adds, however, that "this need not altogether exclude that, for an Israelite ear, there was an element of word play" of the name "Oholibah" with the phrase "my tent is in her," the latter to be interpreted in accord with the "tent of meeting" [297]. We may take this rather surprising reversal as Zimmerli's confession that, whatever its defects, the traditional etymology of the names is too useful to be discarded. The front door having been slammed in its face, it is quietly allowed in through the back.

Do we need to close the door at all? The absence of the *mappiq* from the Masoretic Text is not much of an objection. It is hardly astonishing that transmitters of the text assimilated "Oholah" and "Oholibah" (but not the analogous "Hephzibah") to the normal form of a feminine noun, especially since this required no change whatever in the consonantal text and only a barely audible change in its pronunciation. Ezekiel's failure to use the word *'ohel* (disregarding 41:1) is inconvenient, but hardly overwhelming. Given the frequency of the word in biblical usage, both in its ordinary meaning and in that of "sanctuary" [30], it is difficult to imagine Ezekiel can have been unfamiliar with it.

If, however, we are fully to understand why Ezekiel chose these names for his "lewd women" (23:44), we must combine the traditional interpreta-tion with a psychological one. We must suppose that "tent" meant for Ezekiel, not only the Temple, but the female sexual organs.[9] We may

---

9. I cannot point to any clear attestation in the Bible of this symbolization of *'ohel*. But the idea that an ancient Jew might have used "tent" to represent the female sexual organs

assume that Ezekiel was consciously aware of the former significance. The latter operated, far more powerfully, within his unconscious.

"My tent is in her" will then express Yahweh's claim (which Oholibah obviously rejects) that the woman's genitals are for his exclusive use. But the name has a yet deeper meaning, which points specifically to the womb, and expresses Ezekiel's disappointed expectation that in Oholibah he will find security.[10] The horrid corruption of this enclosure (8:10), and its penetration by aliens (8:11, and chapters 16 and 23 throughout), mark the frustration of both expectations. The frenzied rage of Ezekiel 16 and 23 is the result.

So interpreted, Ezekiel's name "Oholibah" for Jerusalem reinforces his unconscious equation of the Jerusalem Temple with the female organs. It conveys, yet more clearly than we have seen so far, the meaning of his outrage at this Temple's imaginary pollutions.

4. Polluted Woman, Menstruous Temple: Ezekiel 7:20–22

These considerations are particularly relevant to the prophecy of 7:20–22. The Masoretic Text reads as follows.

---

seems inherently plausible, and can be buttressed by the following argument: In Numbers 25:6–8, an Israelite man uses a *qubbah* ("large vaulted tent" [30]) as a place in which to engage in semipublic sex with a Midianite woman. Phinehas takes a javelin to the *qubbah* and runs them through with it—"the man of Israel, and the woman *'el qobatah* [through her belly, or her genitals; see the rabbinic exegesis of this passage, found in Babylonian Talmud, Sanhedrin 82b]." *Qubbah* and *qobatah* (= *qebah* [Deuteronomy 18:3] + feminine suffix?) are presumably from different roots [30]. But the author's juxtaposing these two very rare words, which sound so much alike, suggests that he intended a wordplay linking the literal tent with its counterpart inside the woman's body. A tent like that of Numbers 25:6–8 could also be called by the familiar word *'ohel*, as the very similar scene in 2 Samuel 16:22 testifies. May we not suppose, then, that the symbolic association of "tent" with "female genitals" (*qubbah–qoba[tah]*) would have operated in the individual's unconscious, regardless of whether the "tent" was an exotic *qubbah* or an ordinary *'ohel*? We may compare the recent remarks of Danna Nolan Fewell and David M. Gunn, on Judges 4:17–18: "Like a persuasive Leah coming out to 'hire' Jacob's sexual services, Jael comes out to meet Sisera and to invite him into her tent. And like an obedient Jacob, Sisera complies. This analogy reminds us that, at least in biblical literature, a man seldom enters a woman's tent for purposes other than sexual intercourse. The woman's tent is symbolic of the woman's body" [75]. Cf. also the exegesis of Psalm 91:10 in Babylonian Talmud, Berakhot 55b.

10. This same yearning, I suspect, finds expression in 44:1–3. In a "closed gate" within Ezekiel's ideal Temple (= good mother), "the prince" shall sit, "eating bread before Yahweh." I discuss this point further in the Excursus.

[20]He established his lovely ornament to be a [source of] pride; yet they made [or, "did"; *'asu*] in it the images of their abominations, their detestable things [*salme to'abotam shiqqusehem*]. Therefore I have made it menstruous [*niddah*] for them. [21]I will give it as booty into the hand of strangers; as spoil, to the wicked of the earth. They shall profane it [*wehilleluhu*]. [22]I will turn my face away from them, and they shall profane my hidden place [*sefuni*]. Violent men [*parisim*] shall come into her, and profane her.

Given this text, the best interpretation of verse 20 seems to be that of Rashi and Kimhi [212]. Following this interpretation, we will suppose "he" and "his" in verse 20 refer to Yahweh, whom the preceding verse has explicitly mentioned in the third person. His "lovely ornament" is the Temple, with which he intended to adorn his people (cf. 16:11). As in 24:21, it is their "pride" (*ga'on*). But the Jews have corrupted it—as chapter 8 describes in detail—by "doing" in it "the images of their abominations."

Most moderns have, for good reason, preferred to interpret the text of the Septuagint. The translators evidently read the first verb of verse 20 as plural instead of singular. Its subject ("they," not "he") will then be the Jews themselves, who have wickedly used their gold and silver jewelry as a source of pride.

The advantages of this reading are clear. No longer does the prophet awkwardly shift from third into first person while speaking of Yahweh. Significantly, the Septuagint text omits the only other third-person reference to Yahweh in this chapter: in verse 19, "Their silver and their gold will not be able to save them in the day of Yahweh's wrath." These words are quoted almost verbatim from Zephaniah 1:18. It is natural to suppose that some later glossator copied them into the Masoretic Text tradition of Ezekiel.

Read in the light of chapters 16 and 23, however, the Masoretic Text of 7:20–22 has a certain plausibility.

Regardless of which text we follow, we must certainly understand verse 22 as referring to the Temple. On this interpretation, however, the feminine pronouns at the end of the verse are puzzling. They have no antecedent in the text; and the word "Temple" is in any case grammatically masculine. They make sense only if Ezekiel unconsciously perceived the Temple as a woman, whose "hidden place" is to be penetrated by alien males. We notice that Yahweh speaks of this "hidden place" as "*my* hidden place," just as he speaks of the "tent" that is within Oholibah as "*my* tent."

The alien males are called *pariṣim;* literally, "those who burst through." In the present context, it may also be possible to think of them as rapists.[11] They are also "strangers" (*zarim*) and "the wicked of the earth." Clearly enough, they are entering Yahweh's woman/Temple against her will, in punishment for her earlier sins.

But, when we compare this passage with Ezekiel 16 and 23, it begins to appear that their entry is her sin as well as her punishment. Like chapter 23 (below), 7:20–22 condenses sexual crime and sexual punishment into one.

Thus, in 16:32, the "strangers" enter Yahweh's wife with her enthusiastic consent. And 23:37–39, as we have seen, indicts Oholah and Oholibah for a crime that strikingly resembles the punishment threatened here:

> They have committed adultery with their *gillulim.* . . . This also they did to me: they polluted [*ṭimme'u*] my sanctuary on that day, and profaned [*ḥillelu*] my Sabbaths. When they slaughtered their sons for their *gillulim*—on that day they entered my sanctuary to profane it [*leḥallelo*].[12] That is what they did [*'aśu*] in my own house.

This passage, as I have remarked, looks back to the "abominations" of Ezekiel 8. But it is also linked to 7:20. In the light of the use of the verb *'aśu* ("did") in 23:37–39—which itself echoes the repeated use of this root in chapter 8[13]—it does not seem strange to think of the Jews "doing" the "images of their abominations" in the Temple (7:20). We recall that Ezekiel uses the word for "images" elsewhere only in 16:17 and 23:14, for the phallic "images" on which Yahweh's wife masturbates and for the sexually arousing "images" of Chaldean men. The underlying thought in 7:20 is not the simple placement of idolatrous objects in the Temple, but the "doing" of misdeeds whose fundamental meaning is sexual.

The woman's "lovely ornament"—which, like her "hidden place," Yahweh thinks of as his own—has become "menstruous." We may interpret:

11. I admit that I can offer no evidence outside this passage in support of this interpretation. Ezekiel uses the word *pariṣ* again in 18:10, evidently with the generalized meaning of "hoodlum."

12. The language of this verse is almost exactly parallel to that of 7:22. Cf. *weḥillelu 'et ṣefuni uba'u bah pariṣim weḥilleluha* of 7:22 and *wayyabo'u 'el miqdaši bayyom hahu' leḥallelo* of 23:39.

13. Verses 6, 9, 12, 13, 17, 18.

her genitals are drenched in blood.[14] Once we accept that Ezekiel unconsciously equated the Temple with the female genitals, we may see here an allusion to its anticipated punishment. The Temple, like the rest of Jerusalem, will be awash in blood.

But the "menstruous" Temple contains within itself a reference also to the crime: the "blood" with which, Ezekiel never tires of insisting (7:23, for example), Judah and Jerusalem have become filled. Passages like 8:17, which denounces "violence" in the same breath as the Temple "abominations," have troubled modern scholars. What connection can Ezekiel have made between these two accusations? They are in fact intimately linked. What binds them together is the nexus, stated plainly in chapters 16 and 23—and presently to be examined in detail—of sexual betrayal and the slaughter of children.

5. Punishment and Its Agents

In chapters 16 and 23, Ezekiel imagines the women's lovers as executing God's wrath upon them. This of course reflects the historical reality. It was the Assyrians who destroyed the kingdom of Israel, the Babylonians who were to destroy the kingdom of Judah. But it also reflects, as I have already suggested, a fusion of sexual sin and sexual punishment in Ezekiel's own mind, and, corresponding to this, a deeply ambivalent attitude toward his own sexual competitors.

What exactly are the punishments? In chapter 16, Yahweh begins by reducing his wife's allowance and exposing her to the sanctimonious abuse of the neighbor women (Philistines; verse 27). These moves seem to have no

14. The language of 16:7 confirms that Ezekiel might use *'adi* ("ornament") for the vulva: "[Y]ou grew and matured, and developed the loveliest of adornments [*'adi 'adayim*]—your breasts were well formed and your hair had sprouted; but you were stark naked" (Greenberg's translation). Greenberg is surely right in supposing that these "adornments" are the signs that the young woman is sexually ripe [104]. They include, but are hardly restricted to, her breasts. (We might think, in this connection, of the young Inanna glorying in her vulva, "wondrous to behold" [292], or of Marvin Pope's interpretation of Song 7:3 as praise of the beloved's vulva [230].) Greenberg argues, against Rashi and Kimhi's identification of the "ornament" of 7:20 with the Temple, that the preceding verse threatens that the Jews' precious metals will become "menstruous"; surely the "ornament" of verse 20 must be these same metals [104]? I acknowledge it as a disadvantage that we are obliged to apply the threat of *niddah* to two distinct objects in two successive verses. I believe this disadvantage outweighed by the very substantial advantages of the "Temple" interpretation.

deterrent effect, perhaps because she is economically independent (verse 30, *shallatet* [120]). So he assembles her lovers, exposes her naked before them, and judges her as an adulteress and a murderess (verses 37–38).

This is not, of course, the first time they have seen her naked. Verse 36 indicts her precisely for the crime of having exposed herself to them. But now the sight seems to move them to murderous fury. They destroy the structures she has set up for her pleasure (and theirs! verse 24), strip her of clothes and ornaments. They raise a mob (*qahal*), which proceeds to lynch her. She is stoned, hacked to pieces, her houses burnt. "They shall execute judgments upon you in full view of many women." Thus Yahweh will put an end to her whoring (verses 39–41).

It seems curious that, after Yahweh has exposed his wife naked to her lovers' view (verse 37), she seems still to have clothes for them to tear off (verse 39). It is no doubt this inconsistency that moves Zimmerli to treat verses 36–38 as an editorial addition. Greenberg tries to harmonize the two passages by supposing that verse 37 describes only "turning back clothing . . . distinct from the stripping of the adulteress, which occurs after her conviction" [104,297]. (Yet verse 37 speaks of exposing "*all* your nakedness.")

Neither solution is justified. The contradiction is real, but can be traced back to tension within Ezekiel himself. Yahweh's action, and that of the lovers, are two variants of the same sadistically exciting fantasy of tearing off the clothes of the desired woman. It will follow from this—and we shall presently see more evidence of it—that Ezekiel uses Yahweh and the lovers as representations of the same aspect of himself. This will explain why Yahweh's rivals can so easily function as his agents; why, indeed, he and they are interchangeable.

The retributions inflicted on Oholah and Oholibah are yet more ghastly than those of chapter 16. Oholah's Assyrian lovers strip her, take away her children, and kill her (23:9–10). An "international mob" (*qehal 'ammim*) of Oholibah's rejected lovers mass themselves against her and pass judgment on her. They cut off her nose and her ears, kill her children,[15] strip her of clothes and jewelry (verses 22–26, 29). In a drunken fit, overwhelmed with grief and self-disgust, she slices off her own breasts with pottery fragments (verses 32–34).

Finally, "righteous men" judge Oholah and Oholibah as adulteresses

15. Understanding *'aharit* as "posterity" [30]. The point is stated more explicitly in verse 47.

and murderesses (verse 45). A mob (*qahal*) gathers against them, stones
them, hacks them to pieces, kills their sons and daughters, burns their
houses (verses 46–47). This, God assures Ezekiel, will teach women their
lesson (verse 48).

Much as chapter 16 blurs the boundaries between Yahweh and the
lovers, chapter 23 tends to interchange the lovers and the "righteous men."
The actions performed by the lovers, in verses 22–29, correspond fairly
closely to the actions performed by the "righteous men" in verses 45–47.
(The use of *qahal* in verses 24 and 46–47 is particularly striking.) Further,
the lovers of chapter 16 behave almost exactly as do the "righteous men" of
chapter 23.

16:37–41	23:45–48

³⁷Therefore, behold, I am gather-
ing all your lovers to whom you
were so sweet—all whom you
loved, and all whom you hated—
and I will gather them against
you from all around.¹⁶ And I will
bare your nakedness to them, and
they will see all your nakedness.

³⁸And I will judge you as women   ⁴⁵It is righteous men who shall
who commit adultery and shed   judge them, as women who com-
blood are judged [*mishpeṭe no'afot*   mit adultery and shed blood are
weshofekhot dam], and I will set   judged [*mishpaṭ no'afot umishpaṭ*
upon you the blood of fury and   *shofekhot dam*], for they are adulter-
jealousy.   esses and there is blood on their
                                         hands.

³⁹And I will give you into their
hands, and they shall tear down
your raised place and smash your
lofty places into bits. And they
shall strip your clothes off you,
take your jewelry, and leave you
naked and bare. ⁴⁰And they shall   ⁴⁶For thus says the Lord Yahweh:
raise a mob against you, and they   [They shall?] raise a mob against

---

16. The language is closely parallel to that of 23:22.

shall stone you, and chop you in pieces with their swords.

41They shall burn your houses,

and execute judgments upon you in full view of many women. And I will stop you from being a harlot, and you will give no more gifts [to your lovers].

them, make them a trembling and a spoil. 47The mob shall stone them, hack them to pieces with their swords.17 They shall kill their sons and daughters, burn their houses.
48And I will stop there from being promiscuity in the land; and all women will be taught a lesson, and will not be promiscuous like you.

"Both content and linguistic usage," says Zimmerli, "show [23:]36–49 to be a secondary section, strongly affected by quotations" [305]. It is true that this passage is inconsistent with the earlier parts of the chapter, in that it presupposes that Oholah and Oholibah are yet to be judged, whereas Oholah is in fact already dead and Oholibah horribly mutilated [56]. To this argument, Zimmerli adds the rather paradoxical assertion that "a new level of independence from the original text is evident both in the language and the extent of the dependence on Ezek 16 (and 23)." In other words, 23:36–49 so closely resembles other parts of chapters 16 and 23 that it must have been added on by some imitator of the genuine Ezekiel. "In detail," moreover, "the style has strikingly run wild. . . . The text cannot be from one hand but is broken up by additions . . ." [297].

None of these points seems to me compelling. The stylistic wildness of the passage, which is undeniable, does not point to the piling up of editorial accretions, but to the ill-disciplined outpourings of a human being in nearly unbearable psychic pain. Its close resemblance to chapter 16 is rooted, not in literary dependence, but in a single obsession that drives

17. The verb sequence in verses 46b–47a is very strange. *Ha'aleh* ("raise") could be either a masculine singular imperative or an infinitive absolute; *naton* ("make") is certainly an infinitive absolute; *weragemu* ("stone") is a third-person-plural perfect with *waw*-consecutive; *bare'* ("hack") is usually treated as an infinitive absolute, but its vocalization would better suit a masculine singular imperative (as in 21:24, where Ezekiel is the recipient of the command). The two verbs of verse 47b are, as one would expect, third-person imperfect plurals. Since the Hebrew infinitive absolute is capable of substituting for any conceivable tense, mood, gender, person, or number, it is possible to translate all the preceding verbs as third-person imperfect plurals as well; and the parallel in 16:40 would encourage us to do so. Yet the repeated lapse into infinitive absolute, with a strong hint of the imperative, is troubling. It suggests that Ezekiel perceived himself as one of the "righteous men," charged with executing vengeance upon Oholah and Oholibah.

both prophecies and finds parallel expression in both. And the repeated judgments of the "lewd women" are the effect, not of textual expansion, but of a rage so overwhelming that it cannot punish its victim and then dismiss her, but must bring her back again and again to face ever more hideous revenge.

In Ezekiel's fantasies, the "righteous men," the mob, the lovers,[18] and Yahweh himself all blend together into one great mask of fury. The face behind this mask, we may presume, is Ezekiel's own.

Thus, in 16:2, Ezekiel is called upon to be Jerusalem's prosecutor. In 23:36, he is judge as well. "Yahweh said to me: Son of man, will you judge Oholah and Oholibah, and tell them their abominations?"[19] The peculiar verbs of 23:46b–47a (see note 17) suggest a still more active role. They hint at a barely repressed fantasy in which it is Ezekiel who leads the mob against the wicked women, Ezekiel who hacks them into pieces with his sword—much as, in reality, he had once vented his rage on clumps of his own hair (5:1–4).

At the beginning of this section, I referred to a certain measure of identification, in Ezekiel's mind, of the women's sins with their punishments. Let us now consider some examples.

Because "Jerusalem" stripped herself for her lovers, Yahweh will punish her—precisely by stripping her before her lovers (16:36–37). Her lovers themselves will strip off her clothes, leaving her "naked and bare"—as she was when her nudity seduced Yahweh himself (16:39; cf. verses 7, 22). Oholibah, too, both sins and is punished by the revealing of her nakedness (23:18, 26, 29; cf. 10).

Ezekiel begins his account of Oholibah's punishment with a long description of the martial magnificence of her lovers-turned-persecutors (23:23). The language repeats that of verses 12 and 15, which describe the splendors that first ignited Oholibah's lust. The lovers come in their wrath, then, much as they once came in their desire.

"They shall deal with you [*we'aśu 'otakh*] in fury . . . and they shall deal with you in hatred" (23:25, 29). We must grant that this use of *'aśah 'et* ("deal with") is entirely in keeping with Ezekiel's language (cf. 17:17, 20:44, 22:14). It is nevertheless striking that he uses the same root in verses

18. Who are called an "international mob" (*qehal 'ammim*) in 23:24.

19. Significantly, Ezekiel is also called upon to judge the elders of Israel (20:4), and the "bloody city" of Jerusalem (22:2). We will presently examine these passages.

3, 8, 21, to speak of some manipulation (pressing?) of the sisters' nipples by their early lovers.[20] We may guess that, with this repetition of the verb, Ezekiel intends to recapitulate the sin in the punishment. Once, the girls' lovers had "pressed" them in passion. Now, they do it in "fury" and "hatred."

Most significantly, Ezekiel represents the women's children, and particularly their sons, as victims both of their wickedness *and* of its retribution.

Chapters 16 and 23 agree that the wicked women kill their own children, for the pleasure of their lovers. Not content with her infidelities, Yahweh's wife "took your sons and your daughters whom you bore to me, and sacrificed them to [your lovers] to eat. . . . You slaughtered my sons and made gifts of them, passing them over to [your lovers]" (16:20–21). Her promiscuity, and "the blood of your sons which you gave [your lovers]," are grounds for her to be judged "as women who commit adultery and shed blood are judged" (verses 36–38).

Oholah and Oholibah, too, "have committed adultery, and there is blood on their hands. They have committed adultery with their *gillulim;* and have even given them their sons, whom they bore to me, for them to eat. . . . They slaughtered their sons for their *gillulim;* and, on that day, entered my sanctuary to profane it. That is what they did my own house" (23:37–39).

The women, however, are not the only child killers. So, in chapter 23 (though not 16), are the males who condemn them. The "righteous men" of 23:45, who judge Oholah and Oholibah "as women who commit adultery and shed blood are judged," shade into the "mob" who "kill their sons and daughters" (verse 47). Historical reality intrudes upon Ezekiel's fantasy in verses 9–10, in which Oholah's Assyrian lovers "take away" her sons and daughters. In verse 25, Oholibah's lovers do the same to her. "Your posterity [*'aharit*] will fall by the sword . . . be devoured in fire."

Once again, the "righteous men," the mob, and the lovers turn out to be the same. Yahweh, the ultimate mover in all these atrocities, is one with them all.

Generally speaking, we may account for this identity of sin and punishment by supposing that, in Ezekiel's psyche, sexual desire and rage were largely fused. He could satisfy both by sadistic fantasies, in which one brutal male or another served as surrogate for himself.

20. Pi'el in verses 3 and 8, Qal in verse 21.

But the last detail, the killing of the children, hints at something more complex. Here it is possible to conceive that Ezekiel takes on, at least in part, the perspective of the victimized child. This sets him apart from, indeed in opposition to, the murderous male figures (from God on down) whom he describes.

If this supposition proves justified, it promises to lead us straight to the historical root of Ezekiel's pain and rage. It therefore demands our closest scrutiny.

6. Child Sacrificed: The Crime of the Woman

Ezekiel's women are "shedders of blood" (16:38, 23:45); and their blood-shedding is bound up somehow with their wild sexuality.

The blood, as we have seen, is that of their children—normally, of their sons. Ezekiel 16:20, to be sure, represents "Jerusalem's" daughters also as innocent victims of their mother's cruelty. Other passages, however, seem to implicate the entire female sex in her crimes. Her mother and her sister, too, loathed their husbands and their sons (verses 44–45). Their daughters stand condemned with them (verses 46–49), for, as the proverb says, "Like mother, like daughter" (verse 44). It is no accident that the women's daughters, who hardly appear as victims of their sins, are present in full force as recipients of their punishment (23:10, 25, 47).

Can we suppose that these accusations refer, not to the alleged female evil that serves Ezekiel as metaphor, but to some historical reality for which the metaphor stands?

Certainly, Jerusalem is for Ezekiel what Nineveh had been to Nahum (3:1), the "city of blood" (22:2, 24:6, 9), a "city that sheds blood[21] in its midst" (22:3). Its princes and people are bent on bloodshed (22:6, 9, 12, 27). The land, too, is "filled with blood" (9:9, cf. 7:23).

This portrayal, however, can hardly be treated as sober and objective reportage. Sixth-century Jerusalem was surely, like most cities ancient and modern, home to a fair amount of violence and lawlessness. But no other biblical writer seems to react quite so vehemently to the city's misdeeds, or, as Yehezkel Kaufmann points out, to generalize them into an unrelieved denunciation of the "city of blood." (Ezekiel's "fierce antipathy," Kauf-

---

21. *Shofekhet dam;* the same phrase is used in 16:38 and 23:45.

mann astutely remarks, ". . . leads one to suspect some personal provocation is involved" [163].) Blood is a standard preoccupation of Ezekiel's, as a glance at a concordance will show.[22] Undeniably, Ezekiel's harsh judgment of Jerusalem had some basis in reality. But, just as undeniably, his peculiar psychic bent refracted and distorted that reality.

Ezekiel 22, the most sustained denunciation of "bloody" Jerusalem, opens with the call: "You, son of man—will you judge, will you judge the city of blood? Make known to it, then, all its abominations" (verse 2). This invitation to judgment, as we have seen, echoes 23:36; and, more distantly, 16:2.[23] We may infer that Ezekiel's denunciation of the wicked city is closely tied to that of the wicked women. We may further suppose, in the light of what I have said above, that his more or less pathological convictions about female evil conditioned his perception of the city's wickedness, and not the other way round.

Shall we say, then, that Ezekiel's accusations refer less to Jerusalem's generalized "bloodshed" than to the specific practice of ritual child sacrifice? This view has much to recommend it. Ezekiel certainly intends the reader to understand that this is what he means by the women's child killing. Speaking of these murders, he uses the verbs *natan* ("to give"; 16:21, 37) and *he'ebir* ("to pass over"; 16:21, 23:37). Both verbs are connected, in other biblical texts, with the Molech cult [139,187]. In 16:20–21, he emphasizes this allusion with the verbs *zabah* ("to sacrifice") and *shahat* ("to slaughter"; also 23:39), normally used for animal sacrifice. Ezekiel's claim that the women's lovers eat the children (16:20, 23:37) may, as George C. Heider thinks, hark back to Jeremiah 3:24, which apparently speaks of Baal "eating" the Jews' sons and daughters [139].

As in the case of "bloody" Jerusalem, we are dealing with historical reality viewed through "Ezekiel's ever-peculiar perspective" (Heider). Once again, our concern is with the perspective rather than the reality. We cannot doubt that Judean children were at times sacrificed, as part of a cult (pagan? or possibly Yahwistic?) which was associated with the name "Molech." Ahaz and Manasseh, if we are to trust the author of 2 Kings, institutionalized this cult (16:3, 21:6). Josiah put an end to it, when he "defiled Topheth, which was in the valley of Ben-Hinnom, so that no one

22. The Book of Ezekiel contains far more occurrences of the word "blood" than any book of the Bible except Leviticus. If we disregard passages that speak of blood as the object of ritual manipulation, Leviticus too falls far behind.

23. Also 20:4, which introduces Ezekiel's harangue against the "elders of Israel." We will presently see how chapter 20 belongs in the same context with 16, 22, and 23.

could make his son or daughter pass [*leha'abir*] through the fire to Molech"
(23:10). The Book of Jeremiah, as we saw in Chapter 2, refers back with
horror to the sacrifices that had once been performed in the Hinnom valley
(7:30–34, 19:1–13, 32:26–35).

Scholars continue to debate, with considerable vigor, the nature of the
"Molech" cult [68,135,187,251,288]. They dispute how deep its roots
were, and how widely it was practiced. Kaufmann, for example, insists on
its alienness, its lateness, and its rarity: "Child sacrifice was not normally
practiced (under foreign influence, it was present during the reigns of
Ahaz and Manasseh . . . no northern king is ever blamed for this sin). . . .
It is characteristic of [Ezekiel's] exaggerated generalizations that he does
not mention Topheth or the valley of Ben-Hinnom, but speaks as if the
burning of children took place everywhere and at all times" [163].

Against this, Heider speculates that the cult performed at Topheth was
entrenched in Jerusalemite Yahwism at least since the time of Solomon, and
possibly since the conquest. He must admit, of course, that 2 Kings attributes it only to Ahaz and Manasseh. He explains this—unconvincingly, in
my opinion—as due to the Deuteronomistic author's aim of heightening
the contrast between these two arch-villains and the shining knights of
faith, Hezekiah and Josiah, who succeeded them. Yet, while rejecting Kaufmann's argument from silence with regard to Judah, Heider accepts it for
the North. Children were not sacrificed in the Northern Kingdom, from
which, indeed, the Deuteronomic critique of the cult may have originated
[137]. Ezekiel's charge, therefore, that both Oholah and Oholibah "slaughtered their sons for their *gillulim*" (23:39), must not be taken at face value
[139]. On Heider's view, as well as on Kaufmann's, Ezekiel will be guilty of
exaggeration and overgeneralization.

We must grant, with Baruch Levine, that "definitive judgments concerning the extent of the cult of Molech in biblical Israel will have to await
further evidence" [187]. It is nonetheless hard to imagine that the cult had
the currency to justify Ezekiel's obsession with it, if that obsession had not
drawn its power from something in Ezekiel's own psyche. We must suppose that Ezekiel harped as he did upon Judean child sacrifice, not because
it was widespread even before Josiah's reformation—far less in Ezekiel's
own time—but because it served him as a vehicle for objectifying some
horribly painful aspect of his private experience.

Here, as usual, Ezekiel's metaphor is truer to the reality of the experience than is the history it claims to depict. The "bloodshed" with which he
charges his wicked women is their outrages against their helpless male

children. Their crime will become most fully intelligible if we assume he himself is the outraged and sacrificed child.

To understand the nature of the outrage, we must look more closely at Ezekiel's imputation of "blood" to his villainesses.

In chapter 16, Yahweh's wife is "bloody" in the most literal sense. She is drenched in blood from her infancy. "On the day you were born, your navel-string was not cut. You were not washed with water . . . ;[24] you were not rubbed with salt; you were not swaddled. . . . You were cast out in the open field, in your loathsomeness [go'al nafshekh], on the day you were born. I passed by you and saw you wallowing in your blood. And I said to you, 'In your blood, live.' And I said to you, 'In your blood, live' " (verses 4–6). She apparently spends her girlhood soaked in her own blood, for Yahweh must wash it away when he is ready to take her to bed (verse 9). Much of this blood, we may assume, is menstrual. Verse 7 makes the point explicitly, provided we are prepared to emend 'ade 'adayim to 'iddim ("menses") [56,297].[25] Later, contemplating his wife's sexual excesses, Yahweh can remind her of "the days of your youth, when you were stark naked, wallowing in your blood" (verse 22).

The passage reflects a horror of menstruation, and of the female as a creature of loathsome fluxes. This horror, as we have seen (Chapter 3), was particularly strong in Ezekiel's circles, which were also the circles that produced the Holiness Code. Ezekiel here gives it his characteristic imprint, with an eerie, incantation-like pronouncement. "And I said to you, 'In your blood, live.' "

The doubling of this sentence has troubled commentators. The Septuagint has it only once. What is more, the text that lay before the translator evidently extended the pronouncement into the beginning of the next verse: "In your blood, live *and grow*."[26] This reading is attractive. It is

24. I omit any translation of *lemish'i*, a word "of unknown meaning and dubious form" (Cooke [56]), which has baffled all commentators.
25. Greenberg, however, offers good reasons for hesitating to emend [104].
26. Evidently reading *urebi* for the Masoretic Text's *rebabah*, at the beginning of verse 7. Cooke and Zimmerli follow the Septuagint on this point, but go beyond it in deleting *netattikh* from verse 7. They consequently read Yahweh's pronouncement as (*bedamayikh*) *ḥayyi urebi keṣemaḥ haśśadeh*, "(In your blood) live, and grow like a plant of the field." But the Greek translator plainly had *netattikh* in his text, and it is not clear why anyone should have added this word. (Zimmerli's claim that "[i]t became necessary after the erroneous writing of רבי" [297] overlooks the fact that it was added to the Septuagint *Vorlage before* this "erroneous writing" had taken place.)

possible to imagine an original text in which Yahweh first says, "In your blood, live," and then, "In your blood, live and grow."

But, even as it stands in the Masoretic Text, the repetition is psychologically appropriate. The shorter text's abbreviation of this uncomfortably revealing utterance is likewise intelligible.[27] With the twice-pronounced *In your blood, live!*, Ezekiel conveys the fullness of his mingled desire and loathing. The female is immeasurably appealing to him, with her firm breasts and flowing hair (verse 7), her jewelry and her lovely clothes (verses 10–13, 18). Yet, beneath all these seductions, she is a creature of blood—wallowing in blood, growing in blood, spilling blood.

This enticing being is irresistibly powerful. She is the source of ominous and terrifying fluids. She can arouse the little boy. Yet she will abandon him to sleep with another male, with whose genitalia he cannot hope to compete. In his rage, he wants to slaughter her and gobble her up. Projecting his murderous feelings onto her, he imagines her doing the same to him.

So far, we seem to be dealing with some standard variety of the Oedipus complex. Yet surely we require something more to explain the tenacity and the intensity of Ezekiel's rage and horror. After all, if Freudian theory is right, almost every little boy must cope with frustrated desire for his mother and hopeless competition with his father. The pathological misogyny of an Ezekiel is, one hopes, rare. Something must have gone dreadfully wrong in Ezekiel's upbringing.

In Chapter 3, I detected a few hints in his hallucinatory "abominations" that Ezekiel had at some point been sexually victimized by an adult male. (We shall presently see further evidence of abuse and neglect by Ezekiel's adult caretakers.) I now propose that we interpret these hints of sexual abuse in the light of Ezekiel's repeated accusations that the wicked women offer up their sons for their lovers' pleasure. These accusations may easily be translated into the language of Ezekiel's individual experience. He not only perceived his mother as having behaved seductively toward him, then having preferred to share her bed with her husband or her lover. He

27. What the Septuagint actually says is: "Out of your blood, life," or, following Codex Alexandrinus, "Out of your blood, your life." Given that the translator rendered the next word as an imperative, it is strange that he did not do the same for *ḥayyi*, if that were indeed the word he had before him. Might we imagine that his *Vorlage* had *bedamayikh ḥayyim* or *bedamayikh ḥayyayikh*, in place of the Masoretic Text's *bedamayikh ḥayyi?* The shorter text of Ezekiel 16:6 would then be very reminiscent of Leviticus 17:11–14. We might conjecture that Ezekiel, revising his sometimes embarrassing outpourings, was influenced at this point by his familiarity with some version of the Holiness Code.

believed that she had colluded in his sexual abuse at the hands of that husband or lover.

Naturally, we have no way of verifying the child's perceptions—we have no independent information on Ezekiel's mother. But, given what we know of the appalling frequency with which children are sexually abused even in our own enlightened society [321], we cannot claim there is anything even slightly implausible about them. When Ezekiel accused his mother of sacrificing her son to her lover's appetite—this is, at bottom, what his charges of child sacrifice are about—we have no reason to doubt that he spoke an only thinly disguised version of the literal truth.

The paradoxical implication is that the key to Ezekiel's profound and enduring loathing of female sexuality lies less in the failings of his mother than in those of some significant adult male in his early life. Whether this male was his father, his stepfather, or his mother's lover, is a matter of slight importance.

Freudian theory holds that the normal boy works through his Oedipus complex by identifying himself with his father. He can therefore give up his attachment to his mother by assuring himself that someday he will grow up to be *like* his father, and thus have a woman *like* his mother. If something intervenes to block this identification, he will have no choice but to force the Oedipus complex into his unconscious. It will then remain to torment him.

If Ezekiel's father (or other dominant adult male) was an unloving man who did not truly care for him, who saw him primarily as an alternative sexual object, surely this standard path toward resolution will have been blocked. Ezekiel will then have grown to manhood burdened with all the child's frustrated desire, thwarted rage, agonized sense of betrayal.

He cannot have allowed himself to be aware of these feelings. To do so would have transgressed one of his culture's most insistent taboos. "Each of you shall fear his father and his mother," the Holiness Code intoned (Leviticus 19:3), following the older laws of Exodus and Deuteronomy. According to the Covenant Code, "He who strikes" or even "curses his father or his mother shall surely be put to death" (Exodus 21:15, 17). Ezekiel obviously internalized these demands. "In you," he was later to tell Jerusalem, "they have made light of father and mother" (22:7); his language echoes Exodus 21:17, Deuteronomy 27:16, and the Fifth Commandment.[28]

28. Hiph'il *qll* ("to make light") is from the same root as Pi'el *qll* ("to curse"), used in Exodus 21:17. It is cognate to Hiph'il *qlh*, used in Deuteronomy 27:16. It is the opposite of Pi'el *kbd* (literally, "to make heavy"), used in Exodus 20:12 and Deuteronomy 5:16.

What could Ezekiel, trapped in this dilemma, have done? Several psychological devices for disowning his feelings were available to him. He could, and did, project his feelings onto their object. No longer was the furious child aware of wanting to kill his faithless mother. Rather, it was *she* who wanted to kill *him*. He combined this perception with awareness of the physiological reality that his mother monthly spilled blood, and of the probable historical reality that she had sacrificed his welfare to the convenience of her husband or lover. Thus the child Ezekiel created his image of a bloodshedding, child-murdering female; her "bloodiness," her ruthlessness, her danger all bound up with her sexuality. This image was later to become his model for the political and religious history of Israel and Judah.

He might combine this solution with a projection of a different sort. In this version, his rage could retain its original object, the female. But its subject was now the adult male, whether seen as "lover," "righteous man," or Yahweh (= both husband and father). Identified with the aggressor, Ezekiel could safely indulge his rage at his mother—while convincing himself that his rage was not his own but that of the father-god who spoke through him.

Finally, he might repress his rage outright. This, I will argue in Chapter 5, was the principal function (and thus the primary explanation) of Ezekiel's dumbness. Speechless, he could hardly give rein to his impulse to curse his mother. He could curse her only indirectly, symbolically, using Yahweh's voice. [29]

29. "A repeatedly abused or sexually misused child"—writes Lenore Terr, child psychiatrist and leading expert on the effects of childhood trauma—"may fall upon one of three pathological ways to express anger, that is, if the rage turns out to be the primary emotion stimulated by the abuses. The child may, for one, 'identify with the aggressor' or 'turn passive into active,' leading at its most extreme to a cruel, bullyish, abusive, and even criminal personality. Many child abusers, for instance, were originally child-abuse victims. The abused child may, secondly, retreat into passivity out of habit, a 'reenactment' of old victimizations, in other words. Such a child may well retain the victim stance for life. The child could, as a third option, continue to act in an acceptable fashion, flaring into wild rages and self-destructive sprees whenever frustration hits. One woman I treat, for example, is a successful banker and a respected community leader, but she occasionally attacks her intimates with fingernails or an open palm. She also cuts herself at unpredictable times with razor blades. The woman feels sexually numb. But she is exquisitely sensitive to small insults and to attempts by others to control her. She told me that for ten years of her midchildhood her father forced her repeatedly into brutal and repulsive sexual acts. At age sixteen she ran away from home, never to return. The main feeling she now experiences is an unquenchable rage" [402]. The relevance of Terr's remarks to Ezekiel will become increasingly clear as we go on. Her patient's attacks on herself with razor blades, for example, are suggestive of the peculiar abuses Ezekiel inflicts on himself in chapters 4–5 (especially 5:1–4), about which we will presently have more to say.

Ezekiel's repressed feelings toward his mother emerged in a recurrent fantasy of women as monsters of cruelty and lust. They also emerged, in deeper disguise, in a powerful hallucination of a sanctuary so corroded by monstrosity that Ezekiel imagines Yahweh responding to it as any sensible male would. He withdraws.

We will now understand Ezekiel's apparent digression, at the climax of his account of the Temple abominations, to complain that the Jews "have filled the land with violence [*ḥamas*]" (8:17). Greenberg calls this an "unexpected shift to denunciation of social wrongdoing," and cites the judgment of earlier commentators that it ought to be excised. He himself would retain it, and use it to support Sarna's view (see Chapter 3) that the *zemorah* of 8:17 ought to be linked to violence and social injustice rather than to the Temple abominations [104,246]. But, once we grasp that the "abominations" are a symbolic representation of sexual evil (mostly female), their link to the "violence" will become clear.

Accusations of violence and bloodshed are equivalent for Ezekiel. So we learn from 7:23: "The land is filled with the judgment of bloodshed [*mishpaṭ damim*], and the city is filled with violence [*ḥamas*]." As Greenberg points out, 9:9 takes up the charge of 8:17, but replaces "violence" with "bloodshed."[30] For Ezekiel, idolatry in the Temple and violence/bloodshed in the land are hallucinatory counterparts to the adulteries and bloodlettings of Oholah and Oholibah.[31] The first pair of charges is held together, by virtue of its mirroring the second.

At bottom, Ezekiel 8 and Ezekiel 23 reflect the same primitive longing, rage, and horror. The essential difference is that, in chapter 8, the mirror is vastly larger and more distorted. The brutal sexual imagery of chapters 16 and 23 depicts, with far greater clarity, Ezekiel's image of the woman who had dominated his early years.

7. Child Sacrificed: The Crime of the Man

Where, then, shall we look for Ezekiel's image of the dominant male?

We may reconstruct it by synthesizing the male figures who appear in

30. Some manuscripts, perhaps influenced by 8:17, read *ḥamas* for *damim* in 9:9.

31. We recall that 7:20–22, as interpreted by Rashi and Kimhi, explicitly declares the Temple to be menstruous (see section 4).

his fantasies and hallucinations, and whom we have already seen (above, section 5) to fade into one another. These are the lovers of Yahweh's wives, the "righteous men" (23:45), the "mob" (*qahal*, 16:40, 23:46–47), and Yahweh himself.

To this cluster of imaginary beings, we must add a group of males who actually existed in Ezekiel's surroundings. These were "righteous men" by social definition. Their social functions established them as potential leaders of the *qahal*; and, by virtue of these functions, they may easily have served Ezekiel as unconscious father surrogates. These were the exiled "elders of Israel."[32]

Toward this constellation of male figures, as I have indicated, Ezekiel felt a range of emotions that shaded from love, through homosexual desire and heterosexual envy (mingled with awe at the adult male's sexual powers), into fear and hatred. Naturally enough, he tried to make sense of his contradictory feelings by breaking up the constellation and attaching different feelings to each of its components. But he was unable successfully to maintain this distribution of feelings. We learn as much from his repeated blurring of the boundaries between lovers, "mob," "righteous men," and Yahweh.

The effect was that Ezekiel was sometimes able to identify himself with his composite male image. At other times, he stood over against it, in dread and loathing. In his sexual jealousy for his mother and his rage at her betrayal, he could take on the perspective of her spurned lovers = righteous men = mob = God. But these were also his rivals and his victimizers. As such, they become the objects of his rage and terror. It is they who demand what the wicked woman so readily grants; that she, Inanna-like, yield over to their cruel appetite the helpless body of her only true lover, the child Ezekiel.

32. This suggestion will accord with Jacob Milgrom's argument that Ezekiel is the earliest surviving writer to attest a shift in the meaning of the word *qahal*, which turned it into a synonym for *'edah*. In pre-Exilic times, Milgrom thinks, only *'edah* could function as a technical term for "the people's assembly." This is why we find titles of official functionaries used in construct with *'edah*, not *qahal*: *ziqne ha'edah*, "the elders of the *'edah*" (Leviticus 4:15, Judges 21:16), not *ziqne haqqahal*. Ezekiel, by contrast, never uses the word *'edah*, and he assigns the full range of its meanings to *qahal* [209]. It follows that, in Ezekiel's mind, "elders" and *qahal* will have been linked. Jeremiah 26:17 confirms this supposition. In this passage, which is presumably more or less contemporaneous with Ezekiel, some of "the elders of the land" (*ziqne ha'ares*) address "the assembly of the people" (*qehal ha'am*) and dissuade them from lynching Jeremiah. This surely implies that, on less happy occasions, "elders" might stir up and organize the *qahal* to perpetrate such a lynching. Ezekiel, therefore, might easily have conceived them as stepping into the role of the "lovers" of 16:37–40 or of the "righteous men" of 23:46, and instigating the *qahal* against its female victims.

The child-become-man lashed back, furiously. "Son of man, speak to the elders of Israel. . . . Will you judge them? Will you judge, son of man? Tell them the abominations of their fathers!" (20:3–4). Fittingly, Ezekiel opens his massive indictment of the father by representing him doubly, in the persons of the "elders" and of *their* fathers. The formula he uses follows, as we have noted, the pattern of similar formulae in his indictments of his mother: "Jerusalem" in 16:2 and 22:2,[33] Oholah and Oholibah in 23:36.

In the light of what we have seen in this chapter, it will not surprise us that Ezekiel climaxes the indictment with the charge of child sacrifice. "Are you polluted," he demands of the elders, "in the way of your fathers? Do you go whoring after their despicable things? By offering your gifts, by causing your sons to pass through the fire, do you pollute yourselves for all your *gillulim*, to this day?" (20:30–31).[34]

The accusation has taken most commentators aback. "It is most improbable," says Cooke, "that the exiles, if they are referred to, were guilty of child sacrifice in Babylonia; the words are probably a gloss" [56]. Zimmerli finds here "a piece of later exaggerated elaboration. . . . A still later hand has then very clumsily . . . felt it necessary to refer here again to the practice of child sacrifice, which, so far as we can see, was connected with a place of sacrifice in the valley of Hinnom near Jerusalem" [297].

Heider is not so sure. He grants it is unlikely that Ezekiel's fellow exiles were sacrificing children. Still, Ezekiel does not sharply distinguish the exiles from those left behind in Judah, and may be referring here to the (alleged) revival of the Topheth cult after Josiah's death [139]. For Kaufmann, however, the accusation is just one more example of Ezekiel's "penchant for inventing sins" [163].

In the light of our argument, the charge of child sacrifice will appear natural—indeed, all but inevitable. Its real object is the cruel and destructive father figure of Ezekiel's past, whose image he now displaces onto the unfortunate elders. As I suggested in Chapter 2, his use of insinuating questions to phrase the charge reflects the tension between his unconscious certainty that the elders must (almost *ex officio*) be sacrificing children, and his conscious knowledge that they were doing no such thing.

33. Whose identity with the mother was long ago perceived by Rabbi Eliezer, as we saw at the beginning of this chapter.

34. On the reading of verses 30–31a as a series of questions, see above, Chapter 2, note 21. Here, as in 16:36 and 23:37–39, it is the *gillulim* (idols) who receive the child sacrifices.

Ezekiel's conviction, that he is the child sacrificed to the adult male's appetite, finds more appropriate expression in 20:25–26. Here he attaches it to the cardinal figure in his male constellation.

"It was I," says Ezekiel's God, "who gave them [the Israelites] laws that were not good, statutes by which they could not live. And so I polluted them through their gifts, through their passing every first-born [through the fire, as a sacrifice]; so that I might devastate them; so that they might know that I am Yahweh."

Commentators have long struggled to make moral sense out of this hideous assertion. They have often (most recently, Heider [140]) invoked God's hardening of Pharaoh's heart as a precedent. Their efforts have not carried conviction. Ezekiel's claim, writes Ellen F. Davis, "resists all efforts at domestication. Its power lies precisely in the fact that it cannot be conformed to human reason. This verse reasserts, indeed, carries to its illogical extreme what is Ezekiel's constant theme: the indisputable authority of God to determine and interpret the course of human history" [66].

Considered from a psychoanalytic perspective, however, Ezekiel 20:25–26 is perfectly logical, perfectly conformable to human reason. In the unconscious thoughts that underlie Ezekiel's fantasies, Yahweh is equated with the lovers of the wicked women. He therefore demands, just as they do, that children be sacrificed to his pleasure. That he then proceeds to "devastate" his own children for the crime of destroying theirs, is simply an extension of this demand. It is of a piece with his killing the sons and daughters of Oholah and Oholibah (23:47), in order to punish Oholah and Oholibah for the crime of killing their sons and daughters.

Of course, Yahweh will then emerge as a monster of cruelty and hypocrisy. But surely this is an accurate statement of Ezekiel's unconscious perception of his God. How else are we to understand the revolting bloodthirstiness, the absence of the most elementary compassion or decency, which Ezekiel throughout attributes to him?

It is hard to find a passage in the book in which Yahweh, even when he acts for people's good, is motivated by genuine concern for their welfare. He will restore errant Jerusalem—precisely in order to humiliate her and make her perpetually miserable (16:59–63). In 20:32–44, he will restore Israel to its land, "not as a longed-for release, but as a compulsory, wrathful redemption 'with a strong hand and an outstretched arm.' Willy-nilly the people shall be restored in the sight of the nations for the glory of God" (Kaufmann [164]).

In 36:22–32, Yahweh angrily rejects the notion that, in restoring his people, he is motivated by any selfless concern for their good. What drives him is his thirst for self-aggrandizement, his obsessive fear that no one is going to know who he is.[35] *Then* the nations will know that he is Yahweh, when he uses Israel as a tool for "sanctifying my great name" (verse 23). The Jews themselves he will abandon to shame and self-loathing. For—as he admits with a candor that is perhaps the closest thing he has to an endearing quality—"It is not for your sakes that I am acting" (verse 32).

At times, to be sure, Ezekiel's God can speak in a tone of reassurance. In 18:23, 31–32, 33:11, he eloquently protests that he does not enjoy killing the disobedient; he would much prefer they submit to his dictates, and live. (But 3:20, "I place a stumbling block before him," undermines this disclaimer.) Here and there, some faint note of tenderness is perhaps audible (39:25–29).[36] Yet this God, at his kindest, is a being far different from the Yahweh depicted in Jeremiah 31, who practically bursts with long-suppressed love and yearning to do good. The contrast between these two more or less contemporary prophets, who otherwise have so much in common, is overwhelming. This does not mean that Ezekiel was a worse man than Jeremiah, but only that his God was worse. That is to say, Ezekiel's childhood wounds were vastly more cruel than Jeremiah's. The image of the ideal adult male that he incorporated, therefore, could not be other than debased and vicious.[37]

35. Zimmerli counts no fewer than fifty-four occurrences in Ezekiel of the phrase, "You [or, "they"] shall know that I am Yahweh." Related expressions occur an additional twenty-six times [299].

36. Ezekiel 39:25 contains the only occurrence of the root *rḥm*, "to have mercy," in the entire book. But RSV's translation of the beginning of verse 26, "They shall forget their shame . . . ," probably exaggerates the passage's gentleness. In the light of Ezekiel's repeated usage (16:52, 54; 32:25, 26, 31; 34:29; 36:7, 8, 16; 44:13), surely we are to read *wenaśu* as if it were *wenaśe'u*, "*they shall bear* their shame . . ." [56]. Perhaps it was some copyist, unable to tolerate the relentless vindictiveness expressed here, who partly assimilated the verb to the root *nšh*, "to forget."

37. Ezekiel's characterization of Yahweh is reminiscent of Egyptian novelist Naguib Mahfouz's marvelous portrayal of a malignant narcissist in the person of the paterfamilias Ahmad Abd al-Jawad. Confronted with the prospect of his daughter's engagement, for example, this patriarch thunders: "No daughter of mine will marry a man until I am satisfied that his primary motive for marrying her is a sincere desire to be related to me . . . me . . . me . . . me" [412]. Ezekiel's God resembles Ahmad Abd al-Jawad in the grandiosity of his pretensions, and in his obliviousness to the suffering his tyrannical behavior inflicts on those unlucky enough to be under his influence. Comparable, too, is the victims' response to their tormentor: reverent and loving awe. The rage that Ahmad Abd al-Jawad's children properly feel toward him they turn against themselves, each other, their mother, the female sex. Or they repress it altogether.

It goes almost without saying that Ezekiel could not have allowed himself to become consciously aware of his perception of God as a hateful
being. In reality, the child must have envied and admired, even loved, the
potent male who took his beloved woman and lovelessly used him. His
hatred, unacknowledged, was split off and turned in other directions—
toward pagan cults, toward foreign peoples, and most vigorously, toward
Judah and its elders.

Yet it is hardly possible to doubt that Ezekiel also hated his God. How is
it possible not to feel hatred for a creature whom you believe to have
bound and gagged you, made you a prisoner in your home (3:24–26, 4:4–
8)? Who can be dissuaded only with difficulty from forcing you to eat
excrement (4:12–15)? And who, not content with taking away your childhood love object, must wantonly snatch from you the one beloved of your
adult eyes?

8. Infant Abandoned

We shall return presently to the death of Ezekiel's wife (24:15–27), and
what it meant to him.

We must first, however, conclude our consideration of the sacrifice of
the child, by examining a particularly harrowing account of one aspect of
that sacrifice. I refer to Ezekiel 16's description of the sufferings of an
abused and neglected infant.

I have quoted much of the passage above. It will bear repeating. "On the
day you were born, your navel-string was not cut. You were not washed
with water . . . ; you were not rubbed with salt; you were not swaddled.
No one's eye had pity on you, to do any of these things for you out of
compassion for you. Rather, you were cast out in the open field, in your
loathsomeness [*go'al nafshekh*], on the day you were born. I passed by you
and saw you wallowing in your blood. And I said to you, 'In your blood,
live' " (16:4–6).

In the sequel, the girl lives and grows "like the plants of the field." Her
breasts bud. Her pubic hair sprouts. She remains stark naked. Yahweh,
passing by again, is attracted to her and takes her as wife (verses 7–8).

The commentators are much impressed by Yahweh's graciousness to the
unworthy foundling. Zimmerli speaks of his "unasked for mercy," his

"pitying love," his "free and gracious kindness." He contrasts Yahweh's behavior with that of the callous priest and Levite in the Gospel parable of the Good Samaritan (Luke 10:29–37) [304]. Brownlee makes the same contrast. He is, however, sensitive enough to wonder why Yahweh "does not pick her up and take her to a home where she may be cared for," but instead leaves her, naked and filthy, to the mercy of the elements [31]. I myself, influenced by Yahweh's own highly laudatory evaluation of his conduct, wrote (in an earlier draft) of his having "graciously nurtured" the child.

It was Dexter Hall who pointed out to me that "nurturant" is about the last word to describe Yahweh's behavior. "The male figure," she writes (in a personal communication), "is incapable of indulging in physical contact with the bloody, discarded and pitiful female infant and must urge her into adulthood where she is 'mastered' by means of the sexual act. Only then is the birth blood removed." So little "nurturant" is Ezekiel's God that it does not occur to him so much as to bathe the girl until he is ready to take her to bed (verse 9).

"It would be needless pedantry," Zimmerli thinks, "to ask in detail what had happened between the two occasions" of Yahweh's passing by [304]. Pedantic, perhaps; but let us try. Miraculously, through Yahweh's "gracious" word, the infant lives. She is naked, abandoned, miserable. She suffers alternately from cold and heat. She is perpetually wet; if not from rain, then from her own blood and urine. She has nothing to eat but her own feces, in which she lies. She is too small and weak to move. In any case, she has nowhere to go. Her only conceivable protector has marched away. He will not be back until she is old enough to interest him sexually.

Ezekiel says nothing of the infant's crying. Her implied silence, Hall points out, is wholly unnatural. Surely she must have cried and howled. Just as surely, Ezekiel's God, and thus Ezekiel himself, could not hear her.

This is not the only occasion on which Yahweh makes himself deaf to cries of anguish. "I also will act in wrath," he tells Ezekiel at the climax of the Temple vision. "My eye shall not pity, nor will I have compassion [*lo' tahus 'eni welo' 'ehmol*]; and, when they cry in my ears with a loud voice, I will not hear them" (8:18). The language of this passage links it to 16:5: "No one's eye had pity on you, to do any of these things for you out of compassion for you [*lo' hasah 'alayikh 'ayin . . . lehumlah 'alayikh*]." Comparing the two texts, we learn whose eye it was that did not have enough compassion even to bathe the suffering child. And we may fill in the lacuna of 16:5: *When you cried aloud in my ears, my ears were so tightly shut against your cries that it was as if you had made no sound.*[38]

In all of this, there echoes the pain of a tiny Ezekiel, who wailed and cried for caring attention, yet went unheard.

This assumption, that the dreadful infantile experience described in 16:4–7 was Ezekiel's own, is supported by his reenactment of it at the beginning of his prophetic activity.

Psychiatrist Lenore Terr, drawing upon her years of clinical experience with traumatized children, gives example after example of how children—and sometimes adults—reenact their early traumas. They play weird, monotonous games that replicate or attempt to correct the terrible events that befell them. Or, more subtly, they warp their behaviors into repetitions of these events or attempts to ward them off [404]. "Post-traumatic play," Terr writes, "is probably the best clue one ever gets to the nature of a childhood trauma—that is, if one doesn't get to see the traumatic event itself. This play, when it comes, is absolutely literal. It may reflect a child's compensatory wishes, too. But it will recreate the child's trauma the way a theatrical production recreates a certain mood or a history book recreates a specific happening" (page 248).

In one study, Terr found that children do not seem to retain verbal memories of traumas that happen to them before they are twenty-eight to thirty-six months old. But they do show what she calls "behavioral memory" of much earlier events, going back to the very beginning of their lives. One little girl, who had been sexually abused during the first six months of her life, habitually "piled my office pillows on top of each other as if they were human. When she thought I wasn't looking, she poked a finger into the crotch of the fanciest doll in my office." Terr concludes: "These behaviors turned out to be the truest, most accurate indicators of what traces of

38. The Septuagint omits the second part of 8:18 ("and when they cry . . ."), which closely resembles the beginning of 9:1. It is far easier to imagine it having been accidentally omitted from the *Vorlage* because of this resemblance (Greenberg [109]), than to visualize its having been "accidentally repeated" from 9:1 (Cooke [56]) or "formed in dependence" on it (Zimmerli [297]). Jeremiah's God also threatens that he "will not hear" the Jews' cries of distress (11:11)—after all, they wouldn't listen to *him* (verse 10)—but reverses himself in 29:12. Zechariah 7:13 similarly describes a divine tit-for-tat. All of these prophetic passages are presumably intended to contrast with the traditional conception reflected in Exodus 22:21–26, where Yahweh is never deaf to cries of anguish. "If he cries at all to me, I will surely hear his cry. . . . If he cries to me, I will hear, for I am gracious."

memory still existed in the mind of a child exposed very early to a traumatic event or series of events" [403].

Alice Miller reports a different sort of "behavioral memory," from the experience of psychiatrist William G. Niederland.

> A patient told him he had dreamed he was lying in bed at the North Pole; he became frozen solid in the bed, and then some people came in. The patient was sitting up as he recounted the dream, and at his last words, he turned toward the door. Niederland was struck by this, and he interpreted the movement as that of a child in bed who notices when adults enter the room. During this session they both were intent on discovering the memory behind the dream. Later the same day Niederland received a telephone call from his patient's mother, who reproached him severely for having revealed her secret to her son. It turned out that at the age of eight months the boy had slept by an open window on a very cold New York night and the next morning had to be taken to the hospital with pneumonia. The parents had forgotten to close the window in the evening, and when the baby screamed without interruption, his mother refrained from going in to him because she didn't want to spoil him. Meanwhile, his excreta and vomit had frozen solid. [373]

Ezekiel, too, reenacted his ancient trauma. Bound (3:25, 4:8), restricted to his house (3:24), unable so much as to turn from one side to the other (4:8) for what seemed interminable lengths of time (4:5–6), he acted out again the terrifying immobility and helplessness of his infancy.[39] His impulse to eat excrement, which he was able to restrain only by dint of a compromise measure (4:12–15), similarly recapitulates what must have been the experience of the filthy, untended baby of 16:4–7. And his dumbness—"I will cause your tongue to stick to the roof of your mouth, and you shall be dumb" (3:26)—now takes on a fresh meaning. Surely the infant Ezekiel must have been mysteriously mute? Otherwise, why did no one respond to his cries?

By regressing to his infantile helplessness and state of neglect in the context of his prophetic calling, Ezekiel tried to find meaning for his

---

39. And, perhaps, at the same time partially compensated himself for the neglect he had suffered. According to 16:4, the abandoned infant was "not swaddled" (*hoḥtel lo' ḥuttalt*). Perhaps in compensation, Ezekiel later experienced himself as having been bound.

trauma and thereby to master it.[40] In chapter 16, he took retrospective revenge for his suffering by projecting it onto the woman whom he blamed—with some justice, no doubt—for having caused it.[41] He shielded himself from her retribution by identifying himself with the male parent figure, whom he perceived to be more powerful; who, moreover, could be turned into a vehicle for expressing Ezekiel's own sexual longings and jealousy for the woman.

Ezekiel could not rid himself, much as he surely would have liked to, of the awareness that his male caretaker (to use the term very loosely) had been at least as cruel to him as the female.[42] This awareness occasionally bursts through its heavy repression, most strikingly in 20:25–26. But most of the time he was able to suppress it. He hid behind the Father's mask, while turning the full force of his rage against the Mother. Hence his bitter hatred of women, itself largely unconscious, which reveals itself in diverse forms in various parts of his book.

9. The Death of Ezekiel's Wife

It will surely be objected that the preceding reconstruction of Ezekiel's early experiences is entirely conjectural. We know of Ezekiel's father only that his name was Buzi, and that he was a priest (1:3). Given that the male figure who dominated Ezekiel's childhood may not have been his father (he may have been a stepfather, or a lover of Ezekiel's mother), even this information may not be relevant. About Ezekiel's mother, we know nothing at all.

This objection is legitimate. In the nature of the case, there is nothing we can do to surmount it. Only the most unimaginably improbable of

40. Or, perhaps, to convince himself that next time it would be better, that the parent would come to his aid [389].

41. Michael Fishbane writes, of Ezekiel 16: "[T]he initial image of attempted infanticide re-echoes in verses 20–22, where mother Jerusalem sacrifices her own children. Thus the (attempted) filicide is balanced by ritual filicides as the mother re-enacts her childhood trauma upon her offspring" [79]. Ezekiel's villainess, in other words, is both victim and perpetrator of child sacrifice; and there is a causal link between these two aspects. I differ from Fishbane in reversing the causality.

42. "Here no motive is given for the exposure," says Greenberg of 16:4–5; "from vss. 44f. one may infer only the viciousness of the parents" [104]. The word "viciousness" is not a bit too strong.

chance discoveries could ever yield the missing information about Ezekiel's parents. Our question, therefore, must be this: will my conjectures about Ezekiel's early life help us sufficiently to understand the fantasies and hallucinations of the adult Ezekiel, that we will be prepared to grant, even without direct evidence of their truth, that they are not only plausible but probable? I have tried to show, in my arguments to this point, that our answer to this question must be yes.

We must now consider a fresh, and singularly important, piece of evidence.

It is true that we have no direct knowledge of Ezekiel's parents, or of his relationship with them. But 24:15–27 provides a crucial glimpse of Ezekiel's relation to one flesh-and-blood woman: his wife. If psychoanalytic theory is correct, we may expect Ezekiel to have displaced onto this woman much of the longing and rage he originally felt for his mother.

It is on this supposition that his peculiar response to her death is to be explained.

> [15]The word of Yahweh came to me, saying: [16]"Son of man, I am about to take away from you the desire of your eyes [*mahmad 'enekha*] in one stroke. Yet you must not mourn, you must not weep, and your tears must not come. [17]Groan in deathly silence; do not make lamentation.[43] Put on your turban; wear shoes on your feet; do not cover your lip, and do not eat people's bread."[44]
>
> [18]I spoke to the people in the morning, and my wife died in the evening, and I did in the morning as I had been commanded.
>
> [19]The people said to me, "Won't you tell us what these things you are doing [mean] for us?" [20]I said to them: "The word of Yahweh came to me, saying: [21]Say to the house of Israel: Thus says the Lord Yahweh: I am about to profane my sanctuary—the pride of your

43. *He'aneq dom metim 'ebel lo' ta'aseh.* The meaning of the last three words is clear enough. In translating the first three, I take *dom* as an infinitive construct from the root *dmm*, here in construct with *metim;* literally, "groan, (in) the silence of the dead (ones)." I thereby follow Zimmerli and Shula Abramsky [1,297]. But I see no need to assume, with Zimmerli, that *dmm* here has the meaning of immobility rather than silence. We will presently elucidate the paradox of the silent groan.

44. That is, do not observe any of the customary mourning practices. "People's bread" (*lehem 'anashim,* here and in verse 22) is presumably food prepared for the mourners by their friends and relatives. Zimmerli emends to *lehem 'onim* ("bread of mourning"), following Hosea 9:4; Cooke prefers the more difficult text that lies before us [56,297]. Either way, the point remains the same.

power, the desire of your eyes, the object of your compassion. Your sons and your daughters whom you left behind will fall by the sword.

²²"Then you will do as I have done. You will not cover your lip, and you will not eat people's bread. ²³Your turbans will be on your heads, your shoes on your feet. You will not mourn and you will not weep. You will waste away in your sins, and you will moan to one another. ²⁴So Ezekiel shall be a token for you. All that he has done, you will do. When this comes, you will know that I am the Lord Yahweh.

²⁵"And as to you, son of man: Surely, on the day that I take away from them their safe refuge, their splendid joy, the desire of their eyes, that on which they have set their hearts, their sons and their daughters—²⁶on that day, the fugitive will come to you to let you know. ²⁷On that day, your mouth shall be opened with the fugitive, and you shall speak, and shall be dumb no more. And you shall be a token for them, and they shall know that I am Yahweh."

I can see no reason to question the authenticity or the accuracy of any detail of this narrative. In places, to be sure, it is problematic. What did Ezekiel say to the people on the first morning (verse 18a)? Why does he fluctuate, in verses 21–24, between speaking in Yahweh's name and in his own?[45] Verses 25–27 are particularly troublesome, debouching as they do onto the long-standing crux of Ezekiel's dumbness. (We will consider this problem in detail in Chapter 5.)

Yet Zimmerli's procedure, of writing off as insertions—often, "clumsy" insertions—those features of the text that trouble him, seems misguided. It would be even less appropriate to question the truthfulness of the passage as a whole, or to deny its relevance to the understanding of Ezekiel's personality.

This last assertion brings us into direct collision with G. A. te Stroete's analysis of Ezekiel 24:15–27. "Since the behaviour of the prophet only retains its importance in as much as it points to the same act of not-

45. It is worth recalling Ellen F. Davis's explanation of a cognate tension, Ezekiel's inconsistent use of second- and third-person address in 13:2–16. "The prophet's disposition vacillates between that of the orator and that of the writer, respectively engaged in direct confrontation and exposition" [60]. Here we may imagine Ezekiel vacillating between awareness that it is his own unconscious that speaks under the name of "Yahweh," and his indispensable fantasy that some external being is speaking to him and through him.

mourning on the part of the exiles (for this reason various psychological considerations with regard to the experience and the emotions of the prophet are out of part), our question can be formulated finally as follows: Why are the exiles unwilling or why are they not allowed to mourn, when the temple is destroyed and Jerusalem has fallen?" [261]. In other words, Ezekiel's expectation of the people's behavior is the primary datum requiring explication. His personal experience, as he describes it, was manufactured in the service of this expectation.

For all te Stroete's assurance, however, the principle from which he proceeds is far from self-evident. It in fact fails to yield any good result. We have no reason to believe that Ezekiel's expectation of the exiles' behavior had any grounding in external reality—that the Jews already in Babylonia were any less disposed than were their Palestinian cousins to mourn the loss of city and Temple. (Jeremiah 41:4–5, and the entire Book of Lamentations, bear sufficient witness to the Palestinians' responses to the calamity.) Their "act of not-mourning" existed only in Ezekiel's imagination, and must be explained with reference to Ezekiel himself.

Te Stroete's effort to answer his own question, in terms of Ezekiel's historical theology, is unconvincing. The exiles are not to mourn, he says, "because they know that a new era is dawning through the catastrophe. The messenger of doom who has managed to escape from the city turns into a messenger of joy who announces a new season." But te Stroete's equation of not-mourning with joy has no shadow of warrant within the text of Ezekiel. It is, moreover, entirely false to human psychology. Mourning is a healthy and appropriate response to loss, a necessary precondition of future joy. Inability to mourn means perpetual entrapment in unconscious pain. Verses 22–23, which te Stroete dismisses as an uncomprehending gloss, reflect Ezekiel's profound (though hardly conscious) understanding of this truth, and of its grim implications for his own dilemma.

We must, as nearly as possible, reverse te Stroete's principle. The primary datum is Ezekiel's personal inability to mourn his own loss. His groundless belief, that his fellow exiles would experience a similar block, must be seen as an outward projection and rationalization of his inner experience.

This experience will turn out to be precisely what we would expect from a man whose feelings toward women are those expressed in the fantasies of Ezekiel 16 and 23, and implied in the hallucinatory symbolism of Ezekiel 8.

To understand Ezekiel's experience, we must begin by taking seriously what he says about it.

When Ezekiel, addressing himself through Yahweh's mouth, calls his wife "the desire of your eyes," we must not refuse to draw from this the natural inference that he loved the woman. Zimmerli objects, against these "sentimental considerations," that "Lam 2:4 and Hos 9:16 show that phrases of this kind for a close relative were in general use" [297]. The objection assumes that people will not use hackneyed language to express genuine feeling. This hardly seems true to ordinary human behavior.

George Orwell's observation, on the clichés that have percolated from Kipling's poetry into the English language, is far more perceptive. " *'He travels the fastest who travels alone.'* There is a vulgar thought vigorously expressed. It may not be true, but at any rate it is a thought that everyone thinks. Sooner or later you will have occasion to feel that he travels the fastest who travels alone, and there the thought is, ready made and, as it were, waiting for you" [415]. We may grant that Ezekiel did not invent the phrase *maḥmad 'enayim.* We have no right to conclude from this that it did not express, with painful accuracy, his loving feelings for the wife he had suddenly lost.[46]

But surely these were not his only feelings about her. His inability to mourn her death points to some paralyzing ambivalence. Close comparison of verses 22–23 with 16–17 suggests that guilt played some role in this ambivalence. "Then you will do as I have done. . . . You will not mourn and you will not weep. *You will waste away in your sins, and you will moan to one another.*" Ezekiel's account of his own behavior says nothing about "wasting away." Yet, in the light of his emphatic assurances that the exiles will do precisely as he has done—"You will do as I have done" (verse 22); "All that he has done, you will do" (verse 24)—we can hardly fail to suppose that his expectation of their "wasting away in sin"[47] reflects his own powerful sense

46. Zimmerli is not the only modern commentator to use this reasoning. Robert P. Carroll comments on Jeremiah 3:1–5: "If the language were not so stereotypical (cf. Hosea and Ezekiel), its verisimilitude would suggest that it is derived from the timeless quarrels of husbands and wives" [44]. I submit that this sentence will be more persuasive if rewritten: "*Precisely because the language is so stereotypical* . . . its verisimilitude will suggest that it is derived from the timeless quarrels of husbands and wives." Endlessly recurrent human situations—"timeless quarrels," sexual yearning and betrayal, loss of a beloved object—are the stuff of which stereotypes, and stereotypic language, are made.

47. *Unemaqqotem ba'awonotekhem.* Similar phrases, using the Niph'al of *mqq*, occur in 4:17, 33:10, and Leviticus 26:39 (H). Ezekiel 33:10, which projects onto the exiles the prophet's own sense of unforgivable and unendurable sin, vividly conveys the quality of his feeling. Ezekiel uses the similar phrase *wenaqoṭṭu / uneqoṭotem bifeneheml-khem* (Niph'al of *qwṭ*; 6:9, 20:43, 36:31) to convey a nearly identical feeling of guilty self-loathing.

of guilt. He was not consciously aware of his guiltiness, however, and therefore does not mention it in connection with himself.

Ezekiel's guilt over his wife's death will be intelligible only if we suppose that he had unconsciously wished for it. However much he loved his wife as an individual, he cannot have failed to transfer to her his ancient and powerful image of the female as seductive monster, with all the murderous fury that image aroused in him. His eager expectation of the gruesome deaths of Oholah and Oholibah thus became a wish for his wife's death as well.

Seen from this perspective, Ezekiel's conviction that he had predicted her death in advance turns out to have been justified. His speech "to the people" on the first morning was perhaps some variant of his bloodthirsty harangue against the "lewd women." His longing for their punishment was then abruptly fulfilled, in a dreadful and unexpected way. He responded with real grief, but also with unconscious glee and equally unconscious guilt. Crippled by contradictory emotions, he could not give appropriate expression to his grief. He could only "groan in deathly silence" (verse 17).

A silent groan is of course a paradox. But it marvelously expresses the theme of the whole passage—if not the entire book—of intolerable pain for which the sufferer can find no satisfactory expression. It fits in well with the recurrent motif of dumbness, which Ezekiel takes up at the end of the passage.

The people said to me, "Won't you tell us what these things you are doing [mean] for us?" (24:19).

This passage is among the few in which Ezekiel describes real or imagined responses to his speeches and behaviors. Its closest parallel is 12:9–11.[48] Yahweh has commanded his prophet to anticipate, in pantomime, the exile of the Jerusalemites. He must prepare his "exile's pack" (so Greenberg translates *kele golah* [104]) during the day; in the nighttime, he must mimic the exiles' departure. In the morning, Yahweh addresses him: "Son of man, have not the house of Israel, the rebellious house, said to you, 'What are you doing?' . . . Say: 'I am your token.[49] As I have done, so shall be done to them.' "

It seems clear from 12:9 that the exiles have actually asked Ezekiel their question. In 37:18, he anticipates a similar question. In 17:12, he tries to

---

48. More fully examined in the Excursus.
49. *Mofet*, as in 24:24.

evoke it with a challenge. "Say to the rebellious house: 'Don't you know what these things [mean]?' "[50]

In 21:5 (Masoretic Text) and 33:30–33, Ezekiel summarizes what he imagines to be the public response to his preaching overall. (People see him as a maker of parables, a singer of love-songs.) But, to the best of my knowledge, the only further example he gives of a reaction to some specific speech or action of his is Pelatiah's dropping dead, in 11:13.

It follows that Ezekiel's report in 24:19, although certainly not unique, is just as certainly unusual. Ezekiel's behavior at his wife's death, it seems, had an impact on his fellow exiles that went beyond what he was normally able to achieve. Their reaction thus impressed him enough that he recorded it.

What does this reaction express? Surely, it is the frightened bewilderment of people confronted with behavior which they intuitively understand to be significant, but which they see as bizarre to the point of incomprehensibility. As such, it contradicts the notion, which we have seen Howie advance against Broome (see Chapter 1, section 3), that Ezekiel may have been perfectly normal by the standards of his own time and place [143].

How does the shaman (in what we call "primitive" cultures) differ from the schizophrenic? Julian Silverman has explored this question.[51] Both shaman and schizophrenic, he argues, exhibit similar behaviors, which originate in parallel psychological dynamics. The difference is that the shaman, occupying a recognized and indeed honored place in his society, is able to turn his psychic pain toward the creation of valued cultural products. His suffering itself, moreover, will be less acute than the schizophrenic's; since his peculiarities do not aggravate his pain by isolating him from other people [392].

If we had to classify Ezekiel as one or the other, surely we would place him with the shamans rather than the schizophrenics. The cultural yield of his pain is obvious: we see it in the book that carries his name. His contemporaries seem normally to have assumed that they knew what kind

50. *Halo' yeda'tem mah 'elleh.* Cf. the questions of 12:9, *mah 'attah 'oseh,* 24:19, *halo' taggid lanu mah 'elleh lanu ki 'attah 'oseh,* and 37:18, *halo' taggid lanu mah 'elleh lakh.*

51. I am grateful to Daniel Merkur and Robert Segal for insisting on the importance of this issue, and to Robert Segal for referring me to Silverman's article. After I had completed this manuscript, my colleague Hector Avalos called my attention to an important parallel study: Jerome Kroll and Bernard Bachrach, "Visions and Psychopathology in the Middle Ages," *Journal of Nervous and Mental Disease* 170 (1982): 41–49.

of person he was (Masoretic Text 21:5, 33:30–33), and that such a person deserved at least some respect. The leaders of the exiled community thus seek out his opinions (8:1, 14:1, 20:1) and sit respectfully through his trances (11:25).

In 24:19, too, the people assume that Ezekiel's actions have some significance *for them*. Yet the perplexity and the fear expressed in this passage suggest that they had begun to wonder if they indeed understood the man before them; that, in his inability to grieve over his wife's death, Ezekiel had gone beyond what might be expected of a Jewish "shaman."

By the standards of his age as well as our own, his behavior had passed from the "shamanic" into the pathological. His contemporaries knew this. What they did not know was how to interpret it.

In 24:15–27, Ezekiel makes entirely clear his equation of the woman with the sanctuary. He applies *maḥmad 'en[ayim]* to the one in verse 16, to the other in verse 21 (and, presumably, 25 as well). What had been implicit and unconscious in 7:20–22, and in chapter 8, is here wholly conscious and explicit.

The fundamental premise of my analysis of the Temple "abominations" is thereby validated.

5

Ezekiel's Dumbness

Each patient has an individual way of defending
against the cannibalistic intensity of his or her ag-
gression, and this way is almost always massive
and crippling.
—Leonard Shengold, *Soul Murder* [391]

Ezekiel 24:25–27 links the death of Ezekiel's wife, and the anticipated
destruction of the Temple, with Ezekiel's expectation of relief from his
mysterious "dumbness." The text thus forces us to confront, from our
newly acquired psychoanalytic perspective, one of the most difficult and
heavily debated problems of the Book of Ezekiel.

Klostermann, as we saw in Chapter 1, enrolled Ezekiel's dumbness
among the symptoms of his "catalepsy" [176]. Broome spoke of it only in
passing, as a characteristic of a psychotic experience [28]. Clearly, we must
do more than this. Given our approach, we can hardly avoid speaking of the
dumbness as a symptom. But we cannot content ourselves with using it as
an indicator of one medical condition or another. We must provide some
explanation of its meaning for Ezekiel, and of its role within his psychic life.

If we can do this successfully, and at the same time solve the long-
acknowledged problems of the pertinent biblical texts, we may judge that
our method has validated itself.

1. The Problem

The problem of Ezekiel's dumbness turns on three key passages, of which
24:25–27 is the most perplexing.

[3:22–27] ²²The hand of Yahweh was upon me there. He said to me,
"Rise, go forth to the plain, and there I will speak with you." ²³So I
rose and went forth to the plain, and there stood the glory of
Yahweh, like the glory that I had seen on the river Chebar. I fell on
my face. ²⁴And a spirit entered me and set me on my feet; and he
spoke with me, and said to me:
"Come, shut yourself up inside your house. ²⁵And as to you, son
of man, they have fastened ropes upon you, and have bound you
with them, so that you might not go forth among them. ²⁶And I will
fasten your tongue to the roof of your mouth, and you shall be
dumb, and shall not be a reproving man [? 'ish mokhiaḥ] for them; for
they are a rebellious house. ²⁷And when I speak with you, I will
open your mouth, and you will say to them: 'Thus says the Lord
Yahweh.' Whoever wants to hear, may hear; and whoever wants to
forbear, may forbear. For they are a rebellious house."

[24:25–27] ²⁵"And as to you, son of man: Surely on the day that I
take away from them their safe refuge, their splendid joy, the desire
of their eyes, that on which they have set their hearts, their sons
and their daughters—²⁶on that day, the fugitive [happaliṭ] will come
to you to let you know. ²⁷On that day, your mouth shall be opened
with the fugitive, and you shall speak, and shall be dumb no more.
And you shall be a token for them, and they shall know that I am
Yahweh."

[33:21–22] ²¹In the twelfth year of our exile, in the tenth month, on
the fifth day of the month, the fugitive [happaliṭ] from Jerusalem
came to me, saying: "The city is destroyed." ²²Yahweh's hand had
been upon me in the evening, before the fugitive's coming; and he
opened my mouth until [? 'ad] he came to me in the morning. Then
my mouth was opened, and I was dumb no more.

The Book of Ezekiel, as it now stands, claims that the prophet received
the oracle of 3:16–21 seven days after his inaugural vision at the river

Chebar. (In 1:1–2 the inaugural vision is dated to the fifth year of Jehoia-chin's captivity, fourth month, fifth day; that is, the summer of 593 B.C.) In 3:22 it is plainly implied that he received the command to "go forth to the plain" at about the same time. The dumbness that then falls upon him lasts until he hears word of Jerusalem's destruction, in the tenth month of the twelfth year (the end of 586 or beginning of 585). At some point in between,[1] Ezekiel has an anticipation of impending relief. This anticipa-tion is linked in some way with the death of his wife.

If we are to take at face value both the texts themselves and their current placement in the Book of Ezekiel, we must suppose that Ezekiel was mute for nearly all of the first seven and a half years of his prophetic career. But this assumption involves us in a tangle of difficulties. For the book also claims that Ezekiel said quite a lot during those seven and a half years. Of the fourteen dated oracles in the book, all but four (1:1–2 and 3:16 on the one end, 29:17 and 40:1 on the other) fall within the period of his supposed dumbness. In 3:16–21, moreover, Yahweh has solemnly instructed Ezekiel in his duties as a "watchman for the house of Israel." He must transmit the divine warning to sinners, or himself be held responsible. It would seem odd of Yahweh to strike his "watchman" dumb immediately afterward.

We must, it seems, find some way to modify the book's apparent claims about Ezekiel's dumbness: by declaring it to have been intermittent or conditional (as 3:27 perhaps implies); by finding a way to shorten its duration; or by denying that it happened at all. We shall see that scholars have gone all three of these routes.

Whichever we choose, we must further discharge the obligation of find-ing some *meaning* for Ezekiel's real or fictitious dumbness. A muteness that abruptly disappears as soon as the sufferer receives a significant piece of news is plainly something more (or less, depending on one's perspective) than a physical ailment. No explanation of Ezekiel's alleged dumbness will be satisfactory, unless it can account for why 24:15–27 and 33:21–22 link his relief from this affliction with the death of his wife on the one hand, and with the fall of Jerusalem on the other.

Besides these general questions, the three "dumbness" passages pose a number of specific problems. Can 3:27 be read as a legitimate modifica-

---

1. We do not know when. It is not clear if the date in 24:1 can be extended to 24:15–27, and the authenticity of this date is itself open to some question [88,297]. Te Stroete supposes, on the basis of the sequence within chapters 21–24, that 24:15–27 describes an event that "occurred at a non-identifiable point of time between the commencement of the siege and the actual destruction of Jerusalem" [261], and I will follow him on this point.

tion of verses 25–26, or does it contradict them? The date in 33:21 is a
problem. Jerusalem fell, according to Jeremiah 39:2 and 2 Kings 25:2–12
(= Jeremiah 52:5–16), in the fourth month of Zedekiah's eleventh year.
Why did the news not reach Ezekiel until the tenth month of the twelfth
year "of our exile," presumably a year and a half later? In 33:22, the
meaning of the preposition *'ad*, and its implication for the sequence of
events, are very unclear. Zimmerli, like RSV, translates "*by the time* he
(i.e., the fugitive) came to me in the morning," and takes this to mean that
Ezekiel's dumbness vanished when the fugitive appeared [306]. But Ellen
F. Davis seems to extract, with some justification, precisely the opposite
meaning: "The text specifically designates the opening as having occurred
before the arrival of the refugee . . . this is not Ezekiel's reaction to the
news of the fall" [63].[2]

But the problem posed by 24:25–27 is the most difficult. "*On that day*,"
the very day that Jerusalem (or the Temple) falls, "the fugitive will come to
you to let you know." This passage promises an impossibility. No "fugitive" of the sixth century B.C. could have traveled from Palestine to Babylonia in one day. Moreover, it contradicts 33:21–22, which makes clear that
the fugitive's arrival and the relief of Ezekiel's dumbness did not take place
"on that day," but months afterward. Those commentators who deal with
24:25–27, therefore, normally feel obliged to delete it as inauthentic, or to
alter it in some more or less radical fashion.

2. The Proposals

It would be impossible here to survey every solution that scholars have
offered for this complex cluster of problems.[3] Most of the proposals, however, can be grouped along four main lines.

1. The approach that dominated Ezekiel scholarship, at least until ten or
twenty years ago, runs more or less as follows: We must accept Ezekiel's
dumbness as a fact: 33:21–22 provides a solid datum to this effect, of

---

2. Cooke denies that *'ad* can be given any reasonable meaning at all, and deletes *wayyiftaḥ
'et pi 'ad bo'* as a double gloss. The effect is an interpretation of the text much the same as
Zimmerli's [56].

3. Ellen Davis and Stephen Garfinkel helpfully summarize much of the earlier research
[63,93].

whose authenticity there is no serious doubt [306]. But this dumbness cannot possibly have lasted the seven and a half years that the Book of Ezekiel currently seems to claim. We can and must shorten its duration, by supposing that 3:22–27 has somehow broken loose from its proper place in the book, and that it originally belonged with 24:25–27. Ezekiel was mute, not for years, but for months at most. His muteness fell upon him about the time of Jerusalem's siege and capture.

Naturally, reconstructions of the supposed original text vary in their details. Ernst Vogt, whom we may take as representative of this approach, finds that he can create a coherent narrative by inserting parts of 3:25–26 into the middle of 24:26, and slightly adjusting the result. "Surely, on the day that I take away from them their safe refuge . . . ropes will be fastened upon you[4] . . . and I will fasten your tongue to the roof of your mouth, and you shall be dumb, and shall not be a reproving man for them. And on the day that the fugitive will come to you to let you know, on that day your mouth shall be opened with the fugitive, and you shall speak, and shall be dumb no more."

Ezekiel, Vogt thinks, was seized by paralysis and dumbness on the day of Jerusalem's fall, shortly after telling the exiles, in the words quoted above, that this was going to happen to him. (Vogt does not explain how Ezekiel knew when Jerusalem had fallen. Perhaps he credits Ezekiel's claim to supernatural powers.) The second part of his prophecy, of his release from this affliction, also came true. So he tells us in 33:21–22, which originally came right after 24:27 [284].

We may count Zimmerli with this group of scholars, even though the path he takes toward his result is considerably different from theirs. For him, the original account of Ezekiel's dumbness consists solely of 33:21–22, from which it appears that the handicap lasted only a single night. "The state of rigidity and loss of speech 'fell' . . . on the prophet in the evening, and in the morning, with the exciting event of the arrival of an eyewitness with his message, it left him" [306]. Ezekiel 3:25–27 and 24:25–27 are probably secondary [300].

---

4. So Vogt's translation of 3:25, *hinneh natenu 'alekha 'abotim wa'asarukha bahem*, "wird man dir Stricke anlegen und dich damit binden." Vogt goes on to explain that "man wird dich binden" is impersonal; and, as in the passive "your mouth will be opened" in 24:27, the implied actor is Yahweh. His translation of 3:25 is misleading, to say the very least. The Hebrew strongly suggests that the actors in this passage are very personal, that they are plural, and that they are someone other than God. In the context of Vogt's reconstruction, the lapse into third-person plural is extremely awkward.

Yet Zimmerli seems to waver: "It is a likely assumption that the prophet . . . had to experience over and over again the divinely decreed speech restraint, which was at the same time (3:25f.) also determined by human resistance" [306]. This sounds very much as if Zimmerli was inclined to suspect after all that 3:25–27 was original, and that Ezekiel was troubled by mutism throughout the first part of his prophetic activity. This concession brings Zimmerli close to the second position we have to consider.

2. Greenberg—prompted, he says, by the difficulty of making the scholarly rearrangements of the Book of Ezekiel "plausible to students whose faculties were as yet unused to critical romancing"—proposed in 1958 that the "dumbness" passages might make sense even in their present positions [114]. Ezekiel was indeed "dumb" for seven and a half years, in that he remained shut in his house, speaking nothing but prophecies of doom; disgorging, in other words, the scroll of doom God had stuffed him with (2:8–3:3). Ezekiel 3:27, qualifying this dumbness, seemed to say as much: "And when I speak with you, I will open your mouth, and you will say to them: 'Thus says the Lord Yahweh.' " Ezekiel was nonetheless not a "reproving man" (*'ish mokhiaḥ*, 3:26), because he did not go out among the people. He did not, like the *mokhiaḥ* of Isaiah 29:21, "reprove in the gate."

Greenberg seems originally to have held to as literal an understanding of the dumbness as he could. He admitted that it is hard to imagine a man remaining silent for seven and a half years, interrupting his silence only with prophecies of doom. Yet he was able to point to a story from Josephus suggesting that, before and during the Roman siege of Jerusalem, one Jesus son of Ananias had done precisely that (*Jewish War*, 6.5.3) [114].

By 1983, however, when his commentary appeared, Greenberg had apparently become uncomfortable with the literal interpretation, and shifted his emphasis toward the dumbness as a metaphor. Ezekiel is "dumb" in that he does not have ordinary human contacts with his neighbors. His mouth is eventually "opened," in that the fall of Jerusalem vindicates his claim to address them. Whether Greenberg continued to believe that Ezekiel was mute in any literal sense is unclear [106].

Charles Sherlock's position is very similar to Greenberg's, particularly in its earlier form [247].

3. The views we have considered so far take for granted that at least one of the "dumbness" passages is authentic, and that these texts reflect some

actual experience of Ezekiel's. Robert R. Wilson,[5] however, has argued that all three key passages are the work of an editor of the book, who not only composed them but also placed them where they now stand, in order to convey a subtle message of his own [290].

Extracting this message, Wilson focuses his attention on 3:22–27, and particularly verse 26. Ezekiel is to be dumb, precisely so he should not be an *'ish mokhiaḥ* for the Jews, "for they are a rebellious house." Biblical usage, Wilson argues, suggests that an *'ish mokhiaḥ* is not a "reprover" but a "mediator," an "intercessor." Yahweh does not intend to keep Ezekiel from rebuking his people—that would be absurd—but from interceding on their behalf. The editor, says Wilson, was troubled by the question of why Ezekiel did not discharge this standard prophetic task, so that the holy city and Temple might be spared. Was Ezekiel himself one of the false prophets he denounces in 13:5, who did not stand in the breach for the house of Israel on the day of Yahweh? The editor's answer: Ezekiel did not defend his people, much as he wanted to, because he was under divine restraint. Only when city and Temple had already been destroyed was the restraint lifted.

Wilson thus encourages us to conceive Ezekiel's dumbness, not as a prophetic affliction, but as a literary tactic designed to convey a specific message. Seen from this perspective, the incongruity of a mute prophet is no longer so vexing, and we do not need to relieve it by rewriting the biblical text.

4. Most recently, Ellen Davis and Stephen Garfinkel have tried to read the dumbness as a literary device, while affirming that it was Ezekiel himself who created it [63,92]. Greenberg had perhaps moved toward this position in his commentary, in which, as we have seen, he interpreted "dumbness" as Ezekiel's metaphor for his isolation and impotence [106]. Garfinkel essentially agrees with Greenberg. But, with his suggestion that Ezekiel borrowed the motif from Akkadian incantations and poetry,[6] he shifts Ezekiel's dumbness almost completely from experience to literature.

Davis's treatment of Ezekiel's dumbness is part of her argument for Ezekiel as an innovator who, more than any other single person, reshaped prophecy into a form of written discourse. By speaking of himself

5. Te Stroete follows Wilson on this point [261].
6. I give a fuller summary of Garfinkel's views in Chapter 1, section 5.

as "dumb," he expressed what he perceived as the nature of his prophetic function.

Like Greenberg, Davis links the image of dumbness with that of eating the scroll. "Ezekiel must fall 'silent' and let the scroll which he has swallowed speak through him." Again like Greenberg, she connects both with Ezekiel's social isolation. But, going beyond Greenberg, she sees this isolation as having been, at least in part, the self-imposed seclusion of the writer. It is here that Ezekiel works his great innovation. "The shift from an interactive communications situation to a unidirectional flow represents a major reinterpretation of the prophetic role." The divine book speaks, fixed and unalterable. The people cannot respond, but only hear. Ezekiel's dumbness is his way of representing this "major reinterpretation." Only with the destruction of Jerusalem, when the scroll of woe (2:10) is exhausted, can he again open his mouth.

Each of the proposals we have surveyed has its attractions, and we cannot write off any of them as impossible. Yet none manages to be fully satisfying.

The standard critical tactic of rearranging, recombining, and reconstructing the "dumbness" passages inevitably evokes the suspicion that the commentator has created his own text, which he then has no difficulty interpreting. A procedure like Vogt's, particularly, gives the impression that the critic envisions the text as a jigsaw puzzle that has somehow gotten into the wrong pattern. All the pieces are there, however, and can be properly rearranged if one is only ingenious enough. (The newly rearranged texts often turn out to have problems of their own. See note 4 to this chapter.)

It would not be fair to charge that the critics never explain how (as Greenberg puts it) "an originally continuous and eminently sensible arrangement . . . was . . . violently destroyed by the work of later redactors" [114]. Vogt, for one, makes some effort to explain the editor's motive [290]. Yet it is usually fairly easy to imagine a way in which the editor could have achieved his supposed ends more economically, and with a smoother result than the text that we have. To the question, "Why the current text?" the critic can respond only with a shrug.

Greenberg tried—originally, at least—to stick to a fairly literal reading of the text as we have it, and to show that what it asserts, fantastic as it may seem, is at least not impossible. I am very much in sympathy with this approach, and will presently return to its defense. Yet it has its flaws. Davis objects that the text itself gives no hint that Ezekiel's muteness was interrupted in any way. We can respond by supposing (as Greenberg does) that 3:27 speaks of repeated "openings" of the prophet's mouth, and thereby qualifies what is said in verse 26. But this requires that we play down the tension between 3:26 and 27, which Vogt, with some justice, stresses. Vogt's complaint, that Greenberg wholly ignores the problems of 24:25–27, is also justified [284].[7] And there is a deeper problem with any effort to read the text literally. To the extent to which we insist on the objective reality of Ezekiel's dumbness, we are apt to lose sight of the question of its meaning, to fail to ask what message it conveys.

It is the strength of the last two approaches we have considered that they emphasize the issue of meaning. Their weakness is that the "dumbness" the book describes seems to convey its alleged meaning ineptly and obscurely. Even if we grant Wilson that 'ish mokhiah can mean "intercessor," and that intercession would be a task normally expected of a prophet— both are open to question [16,106]—surely an editor of the Book of Ezekiel would have had more direct ways to make the point that God had restrained Ezekiel from this activity. Jeremiah, or some Deuteronomistic editor of his book, had no difficulty saying this in so many words. "As for you, do not pray on behalf of this people. Lift up no cry or prayer on their behalf, and do not importune me; for I will not listen to you" (Jeremiah 7:16; similarly, 11:14 and 14:11). Why should an editor of Ezekiel have made the same point in a manner so oblique, so easy to misunderstand?

Nor does it seem natural for a writer to choose the image of dumbness to represent literary activity (Davis). The act of writing hardly silences the writer's voice. On the contrary, by Davis's own account, it gives the voice a vastly extended range and increased authority. Davis approvingly quotes Walter Ong to the effect that writers have continued, down to very recent times, to perceive their act of composition as a form of speaking [62,64]. This seems entirely plausible—and entirely opposed to Davis's idea that Ezekiel would have chosen dumbness as a metaphoric representation of the act of writing. The act, indeed, marks a shift from interactive to unidirectional discourse. But it is not Ezekiel who has lost his voice in this shift, but the people he addresses. If Ezekiel wanted to use some physical disability as a metaphor for his alleged transformation of prophetic discourse, deafness would seem far more appropriate.

The hypotheses of Davis and Garfinkel have a further weakness, which

7. Not only with regard to Greenberg. Wilson, Garfinkel, and Davis also leave 24:25–27 unremarked.

Wilson's does not share.[8] They require us to discount, in very large measure, Ezekiel's explicit statements about his own experience. Even Greenberg (in his commentary) will have us believe that, when Ezekiel said he was dumb, he really meant something else. But Garfinkel and Davis go much further in denying the reality of Ezekiel's experience.

Davis does not say in so many words that Ezekiel was never actually mute, but this is the trend of her argument. She similarly proposes an "agnostic" attitude toward the reality of Ezekiel's sign-actions. She points out that "the question of actual performance is certainly muted in Ezekiel's representation, where emphasis falls entirely on the divine instruction" [64]. Whatever legitimacy this observation may have with regard to the sign-actions, it is hardly relevant to Ezekiel's dumbness. In 33:22, which describes the end of the affliction, there is left no doubt that Ezekiel wants us to take it as something he had really experienced. "Then my mouth was opened, and I was dumb no more."

Can we suppose that Ezekiel deliberately fictionalized his own life experience—or, to put it less gingerly, that he lied about it? It is not unthinkable. Certainly the Jewish prophets called each other liars often enough; and, as Morton Smith has remarked, they may often enough have been right [252]. Ezekiel himself, as Kaufmann has shown, was capable of playing fast and loose with Israelite history.

But we should hesitate long before we adopt this solution. When an ancient writer makes a claim about his experience that, as we shall see, involves no significant implausibility; that is, moreover, entirely consonant with everything we can gather about his character—surely it is the wiser course at least to begin by trying to believe him.

3. The Coming of the Fugitive

Let us begin with the chronological problems of 24:25–27 and 33:21–22, and the apparent contradiction between the two passages.

Scholars have proposed two alternative explanations, both of them plausible, for the apparent time lag between the fall of Jerusalem (eleventh year of Zedekiah's reign, fourth month) and the arrival of the news in Babylonia (twelfth year of Jehoiachin's captivity, tenth month). The simpler solu-

---

8. I indicate other objections to Garfinkel's views in Chapter 1, section 5.

tion is to emend "twelfth" in Ezekiel 33:21 to "eleventh." The emendation has some manuscript and versional support. It has the advantage that we can explain the presumed misreading: some scribe expected that the date in 33:21 should be no earlier than that of 32:17, which falls in the twelfth year [306]. If the text had originally used the phrase 'ashte 'esreh for "eleventh" (as it does in 26:1), the corruption is particularly plausible; for 'ashte 'esreh differs by only one Hebrew letter from shte 'esreh, "twelfth."[9]

It is possible, however, to get a similar result from the current Hebrew text. K. S. Freedy and D. B. Redford have championed the view (which goes back, in one form or another, to the seventeenth century [306]) that the Jews in Palestine counted the regnal years of Zedekiah as beginning in the autumn. The exiles in Babylonia, following their neighbors' practice, counted the years of Jehoiachin's captivity as beginning in the spring. Both groups, however, began their sequence of months with the spring. The summer of 586 B.C., therefore, will have fallen in the *twelfth* year of Jehoiachin's captivity (which began in the spring of 586), but in the *eleventh* year of Zedekiah's reign (since his twelfth year would not have begun until the autumn). The tenth month of the twelfth year of the exile, therefore, will have fallen only six months after the fourth month of Zedekiah's eleventh year.

In support of this view, Freedy and Redford point to 2 Kings 25:8 (= Jeremiah 52:12), which has the Temple destroyed in the fifth month of Nebuchadnezzar's nineteenth year; that is, the summer of 586 [87].

We do not need to choose between these two options. The only real consequence of this decision—the dating of the fall of Jerusalem to 587 or 586 B.C.—is of no importance to us. Either way, Ezekiel will have heard of the event six months or so after it happened. Ezra 7:9 suggests that this time lag is reasonable [105]. In one way or the other, the apparent difficulty of the date in Ezekiel 33:21 can be relieved, and the plausibility of the text upheld.

If the eighteen-month gap implied in 33:21 can easily be reduced to six, its reduction to a matter of hours in 24:25–27 is vastly harder to explain. At

---

9. 'Ashte 'esreh also in Ezekiel 40:49 (not a date, however), and in what many scholars suppose to be the original text of 32:1 (currently shte 'esreh [88,105]). Ezekiel 30:20 and 31:1, however, use 'ahat 'esreh for "eleventh." The dates of 32:1 and 17 are both problematic (the month is entirely missing from the Hebrew text of the latter), and most scholars prefer the Septuagint's plausible sequence to the more difficult one found in the Masoretic Text [88,105].

first sight, Vogt does not seem to exaggerate when he says that this passage is "certainly meaningless" (*sicher sinnlos*) as it stands [284]. But the task of constructing a more plausible text, and explaining how it became twisted into the one that lies before us, has so far been beyond scholarly ingenuity.

Cooke suggests reading *beyom* ("in the day") for *bayyom hahu'* ("in that day") at the beginning of verse 26, and treating that verse "as continuing v.²⁵, defining it more closely, and forming the antecedent to v.²⁷, thus: *in the day that I take from them* (v.²⁵) . . . *in the day (when) the fugitive shall come* (v.²⁶) . . . *in that day shall thy mouth be opened* (v.²⁷). . . . Through misunderstanding or carelessness the beginning of v.²⁶ was made to conform to the beginning of v.²⁷" [56]. It is not clear, however, how this would solve the problem, since the "day" of Jerusalem's destruction and the "day" of the fugitive's arrival in Babylonia would still be the same.

Zimmerli, who treats all of 24:25–27 as secondary, regards verse 26 as an addition within it. Its author, he explains, noticed that the prediction of verses 25 and 27 does not suit the event described in 33:21–22. He therefore tried, "in a clumsy way," to bridge the gap [300]. On this hypothesis, the glossator must have been not merely clumsy, but something of an imbecile to boot. For, given the liberties he supposedly allowed himself with the text, he could easily have gotten the effect he wanted without committing an absurdity. All he would have needed to do was change *on the day that I take* to *when I take* in verse 25, and then begin his insertion: *on the day that the fugitive will come to you . . .*[10]

Vogt's hypothesis [284] suffers from an implausibility similar to Zimmerli's. If we are to rewrite 24:25–27 in a more satisfactory way, there is no way to avoid postulating a fantastic degree of ineptitude in the glossators or redactors who put it into its present form. We must ask again if there is really no way to make sense of it as it now stands.

We may freely grant that it is an utter impossibility for any refugee to have covered the distance from Jerusalem to Babylonia in a single day. It will not follow that Ezekiel did not expect, in full faith, that this impossible event would occur. On the contrary, the prophetic traditions he cherished, reinforced by his personal experience, gave him every reason to think that such a thing could and would happen.

10. That is, change *beyom qahti* to *beqahti*, then begin verse 26 with *beyom* instead of *bayyom hahu'* (as Cooke would have done).

Scholars have long observed that the traditions of preclassical Israelite prophecy, such as are found in the stories of Elijah and Elisha, deeply influenced Ezekiel's perception of his own prophethood [40,299]. These stories presuppose that the divine spirit, no doubt perceived as a wind (Hebrew *ruaḥ* has both meanings), can pick people up and carry them to unpredictable places. Thus, Elijah's friend Obadiah worries that, the moment he turns his back, "Yahweh's spirit/wind will carry you I don't know where," and no one will be able to find him (1 Kings 18:12). When a whirlwind carries Elijah to heaven, the "sons of the prophets" suspect that what has really happened is that "Yahweh's spirit/wind has lifted him up and cast him on some mountain or in some valley" (2 Kings 2:16).

We cannot be sure how literally this "lifting" was intended. It is possible to imagine Yahweh's wind actually carrying Elijah through the air (which is more or less how Elijah left this world). Or, perhaps, it filled and inspired him, enabling him to perform feats of locomotion beyond ordinary human powers—as "Yahweh's hand" does in 1 Kings 18:46, empowering Elijah to run before Ahab's chariot from Mount Carmel to Jezreel. We cannot be sure, either, how Ezekiel understood these tales. But it is surely plausible to suppose that he took from them the expectation that supernatural transport is a part of the prophetic life.

What tradition taught Ezekiel to expect, his own experience verified. He had himself been transported from Babylonia to Jerusalem, then back again, in practically no time at all. "A spirit/wind lifted me up between earth and heaven, and brought me to Jerusalem in visions of God" (8:3). At the end of his vision, "a spirit/wind lifted me up and brought me to Chaldea, to the exiles, in a vision, in the spirit of God" (11:24). He knew, to be sure, that this had happened to him only in the spirit, only in a vision. While his spirit traveled, his entranced body continued to interact with the exiled elders in Babylonia. Yet this experience, of being lifted on the wind and carried instantaneously to Jerusalem, must have strengthened his conviction that such things might happen even in the body.

Ezekiel uses very similar language in 3:14–15, to describe his bodily locomotion while in a state of ecstasy. "A spirit/wind lifted me up and took me, and I went bitter in the heat of my spirit, Yahweh's hand being mighty upon me; and I came to the exiles at Tel Abib." Ezekiel knew well enough that he was traveling on foot, yet perceived his experience as one of being lifted and carried. It is possible that he lost all sense of the duration of his trip and perceived it as instantaneous. Significantly, Ezekiel describes all these experiences in language shared with, and presumably drawn from, the Elijah stories [41].[11]

If we can accept that Ezekiel believed that Yahweh's spirit/wind might have whisked Elijah's body to some valley or mountaintop; that he knew from his experience that the spirit/wind had carried him to Tel Abib in the body and to Jerusalem in the spirit—why should we balk at his having expected the same spirit/wind to carry a fugitive from Jerusalem to Babylonia, to bring Yahweh's prophet instant notification that the "splendid joy" of Israel had been taken away?

Nothing of the sort happened, of course. Ezekiel 33:21–22 describes the considerably more prosaic reality. The long-awaited fugitive eventually turned up, several months after the city fell. Upon hearing his news, Ezekiel felt himself relieved of his muteness.

It is not very likely that the fugitive came straight to Ezekiel to deliver his message. No doubt Ezekiel heard reports about his arrival some hours at least before he actually saw the man. This will explain the obscure 'ad ("until") of 33:22. "Yahweh's hand" fell upon Ezekiel "in the evening," when he first learned that what he had so long predicted had indeed come true. It was then that he felt his dumbness begin to leave him. By the time he got to see the fugitive, "in the morning," his disability was gone and he was able to converse. The obscurity of Ezekiel's language reflects the tension between his expectation, that his personal encounter with the fugitive would bring sudden relief, and the actual event.

The contradiction between 24:25–27 and 33:21–22 is nothing more nor less than an example of the "rift between prophecy and reality" (as Yehezkel Kaufmann called it) that makes itself felt throughout the Book of Ezekiel. Ezekiel, his own fond belief to the contrary, had no privileged access to the future. His expectations were frustrated again and again. Yet they did not fail to be faithfully recorded.

The clearest example of the rift is 29:17–21. Here (again quoting Kaufmann) "the prophet himself takes account of the failure of his Tyrian prophecy to materialize." He consequently "announces that Nebuchadnezzar will take Egypt in lieu of Tyre"—which did not materialize either. Yet the original erroneous prediction is also preserved, in Ezekiel 26–28. Kauf-

---

11. Ezekiel 8:3: *wattiśśa' 'oti ruaḥ . . . wattabe' 'oti.* Ezekiel 11:24: *weruaḥ neśa'atni wattebi'eni.* Ezekiel 3:14: *weruaḥ neśa'atni wattiqqaḥeni . . . weyad YHWH 'alay ḥazaqah.* 1 Kings 18:12: *weruaḥ YHWH yiśśa'akha.* 2 Kings 2:16: *neśa'o ruaḥ YHWH wayyashlikhehu.* 1 Kings 18:46: *weyad YHWH hayetah 'el 'eliyahu.*

mann infers that the book preserves Ezekiel's prophetic anticipations much as they came to him, without significant revision by himself or anyone else [163]. Davis draws the same conclusion from this passage [64]. She similarly interprets the tension, in chapter 17, between verses 9 and 17 [65].

To this dossier, we may now add the contrast between Ezekiel's anticipation of how his dumbness *would* end, and the reality of how it *did* end. The gap between the two argues that 24:25–27 accurately reports Ezekiel's anticipation, just as 33:21–22 truthfully describes the reality.

We may consequently take as certain that Ezekiel had been mute before his wife's death. Shortly after her death, he became possessed by the conviction that his muteness would vanish once the Temple was destroyed. Desperately eager for this relief, he persuaded himself that God would bring him a witness to the destruction on the very day it happened.[12]

This was, of course, a delusion. Ezekiel learned of the Temple's fall in an ordinary way, months after the event. His anticipation of relief, however, proved correct. It must, therefore, have been rooted in the same unconscious process that had determined his affliction in the first place.

It was the death of Ezekiel's wife that triggered this flash of insight into the mechanism of his dumbness. Combined with other evidence, which we will presently consider, this will suggest that his dumbness was linked to murderous wishes against a female; and that it served to protect him from these wishes and from their anticipated consequences.

4. Conversion Mutism: The Clinical Evidence

Garfinkel, attempting to define the central questions posed by the reports of Ezekiel's dumbness, asks whether his muteness was "actual or metaphorical . . . a physical disability or a symbol reflecting a socio-political reality" [92].

12. This certainly does not exhaust the meaning that the anticipated "fugitive" had for Ezekiel. For, if his only function was to convey to Ezekiel the news of the destruction, Yahweh could have accomplished this more economically with an oracle. ("Son of man, on this day I have taken away from them their safe refuge, their splendid joy, the desire of their eyes," etc.) In the Excursus, I offer a speculative explanation of the "fugitive's" unconscious significance for Ezekiel—which, if correct, will further clarify why Ezekiel expected him to arrive instantaneously.

Neither alternative, as we have seen, is entirely faithful to the biblical evidence. We cannot dispute the physical reality of the dumbness without claiming either that Ezekiel did not write the pertinent passages, or that, in writing them, he did not really mean what he said. But, if we try to deny the dumbness any symbolic or metaphorical character, we will be left at a loss as to why it suddenly vanished when Ezekiel learned the Temple had been destroyed.

We have no choice, therefore, but to favor a hypothesis that allows the dumbness to have been both actual *and* metaphorical, both a physical disability *and* a symbol. To state this hypothesis, we must perforce use medical language, and describe Ezekiel's dumbness as a conversion reaction.

Conversion reactions are physical symptoms that occur without any discoverable physiological cause. These symptoms may include (to quote Arnold E. Aronson) "loss of general sensation in response to touch, pressure, or pain, or impairment of the special senses of vision or hearing . . . weakness, incoordination, complete loss of movement control ('paralysis'), or unusual or bizarre movements anywhere in the body." They also include voice disorders of various kinds and degrees: hoarseness and disturbances in pitch, inability to speak above a whisper, inability to speak at all [313].

Disabilities of this kind—often, though imprecisely, called "hysterical"—are nowhere near as common as they were a hundred years ago, when the young Sigmund Freud founded his medical practice on them [385]. (At least, they are no longer as frequently reported [386].)[13] But that the phenomenon exists, and that its roots are psychological, there can be no doubt.

What causes it? Freud and his followers explained that an unwelcome feeling—in this case, anxiety—will possess a quantity of psychic energy. This energy can be diverted away from the consciousness by being transformed into a physical symptom. (Hence the name "conversion reaction.") The symptom that is chosen will have some symbolic relationship with the content of the anxiety from which it is supposed to shield the consciousness. That is why it is selected, in preference to some other symptom.

To this, Freud added at one point an interesting qualification. "A hys-

13. According to Ziegler and Imboden, "classical" conversion symptoms are now most common in backwoods areas [409]. Kinzl and his colleagues, basing themselves on work published in the early 1980s, claim they are on the increase [356].

terical symptom develops only where the fulfilments of two opposing wishes, arising each from a different psychical system, are able to converge in a single expression." In other words, the symptom must express both an anxiety-producing unconscious wish, and a tactic used to repress that wish.

Freud illustrated this with the case of a woman whose

> hysterical vomiting turned out to be on the one hand the fulfilment of an unconscious phantasy dating from her puberty—of a wish, that is, that she might be continuously pregnant and have innumerable children, with a further wish, added later, that she might have them by as many men as possible. A powerful defensive impulse had sprung up against this unbridled wish. And, since the patient might lose her figure and her good looks as a result of her vomiting, and so might cease to be attractive to anyone, the symptom was acceptable to the punitive train of thought as well; and since it was permitted by both sides it could become a reality. [338]

In an article that appeared in 1962, Frederick J. Ziegler and John B. Imboden found it necessary to qualify and partially discard the Freudian formulations [409]. The unpleasant feeling "converted" is not necessarily anxiety. Further, in place of some mysterious process of "energy transmutation," we must imagine the individual unconsciously expressing his or her needs through some organ system that can make differentiated responses to demands originating in the cortex (that is, the locus of the higher brain processes).[14] This will encompass all the symptoms listed by Aronson: blindness, deafness, dumbness, paralysis, and so forth.

But Ziegler and Imboden follow the Freudians on the point that most directly concerns us. The conversion symptom, they agree, has a symbolic meaning that links it with the distress that brought it into being. The individual is "symbolically communicating his distress—dysphoric affect and/or unacceptable fantasy—by means of somatic symptoms. . . . Through the conversion reaction, the fact that the patient is in distress is formulated to himself and communicated to others in the ego-syntonic terms of 'physical illness,' and the patient thereby distracts himself (with

14. Yet Kinzl and his colleagues, in an article published in 1988, continue to explain conversion disorders as "caused by the transformation of affective energy to physical impairment; underlying is some unconscious need and its satisfaction, respectively" [356].

varying degrees of success) from the more immediate perception of his dysphoric affect." In other words, the patient uses the symptom as a symbolic representation of inner pain and, at the same time, as a shield against conscious awareness of it.

The choice of symptom, according to Ziegler and Imboden, can be determined by a number of factors. These include the individual's notions of what "illness" is supposed to be like. But, in addition, "specific symptoms may develop or receive prominence because they are especially suited to the symbolic representation of specific fantasies, affects, and motivational conflicts. For example, an ex-secretary of a neurologist, who had intermittently simulated multiple sclerosis for some months, expressed unconscious rejection of her pregnancy with her complaint of progressive weakness of her arms, which she fantasied would prevent her from holding the unwanted baby." On the basis of their clinical experience, Ziegler and Imboden suggest that "unconscious denial of anxiety related to aggressive impulses is apt to be associated with feelings of weakness or numbness." This observation is worth keeping in mind when we consider Ezekiel's feelings of being "bound."

Aronson and his colleagues followed Ziegler and Imboden. They applied their model of conversion reactions to psychogenic voice disturbances, including partial or total voice loss [311,313,315]. Aronson's textbook, *Clinical Voice Disorders*, provides the most accessible statement of his views.

"A conversion voice disorder," Aronson writes, "(1) exists despite normal structure and function of the vocal folds, (2) is created by anxiety, stress, depression, or interpersonal conflict, (3) has symbolic significance for that conflict, and (4) enables the patient to avoid facing the interpersonal conflict directly and extricates the person from the uncomfortable situation" [313]. People suffering from the most extreme such disorder, mutism, share the following characteristics: "(1) A conflict between wanting but not allowing oneself to express anger, fear, or remorse verbally. (2) A breakdown in communication with someone important to that person. (3) Fear or shame standing in the way of expressing feelings via conventional speech and language" [313].

In illustration, Aronson offers a case history, parts of which might almost have been copied from the Book of Ezekiel:

> A 44-year-old female presented with no use of speech structures for communication. All her responses were written. Her history was

one of struggle and deprivation from birth. She was the youngest of ten, her family being burdened by five other children from her father's former marriage. By the time she was 20, her father then dead and most of the children gone, she had been saddled with the responsibility of caring for her aging mother and two older sisters. She lived a Cinderella-like existence, doing the household chores and being dominated by her sisters, who rarely allowed her out of the house. Under these circumstances, at age 23, she had her first conversion symptom, a "paralysis" of the right arm lasting two weeks. Three years later, she became severely depressed and unable to work for several months. Then, at age 27, her mother, "the only person who ever loved me," died. Shortly thereafter, she developed a "paralysis" of both legs and became an invalid for one and a half years. Physical therapy effected a "dramatic cure." Her doctors, who knew of her hostile and dependent relationship with her sisters, urged her to get out on her own. Six years later, at age 35, she married a 27-year-old man with a son from a previous marriage. She had made an adjustment to life. Financial worries and behavior problems in the son were followed by episodes of dysphonia. During the winter prior to the present interview, she had many episodes of intermittently phonated-whispered voice. Her present episode had begun nine months before with a period of whispered speech lasting seven months and finally giving way to muteness and writing notes. [313]

One can easily imagine this unfortunate woman's rage toward her mother, as well as her need to repress any awareness of her rage. (She could hardly have wanted to violate her memory of her mother as "the only person who ever loved me.") Although Aronson does not give us enough information to be sure, we may guess that her loss of voice was connected with this repression, and that it grew worse as she felt more and more driven to utter her forbidden emotions. The relevance of this observation to our understanding of Ezekiel's dumbness will soon become clear.

In our effort to imagine Ezekiel living with his handicap, it is worth recalling that the woman's problems with her voice were to some extent intermittent, and occurred in several different forms. This last characteristic is common, according to Aronson.

Kinzl and his colleagues found that people with conversion voice disorders see themselves as caught in difficult situations, without adequate support from those whom they might expect to give it [356]. Those suffering from mutism, says Aronson, often show "chronic stress, primary and secondary gain, indifference to their symptom, other manifestations of conversion, poor sex identification, suppressed anger, immaturity and dependency, neurotic life adjustment, and mild to moderate depression" [313]. Of these features, the most relevant to Ezekiel is "suppressed anger."[15]

"Indifference to his symptom," on the other hand, would hardly seem to describe Ezekiel, given what we have seen about his eagerness to be rid of it. But Aronson plainly does not claim this as a universal feature. Further: "Once the patient realizes that his voice has returned, there occurs, oftener in women than in men, a fairly sudden expression of relief accompanied by crying, and a facilitation of expression of feelings about the voice loss and the events leading to it" [312]. This description perhaps suggests how we are to envision Ezekiel's mouth being "opened with the fugitive." In any case, dramatic expression of relief would seem to point to a prior yearning for relief, which some sufferers (like Ezekiel) are more consciously aware of than others.

Aronson also observes that one does not have to be in acute psychiatric distress in order to suffer from conversion voice impairment. Of twenty-seven patients in one of his studies, none were worse than neurotic [315].[16] Clearly, one does not have to imagine Ezekiel a raving lunatic to suppose that he suffered from disabling symptoms of psychological origin. Any criticism of our hypothesis that is grounded in such an assumption will be misguided.

The purposes served by conversion voice loss are sometimes fairly obvious. Elspeth and Peter McCue report the case of a middle-aged Englishwoman who, rather like Ezekiel (3:23–26), fell unconscious and awoke totally unable to speak. It came out that she was scheduled to give testimony in court against her husband. Her mutism rescued her from this unpleasant prospect [368]. One of Aronson's patients, who could only speak in a whisper, was a policeman who disliked his job. He feared

15. "Joy and love are emotions to be expressed," Aronson describes one of his patients as saying, "but not anger" [315].

16. Links between conversion reactions and what is conventionally described as the "hysterical personality" exist, according to Aronson, but are not very strong [313,315]. Kinzl and his colleagues come to a similar conclusion [356]. This is the main reason why modern medical writers have broken with the practice of calling conversion disorders "hysterical illnesses."

having to confront speeding motorists, but also feared having to tell his parents about his feelings [312,313]. Rose Shalom, M.D., tells me of a relevant case from her practice. A man had promised his mother that, when her illness reached a hopeless stage, he would tell her doctors to remove her from life-support systems. Confronted with the situation, he lost his voice.

Psychoanalytic case studies, as might be expected, look for deeper meanings in voice loss.

In 1930, the Soviet analyst E. Perepel published an account of a young woman who became completely mute after a quarrel with the manager of the asylum where she worked. "The dumbness lasted for nearly a month and then it ceased." It was followed during the next several years by periods when the woman could only whisper.

Perepel explained the woman's dumbness as her effort to repress her feelings of pleasure at defecation. This was itself tied to her forbidden longings for her father, for whom the asylum manager was a stand-in. Her unconscious had presumably transferred her anal erotic pleasure upward to her mouth. The whispering speech that later developed combined, in good Freudian fashion, "the satisfaction of the anal-erotic and the punishment it deserved." Perepel believed, however, that the symptom had other determinants. Among them was an order she had once received from her mother's lover, never to speak of what she had seen [382].

Another case, described by Edward S. Tauber, involved a housewife who could not speak above a whisper. The aphonia, Tauber thought, may have been connected with the woman's shame and fear of discovery over a minor homosexual affair she had once had with her high-school basketball coach. But, more significantly, it both symbolized and served as a vehicle for her emotional withdrawal from other people (particularly her husband), and her unwillingness to confront them with her needs.

The woman's disability further cemented her relationship with her mentally ill father, with whom she believed she had a special bond that went beyond words. "Her aphonia, which was no hindrance to her in her relationship to her father because they understood each other without words, was to show him that she had relinquished the outside world with which it was necessary to communicate by words." Substitute "God" for "father" in this description, and its relevance to Ezekiel's dumbness will become evident. Sexual frustration surely also played a role of some sort, for Tauber remarks that the woman's "difficulty in speaking was more prominent when she stopped masturbating" [400].

More recent writers have often preferred to generalize from their clinical experience. I have already quoted Aronson's view that voice loss both symbolizes a conflict and "solves" it by giving the individual a way to avoid it. Its most particular function is to block expression of anger [315]. Kinzl and his colleagues support these views, adding that "the conversion reaction is used as a means to express anxiety and maintain self-assertion at the same time." In patients with hysterical personality traits, it has the further effect of "making something undone, of a regression to infantile dependence" [356].

Even in cases where psychogenic mutism provides some obvious advantage (not having to testify against a spouse, for example), we cannot suppose that is the whole explanation. Surely there is something deeper in the individual's psyche that predisposes the person to hit upon just this solution to the immediate problem. It is worth recalling Freud's maxim, that a symptom will come into being only if it can satisfy distinct and perhaps contradictory psychic needs [338]. Without psychoanalytic investigation, it is not clear how this network of intersecting needs might be elucidated.

If we are to follow the example of most Bible scholars, we will be very wary of allowing modern clinical observations of conversion mutism to guide our understanding of the precisely similar phenomena described in the Book of Ezekiel. We will refuse to share what Davis, in her dismissal of Broome, contemptuously calls his "confidence in the exegetical power of medical science" [64]. With Garfinkel, we will eschew the "medical model" in favor of some other approach to the text. This in spite of the fact that it may be the "medical model" that allows us to affirm the text's authenticity, and to grant its words their most evident meaning.

I myself can see no ground for this skepticism other than prejudice. There is not the slightest reason to imagine that conversion reactions are something exclusively modern. Let us grant that the "hysteria" of the ancient Greek physicians—so named on the basis of their theory that it was a female disease caused by a wandering uterus—may not be relevant, since it is very hard to get a clear picture of just what this alleged disease was [386]. Yet inscriptions from the temple of Aesculapius at Epidaurus describe miraculous healings of the blind, paralyzed, and mute [325,406]. It is not easy to explain these healings, except on the supposition that the ailments themselves were conversion reactions. For example:

> A voiceless boy. He came as a suppliant to the Temple for his voice. When he had performed the preliminary sacrifices, and fulfilled the usual rites, the temple servant who brings in the fire for the god,

looking at the boy's father, demanded he should promise to bring within a year the thank-offering for the cure if he obtained that for which he had come. The boy suddenly said, "I promise." His father was startled at this, and asked him to repeat it. The boy repeated the words and after that became well. [406]

Jesus also healed the dumb, according to Matthew 9:32–34 and its parallels. Morton Smith is surely right to suppose that this and other Gospel accounts of miraculous cures cannot all be dismissed as pious fabrications. Some, at least, surely rest upon authentic reports of the relief of conversion symptoms [250].

Once we grant that conversion reactions existed in antiquity, interpreting them in the light of modern clinical evidence is simply a matter of reasoning from the known to the unknown. We have no reason to refuse this tool, or to exempt the ancient Jews in general or Ezekiel in particular from its workings. On what grounds might we refuse to apply to them Aronson's judgment, that psychogenic muteness serves to repress angry feelings that are seen as unacceptable? Do we imagine that they never experienced anger? That they never felt the need to conceal their angers from others and from themselves? That the conflicts such repressions created were less painful for them than for us? Such ideas are, to me, wholly inconceivable. I can as easily imagine Ezekiel and his contemporaries to have been innocent of the love that is strong as death, the jealousy that is cruel as the grave (Song of Songs 8:6).

To be sure, modern medical literature provides only a perspective from which to interpret the ancient data. It will tell us nothing, unless the ancients provide us with material to which we can apply it. Normally, this is hardly to be expected. The mute boy of Epidaurus, for example, provides us with no such material, and we have no way to surmise what it was that he expressed with his dumbness.

But, when it happens that an ancient author does provide us with the evidence we need, we have no excuse for overlooking it. This is the case with Ezekiel.

5. The Solution

Our analysis of Ezekiel 16 and 23 has shown us a man overwhelmed by sexualized rage against females. He perceives them as powerful and cruel,

sexually rampant, seductive and treacherous. Seldom does he openly express his anger against any human woman.[17] Rather, he displaces his
feelings onto personifications of Israel, Judah, and Jerusalem; and, in
deeper disguise, onto the Temple (Ezekiel 8). His rage prevents him from
mourning his wife's death. But he has no conscious awareness of this and
must imagine himself blocked by Yahweh's command. It goes almost without saying, however, that the roots of his anger must lie in a human
relationship; most plausibly, his relationship with his mother.

We have seen traces of an even more deeply buried rage, directed
against the male figure who is likely to have been the worse of his abusers.
Given Ezekiel's association of this male figure with his God, we can understand why he found it safer to turn most of his wrath against the female;
indeed, to identify himself with the male and under this guise to take his
revenge on the female.

Even the female, in her original form, was an unacceptably dangerous
target. Ezekiel's religious culture taught him that his rage against his mother
must be ferociously repressed. "He who curses his father or his mother shall
surely be put to death" (Exodus 21:17). The stronger the impulse to curse,
the more stringent must be the repression. It would be hard to imagine a
more effective way to repress a curse than with muteness.

But the blocked impulse had a way out. Hidden behind the ultimately
powerful male, Ezekiel might dare to proclaim his rage and loathing—
provided that its female object is suitably disguised. He must make absolutely clear that his words are not his own, that he cannot be held responsible for them. "When I speak with you, I will open your mouth, and you
will say to them: Thus says the Lord Yahweh" (3:27).

Let us grant that 3:26 and 27 contradict each other. The one represents
Ezekiel as dumb and therefore unable to reprove. The other has him

---

17. Only, to my knowledge, in 13:17–23: Certain self-proclaimed "prophetesses" have
stitched together some sort of paraphernalia, with which they entrap other people's vital forces
(*nefashot*), "killing people who ought not to die and keeping alive people who ought not to live."
Yahweh, indignant at this, promises to intervene, tear up the women's traps, and set the victims free. "I will . . . save my people from your clutches; they shall no longer be prey in your
clutches, and you shall know that I am YHWH" (verse 21, in Greenberg's translation [104]).
These women surely cut a rather pathetic figure; especially if we suppose, with Zimmerli
[297], that verse 19 intends to say that they perform their sorceries in exchange for "handfuls of
barley and bits of bread." But, for Ezekiel, they are mistresses of life and death, whose sinister
power over God's people can be broken only by God himself. The terrifying image of female
power, which was Ezekiel's childhood burden, will do much to account for his perception of
them. Greenberg remarks that the language of 13:17–23 recalls Proverbs 6:26, which carries us
back to the "strange woman" and the complex of terrors with which Proverbs surrounds her.

speaking the words—reproofs, presumably—of Yahweh. But we may resolve the contradiction without recourse to editorial tinkering, by recalling Freud's story of the borrowed kettle. Eager to deny that he had damaged his neighbor's property, the borrower "asserted first, that he had given it back undamaged; secondly, that the kettle had a hole in it when he borrowed it; and thirdly, that he had never borrowed a kettle from his neighbour at all" [334,340].

Ezekiel, driven to deny that he could ever have cursed his (*ex officio*) loved and revered mother, uses a similar strategy. First, he protests, he is absolutely without speech and therefore cannot possibly curse her. Second, the harsh words he speaks are really Yahweh's, and he cannot be held responsible for them. Third, they are really not directed against his mother at all—as he asserts by the symbolic disguises and displacements of his rage. This threefold protest, to be sure, smacks of the comical. But it can nonetheless aptly describe Ezekiel's unconscious reasoning. The ways of the comic and the processes of the unconscious, Freud has shown, lie very close together [339].

In this way, Ezekiel's conflicting claims that his dumbness was both absolute *and* intermittent become psychologically intelligible. The "doublethink"[18] involved was a necessary response to the otherwise unbearable pressure of contradictory demands.

Once we have allowed that this pressure might to some extent distort Ezekiel's memory of his disability, we may permit ourselves to wonder if it did not work another, fairly slight, distortion. Is it possible that, even apart from his proclamations in Yahweh's name, his dumbness was not always absolute? That, like Aronson's intermittently mute and paralyzed patient, he may at times have been able to communicate in a whisper? This conjecture is not indispensable. Yet it will certainly make living with a seven-year dumbness easier to imagine. No doubt, Ezekiel was entirely mute much of the time. But perhaps it was only in anticipation (3:22–27) and in retrospect (24:25–27, 33:21–22), driven by the need to deny any expression of his hostility, that he conceived himself as *always* entirely mute.[19]

18. Leonard Shengold uses Orwell's word frequently to describe the psychological defenses of those who have endured intolerable childhood abuse. His book, *Soul Murder*, may perhaps orient us to what Ezekiel may have suffered [388].

19. "Patients who present with one form of conversion voice disorder very likely have experienced other forms" (Aronson [313]). The reader may object that I have earlier criticized Greenberg, Garfinkel, and Davis for refusing to take Ezekiel's claims about his experience at face value. Now I seem to be doing the same thing. But the degree of distortion of reality posited by my hypothesis, and that posited by theirs, are of different orders of magnitude.

Exodus 21:16–18, as we have seen, prescribes death for striking as well as for cursing one's parents. Here, perhaps, we have the clue to one meaning of Ezekiel's paralysis. As he made himself mute in order to repress his childhood urge to curse his mother, so he made himself immobile in order to repress a childhood urge to strike her.[20] Like the urge to curse, the urge to attack forced its way out, in an attenuated but unmistakable form. Lying helplessly on his side (4:4–8), Ezekiel nonetheless bares his arm in what is obviously a threatening gesture directed against the mother city. (The commentators agree on this understanding of 4:7 [56,104,297].)

Given this underlying motivation for Ezekiel's paralysis, it is understandable that he may have unconsciously exaggerated its severity. It may originally have been to some extent intermittent. He will have found it inconvenient to remember, and will therefore have forgotten, the times when it was relaxed. We may therefore grant the essential reality of Ezekiel's long-term immobility, without having to take at face value his apparently fantastic claim of having lain continuously on one side for 390 days, forty on the other (4:5–6).

Ezekiel's explanation, that he lay on one side to bear the iniquities of Israel and on the other to bear the iniquities of Judah, is to be considered a *post hoc* rationalization of his behavior. It nonetheless preserves a distorted echo of his real motive: to restrain himself from committing what he perceived to be unbearable iniquity.[21]

Can it be coincidence that Ezekiel's contemporary, the author of Psalm 137, calls upon himself a curse that strikingly resembles what Ezekiel actually experienced?

The psalmist dreads—which is to say, unconsciously desires—that he might forget the mother city, that he might set his own satisfaction above her. He therefore begs that his right hand, which might strike her, may itself "forget" (how to act, presumably). His tongue, which might curse her, is to stick to the roof of his mouth (137:5–6).[22]

---

20. "Unconscious denial of anxiety related to aggressive impulses is apt to be associated with feelings of weakness or numbness" (Ziegler and Imboden [409]).

21. The play on the words "bear iniquity" is valid in Hebrew as well as English. With Ezekiel's *tiśśa' 'et 'awonam . . . wenasa'ta 'awon bet yiśra'el . . . wenasa'ta 'et 'awon bet yehudah,* compare Cain's protest, *gadol 'awoni minneso'* ("My iniquity [or "punishment"] is great beyond bearing," Genesis 4:13).

22. His language is very close to Ezekiel's: *tidbaq leshoni lehikki* (Psalm 137:6); *uleshonekha 'adbiq 'el hikkekha wene'elamta* (Ezekiel 3:26). I have adopted the most conservative interpretation of the difficult *tishkah yemini* ("may my right hand forget," without any direct object).

To "forget" Jerusalem is an expression of hostility. But it may be protective at the same time. For an abused child, repression of memory may be the only way to restrain feelings he cannot tolerate. The psalmist, we may imagine, desperately wants to forget his unbearable rage and pain. He calls upon paralysis and dumbness to enforce his repression.

This conjecture requires us to assume that the psalmist shared with Ezekiel, not only the adult trauma of exile, but certain childhood traumas as well. The two men dealt with their feelings in different ways. The psalmist directs his rage at his "bad mother," and his longing for revenge, toward the "daughter of Babylon." For her brutality toward helpless children, he assures himself, she will be cruelly punished.[23] He turns his yearning for a good mother toward his idealized Jerusalem.

For Ezekiel, by contrast, the "bad mother" is Jerusalem, which he hates with fanatic intensity (chapters 16, 22). His "good mother" is perhaps the fantasy city and Temple sketched in chapters 40–48. The real (= bad) Jerusalem spread her legs for all passers-by (16:25). But the ideal Temple will open her "gate" only to Yahweh, and to the "prince"—surely the infant Ezekiel—who sits nourishing himself within (44:1–3).[24]

Yet both Ezekiel and the psalmist found themselves unconsciously wishing for dumbness and paralysis, to help them control their terrifying rage. Ezekiel, unluckier than his fellow exile, was able to make his wish come true.

So far, I have explained Ezekiel's dumbness and paralysis as protective measures. They held back his urges to avenge himself for his childhood wounds. They consequently had the effect of repressing the memory of these wounds.

In Chapter 4, however, I proposed a different interpretation, no less oriented toward Ezekiel's childhood experience. I suggested that Ezekiel's

---

Many scholars prefer to translate verse 5's second *škḥ* (not the first) as "wither," on the basis of a supposed Ugaritic cognate [11,86]. This interpretation will suit my hypothesis still better.

23.   "O devastated daughter of Babylon, happy is he who pays you back for what you have done to us. Happy is he who seizes and smashes your little ones against the rock" (verses 8–9). *What you have done to us* (understand, *to me*) is the key phrase, which makes intelligible the feelings that underlie this gruesome curse.

24.   The traditional Christian expositors, who saw in 44:1–3 a prophecy of the Blessed Virgin [56,216], were surely wrong in detail but right as to the essentials. Significantly, this same gate later becomes the source of Ezekiel's river of life (47:1–12, especially verse 2). I pursue this line of thought a short distance in the Excursus. I hope others may be encouraged to follow it further. (Julie Galambush [91] now offers some relevant observations.)

immobility reenacted his infantile helplessness, whereas his dumbness repeated his experience of crying out for care and being ignored. (If I cry and no one responds, surely it is because I am unable to make a sound?) Ezekiel's conversion symptoms will then have manifested what Leonard Shengold calls the "mysterious compulsion to repeat traumatic experiences," in the expectation that "this time the contact will bring love instead of hate" [389].[25] They serve as an extreme illustration of Kinzl's observation: in hysterical patients, "functional aphonia has the effect of making something undone, of a regression to infantile dependence" [356].

These two interpretations do not exclude each other. On the contrary, if Freud was right that "a hysterical symptom develops only where the fulfilment of two opposing wishes . . . are able to converge in a single expression" [338], their simultaneous presence is precisely what we would expect. Ezekiel's dumbness and paralysis served at once to *reenact* his early traumas, and to *repress* expression of the hate and rage that these traumas provoked.[26]

I do not exclude the possibility that Ezekiel's symptoms may have had still other functions. Like Edward Tauber's patient, Ezekiel may have used his dumbness to seal his intimacy with a father-God who did not speak in the ordinary sense of the word [401]. But the two complementary interpretations I have proposed are the primary ones. Together, they are certainly adequate to explain how Ezekiel's symptoms came into existence.

But how did the symptoms end? Ezekiel's paralysis seems to have faded after he had finished expiating "the iniquity of the house of Judah" (4:6). His dumbness was more persistent. We may guess that, of the two repressions, that of speech was the more important. Ezekiel could no longer strike his mother. But he could, if he did not check his impulses, defame her memory.[27] His muteness therefore continued to oppress him, until external circumstances brought him relief.

How did this happen? Let us recall, once again, that Ezekiel's strategy for attacking his mother involved identifying himself with the father (Yahweh speaks with Ezekiel's voice). He was then free to persecute the female, in the guise of the righteously inflamed male.

25. Lenore Terr gives many examples of how this "mysterious compulsion" can manifest itself [404] (see Chapter 4, section 8).

26. Somewhat like the hypnoid state Shengold describes in one of his analytic patients; which, he says, "both warded off and repeated the past" [390].

27. The Mishnah, contrasting the prohibitions of striking and of cursing one's parents, makes a similar point (Sanhedrin 11:1).

When we consider that Ezekiel worked this strategy out with Jerusalem and the Temple as his representations of the female, we can understand that which properly puzzled Yehezkel Kaufmann: the unparalleled ruthlessness of Ezekiel's prophecy of doom. "Isaiah steadfastly believed in Jerusalem's inviolability . . . Jeremiah promises to the very last that if the city will submit to Nebuchadnezzar there will be no fall or exile" [162]. "Alone among the prophets, Ezekiel foretells the unconditional destruction of Jerusalem. His prophecy of the destruction of city, temple, and monarchy has no accompanying call for repentance" [163]. (Kaufmann adds, with greater perspicacity than he can have realized: "His fierce antipathy toward Jerusalem . . . leads one to suspect some personal provocation is involved.")

City and Temple fell. A fugitive brought the news to Ezekiel's community. In that instant, Ezekiel must have leaped to the conclusion that *his self-identification with the paternal tyrant had been successful.* In defiance of the devout expectations of an entire nation, Yahweh had shown beyond doubt that he shared Ezekiel's savage hatred of the woman/sanctuary. He who had threatened death for striking or cursing one's mother, now had proved with his actions that such murderous expressions of rage were no crime after all. Ezekiel's guilt was absolved, his fear of punishment relieved.

It would be too much to claim that Ezekiel now allowed himself to become consciously aware of his feelings. On the contrary, in 25:1–7, he disowns his glee over the fall of the Temple by projecting it onto the "bad boys" of Israelite tradition, the Ammonites (cf. Deuteronomy 23:3–6). These wicked heathen will be punished, Yahweh solemnly promises, "because you said, Aha! [*he'ah*] over my sanctuary when it was profaned, and over the land of Israel when it was devastated, and over the house of Judah when they went into exile . . . because you clapped your hands and stamped your feet and rejoiced with all your soul's contempt over the land of Israel" (25:3, 6).

We cannot deny that the Ammonites may indeed have celebrated the news of Jerusalem's destruction. Yet other passages in the Book of Ezekiel leave little doubt that the sadistic euphoria expressed here was, in reality, Ezekiel's own. He it was who cried "Aha!" (*'ah*), clapped his hands and stamped his feet (6:11), while howling damnations against the land of Israel (6:2–3, 7:2) and the soon-to-be-profaned sanctuary (7:20–24).[28]

28. I can see no reason to suppose that *'ah* in 6:11 and 21:20 means anything different from *he'ah* in 25:3, 26:2, 36:2 [107]. Ezekiel attributes similar outpourings of *Schadenfreude* to

Now he had a clear sign that his murderous wishes had divine approval. The unconscious anxieties these wishes had aroused must have been greatly soothed. The elaborate mechanisms he had used to guard against them were no longer required. "Then my mouth was opened, and I was dumb no more."

This denouement, as we have seen, did not come unexpected. The death of Ezekiel's wife had inspired him with the conviction that he would be able to speak freely once he learned of Jerusalem's fall. The event proved that his conviction had been justified. How did this happen?

On the basis of our argument so far, it is easy enough to formulate an explanation. Jerusalem and the Temple were the screen *par excellence* onto which Ezekiel displaced his image of the hated and hateful female. But he must also have displaced something of this image onto his wife. When she abruptly died, and he understood this to be an act of God, he will have responded much as he later responded to news of the destruction. Unconsciously, he must have been aware that his feelings for his wife were linked with his feelings for the Temple. So we must understand the woman-sanctuary equation of 24:15–27. And we must translate his assurance, that "Ezekiel shall be a token for you" (24:24), into the underlying reality. His reaction to his wife's death was a token for *him*, foreshadowing how he would react to news of the Temple's fall.

But, if so, why did he not begin to speak as soon as she died? We must recall that his feelings toward her were far more ambivalent than his feelings toward the Temple. His love for the individual woman countered his hatred for the displaced image of the Female. His emotional paralysis at her death followed, as we have seen, from this ambivalence.

This was hardly a situation likely to relieve Ezekiel's anxieties and release his repressions. His wife's death may indeed have indicated to him that Yahweh hated the Female, and thus helped ease his guilt over his own hatred. But it also had the effect of provoking more guilt, that he should feel joy and satisfaction at the death of that specific female (see Chapter 4, section 9). Further, as a token of the divine will, the death of a human

---

Tyre (26:2), Edom (35:10), "the enemy" (36:2), and an unspecified "they" (36:13). All of these remarks, especially the last, can be interpreted as conveying Ezekiel's own feelings. "You [feminine] eat human flesh, you have deprived your peoples of their children" (*'okhelet 'adam 'at umeshakkelet goyayikh hayit;* 36:13). We are by now familiar with Ezekiel's child-eating females.

being is far more ambiguous (and therefore less reassuring) than God's devastation of his own sanctuary.

The death of Ezekiel's wife therefore could not itself "open his mouth." But it did allow him to anticipate that his mouth would be opened at some future time, when another mother-representation, which he hated with a hatred more nearly pure, would meet her end.

The situation came to pass. He responded as he had expected. The unconscious had prophesied of its own workings. Its prophecy, not unnaturally, came true.

How permanent was Ezekiel's "cure"? Most psychoanalysts, I imagine, would be pessimistic. Ezekiel's dumbness was his desperate yet indispensable device for coping with a painful and deep-rooted conflict. A fortuitous external event like the fall of Jerusalem might provide some relief. But, without any true resolution of the conflict, the relief could only be temporary.

It is hard to imagine that Ezekiel could have resolved his conflict without some measure of insight into its reality. It is harder still to think of any way he could have achieved that insight. It will follow that the dumbness must sooner or later have returned, or been replaced by some other conversion symptom serving the same function.

Clinical evidence, it is true, does not unequivocally confirm these expectations. D. Walton and D. A. Black have reported the case of a woman who suffered for seven years from a conversion voice disorder that left her almost entirely mute. They treated her on the theory that her symptom was a habit she had to unlearn, without even trying to attack its underlying causes. The symptom disappeared. It did not come back, at least for the eleven months they followed her case. No alternative symptom made its appearance. This result, Walton and Black do not neglect to point out, seems to contradict psychoanalytic theory [408].

Aronson also was successful in treating conversion voice disorders on a symptomatic basis. Like Walton and Black, he found that alternate symptoms did not materialize. But Aronson was careful to guide his patients toward psychotherapy, if he suspected that their voice loss was rooted in a deep and serious problem [311,314].

Aronson wrote in 1985, summarizing his years of experience:

> The likelihood of complete return of the voice via symptomatic voice therapy is excellent if the patient is ready to relinquish the voice sign and to bring the problem causing it into the open. The

prognosis is also excellent if the original problem has disappeared, leaving the residual voice sign. The prognosis is poor for patients who are unwilling to face and deal with the underlying problem causing the voice disorder, in which case it will be impossible to improve the voice by means of any therapy or, if improvement does take place, it will be incomplete or short-lived. [314]

It is not hard to guess which of Aronson's categories Ezekiel would have fallen into.

We will therefore not be surprised to find, in the last of Ezekiel's dated oracles (29:17–21; April 571), that he still yearns for "opening of the mouth." Nor is it surprising that he links this yearning with a fantasy of phallic potency. "On that day, I will cause a horn to sprout for the house of Israel. And to you I will grant opening of the mouth, in the midst of them. And they shall know that I am Yahweh" (verse 21).

Conclusion

. . . our tears are always young, the saltwater
stays the same from cradle . . . to grave.
—John Updike, *Rabbit Is Rich* [417]

The central argument of this book lies in the correlation of Ezekiel 8:7–12, chapters 16 and 23, and 24:15–27. These passages express, in three distinct modes, the same emotional stance of their author; namely, dread and loathing of female sexuality.

This stance is expressed very nearly overtly, covered only by a thin veil of historical allegory, in chapters 16 and 23. In 8:7–12, it is conveyed in the symbolic language of dreams. It manifests itself in 24:15–27, in the self-described behavior of the writer. These three modes of expression reinforce one another, and each of the relevant passages confirms the interpretation I have given of the others. They form, together, a threefold cord not easily broken.

My argument presupposes that Ezekiel's account of his own behavior in 24:15–27 is truthful and accurate. It presupposes, too, that 8:7–12 is to be read as a genuine artifact of a hallucinatory experience, which conveys the author's unconscious processes as authentically (and as cryptically) as our dreams convey ours. Both of these premises can be and have been questioned. Neither, however, is in any way implausible. The exegetical gain that we have seen to result from them justifies our adopting them.

We are, consequently, justified in reading the Book of Ezekiel psychologically. That is to say, we may give ourselves permission to understand it as a document created by a being no less human than ourselves; a document no less expressive of his individual humanity than our writings are expressive of ours. We may suppose Ezekiel to have been governed, no less than ourselves, by a stubbornly maintained inner reality. Once we have taken historical and cultural differences into account, we may boldly seek to recognize and comprehend his inner reality on the basis of what we know of ours.

Once we have granted the validity of this procedure, we have warrant to extend it, to probe what lies behind Ezekiel's radical misogyny.

I have thus carried the inquiry from Ezekiel's hated and feared (yet intensely desired) female images, to his more enigmatic and ambivalent images of the dominant male. The need to make these images intelligible demanded speculation: about their genesis in the child Ezekiel's experiences of his adult caretakers, and about how his childhood sufferings shaped his adult disabilities (most obviously, his dumbness).

At every point, I have tested these speculations against the criterion of exegetical gain. Will individual passages, particularly those long recognized as cruxes, now become more intelligible? Will unexpected correlations among different passages of the book now emerge, and the book thus become more coherent and comprehensible? The answers to these questions have consistently been affirmative.

For example: Seen from a psychoanalytic perspective, Ezekiel's seemingly bizarre assertion that Yahweh ordained child sacrifice for the Israelites (20:25–26) can be correlated with his tormented images of evil mothers sacrificing their little boys to their lovers' appetites (16:20–21, 23:37–39). Both reflect Ezekiel's perception of having been "sacrificed" to an adult sexual rival. The phallic "scroll" of one of Ezekiel's hallucinations (2:8–3:3) can be correlated with the phallic "branch" of another (8:17). Taken together, they suggest this "child sacrifice" was real, and that it took the form of sexual victimization. Ezekiel's vivid and troubling portrait of an abandoned infant (16:4–7) can be correlated with his own infantile regressions (3:22–4:17). Together, they point to another aspect of his childhood trauma. Against this background, his dumbness and its vicissitudes become wholly intelligible for the first time.

It is at this point that I stop.[1] The reader may perhaps wonder why. Surely the success of the method so far should embolden us to pursue it until we have achieved an all-encompassing psychoanalytic interpretation

---

1. Leaving aside my speculations about Ezekiel 12:1–16, set forth in the Excursus.

of the Book of Ezekiel? But such a goal, in my opinion, would be neither possible nor desirable.

One reason for this is the limitation of our evidence. I have chosen to call off the inquiry at a place where the ground under our feet is still reasonably firm. In what has gone before, I have been obliged to speculate. But I have been able to defend my speculations by pointing to the advantages they give us in understanding the text. Beyond this point, however, it would be difficult to advance without piling conjecture upon conjecture, and without getting into the position of defending one hypothesis by reference to others.

This is not to say that our arguments so far do not point to the lines along which other long-standing problems might be solved. Commentators, for example, have often puzzled over why Ezekiel consistently imagines Yahweh addressing him as "son of man" (ben 'adam), a form of address practically without parallel in the Hebrew Bible.[2] We may easily imagine that this problem is linked with a question that has repeatedly confronted us, whether the dominant male figure of Ezekiel's early life was his father or his mother's lover. It is at least thinkable that Ezekiel was himself uncertain on this point, and that his strangely vague self-designation expresses his uncertainty.[3] But once one tries to buttress this conjecture, or even to formulate it more concretely, one begins to run into difficulties. I therefore prefer to leave it at the level of a suggestion, and keep it just outside the boundary of our investigation.

The merkabah (Ezekiel 1) must also remain outside our bounds. I do not doubt that a psychoanalytic approach to this text is legitimate, indeed, necessary to reveal its deepest secrets. Broome's efforts in this direction (summarized in Chapter 1), although incomplete and speculative, seem to me plausible and useful. But I do not sense that this chapter affords us any

2. The Aramaic apocalypse of Daniel 7 speaks of the appearance of a being "like a son of man" (kebar 'enash, verse 13). It is not clear if this has any relation to Ezekiel's expression. In the Gospels, Jesus regularly refers to himself as "son of man," an exceedingly mysterious usage that is perhaps rooted in Ezekiel, or Daniel, or both.

3. We may note in this connection the curious name "Buzi," which 1:3 gives for Ezekiel's father. The name is unusual, though not wholly unparalleled. The Brown-Driver-Briggs lexicon lists two individuals and a tribe named "Buz," and notes that Job 32:2, 6, refers to Elihu's father as a "Buzite" (buzi) [30]. "Buzi" is, as both Christian and Jewish commentators have noted (Origen [129], Kimhi [130]), very suggestive of the Hebrew word for "contempt" (buz or buzah). Is it possible that Ezekiel here expresses his feelings about the man he regards as his father, by inventing an abusive name for him, or abusively distorting his real name? I cannot think, by the way, of any passage where Ezekiel speaks of Yahweh as a father, along the lines of Jeremiah 31:9.

basis from which to grasp the meaning of Ezekiel's associations. I therefore have not tried to contribute anything of my own to its explication.[4]

Besides the uncertainty of our knowledge, there is another reason why a purely psychoanalytic interpretation of the entire Book of Ezekiel would probably be invalid.

Psychoanalysis, by its nature, is about the individual mind. It looks for the roots of human expression in a person's inner drives, and in the extremely narrow social context (consisting mainly of one's parents) in which these drives work themselves out during the first years of life. This simplification of the human being serves a useful goal, and is therefore functionally legitimate. But, as a description of any individual or of his or her creations, it is bound to be incomplete. Most people do not live in universes consisting only of themselves, or (after infancy) of themselves and their mothers and fathers. Our worlds are social as well as private. Any interpretation of any one of us that ignores the social reality will be as incomplete as one that ignores the private reality.

Ezekiel, I have assumed throughout this book, was an intelligible human individual, recognizably of the same species as ourselves. But he was also embedded in an ancient society that during his lifetime was experiencing one of the most agonizing crises of its history. When he spoke or wrote, his purpose was not to express his psychic pain to us moderns, but to communicate with his contemporaries about their common crisis.

The burden of my argument has been that Ezekiel's book *does* in fact convey to us the pain of his elemental human wounds. This is our great good fortune. But the reality of this unintended effect is no excuse for neglecting the effects that Ezekiel did intend. Ezekiel was both a private individual and a member of a society. The Book of Ezekiel is both an unwitting expression of private agony, *and* a conscious response to societal concern. No historian who wants to understand the man and the book can pretend that only one aspect or the other is worth paying attention to.

---

4. In my book on the *merkabah*, *The Faces of the Chariot*, I treated Ezekiel 1 as a sort of Rorschach blot onto which later Jewish and Christian expositors projected their own needs and aversions, but whose meaning for its own author remains beyond explication. I did, however, tentatively suggest that one rabbinic exegetical tradition, which links the "calf's foot" and the "ox's face" of Ezekiel 1:7 and 10 with the golden calf of the desert idolatry (Exodus 32), may perhaps make explicit a message which was latent in the text itself [127]. This message, pointing as it does to a fundamental moral ambiguity in God's character, would well accord with what I have here proposed about Ezekiel's highly ambivalent attitude toward his God.

In Chapter 1, I criticized Ellen Davis for her dogmatic and ill-considered dismissal of psychological approaches to the Book of Ezekiel. I would not now retract a word of that criticism. But I must emphasize that this in no way implies a counterdismissal of Davis's own approach, which treats Ezekiel as a writer deeply concerned with his social surroundings and his potential impact upon them [60]. The psychological approach, and the social/literary, do not exclude each other. The positive elements of Davis's program do in fact make interesting reading, and some may prove extremely useful.

The truth is that no historical figure, especially one as complex as Ezekiel—and living in a situation as demanding as Ezekiel's—can be captured with a single interpretative formula. No more than anything else is psychoanalysis an Open Sesame for the entire Book of Ezekiel. The psychoanalytic interpretation that will account for every aspect of the book will never be found because it cannot exist. To try to discredit any psychoanalytic argument, on the ground that it leaves much outside the bounds of its interpretative powers, would be absurd.

What have we gained from our psychoanalytic reading of the Book of Ezekiel? To begin with, simple clarity of exegesis. This is the most basic advantage that can be claimed by any approach to a text. If the claim proves justified, it is the most powerful warrant imaginable for the legitimacy of the approach. I have tried to show throughout that the words attributed to Ezekiel, read from a psychoanalytic standpoint, yield their meaning with an ease and naturalness otherwise impossible.

We have gained a renewed faith in the possibility of understanding Ezekiel as a human being like ourselves, intelligible to us in human terms. This is, at bottom, what we mean by a "psychological" reading of any document. We give it up only at great cost to ourselves. This cost may be unavoidable in regard to many texts, but I have tried to show that the Book of Ezekiel is not one of them.

Zimmerli's concession, that "Ezekiel's personality is hidden by stylized forms and traditions more deeply than any other of the great prophetic figures" [298]—which Davis quotes approvingly, and turns into something like a programmatic statement [67]—turns out to be not only unnecessary, but positively false. We must endorse the contrary judgment of Karl Jaspers (see Chapter 1). Ezekiel has no equal among the prophets, and indeed among the ancients, in the amazing opportunity he offers for psychological interpretation [153]. The first perception most readers have had of the book, that it bears throughout the signs of a powerful and very unusual personality, is very close to the truth.

We have been able to assert, for the most part, the integrity and authenticity of the book as we have it. We need not insist that every line of the Masoretic Hebrew text is, just as it stands, a precise record of Ezekiel's outpourings. Yet, again and again, we have found that we can make better sense of the text by trusting it than by suspecting it. The book's claims to depict objective reality may not always be justified. In the case of the "abominations in the Temple," as we have seen, they are certainly false. But, as a record of Ezekiel's individual experiences, and of his perceptions of reality, the Book of Ezekiel has shown itself almost entirely reliable.

Even the divergences between the Masoretic and the Septuagintal forms of the text leave this assertion unshaken. We have seen that it is possible to treat both as Ezekiel's own work, the differences between them reflecting the degree to which the man was able to distance himself from his unconscious processes.

This has by no means required us to ignore or to play down the tensions and inconsistencies that certainly exist within the Book of Ezekiel. But working with a psychological model that recognizes the contradictory trends operating within a single individual, we have felt no pressure to relieve these tensions by disintegrating the text.

It will follow that one of the most unsophisticated questions that can be asked about a text—"What kind of a person was it who would have written something like this?"—may turn out (as unsophisticated questions often do) to be precisely the right question. We cannot guarantee that it will always be possible to find an answer. Yet given a suitable text, given a suitable method, given the right match of the two, we have every reason to be hopeful. I have tried to show that psychoanalysis is a useful method for understanding writings from the past, and that the Book of Ezekiel is a text to which it may appropriately be applied. If my demonstration is judged valid, the study of literature as human creation will have gained from it.

But the Book of Ezekiel claims to be a great deal more than a human creation. Our study has religious implications, which we cannot afford to ignore. Can we suppose ourselves to have achieved some gain in this sphere?

We must acknowledge that, as far as theology proper is concerned, the effect of our study is wholly negative. Neither our methods nor our conclusions are compatible with the belief that Ezekiel was in contact with a transcendent being; or that his words or actions convey, in however distorted a form, the intent of such a being. Whatever one may say about the biblical God in general (or God in general), the God of Ezekiel was a creation of Ezekiel's own brain. This proposition follows inevitably from the work we have done here.

Given the appalling character of the deity in whose name Ezekiel spoke, this surely represents something less than a catastrophic loss. Yet it remains true that we have lost at least one warrant for the existence of some being greater than ourselves who looks over our affairs. There is in this a sadness that cannot be denied.

The practical consequence of this conclusion would seem to be that we must expel Ezekiel from the canon, if not dissolve the canon itself. It is not at all clear, however, that this will follow, once we recognize that religion encompasses something more than theology.

If the history of the twentieth century has taught us anything, it is that religion is a phenomenon vastly more tenacious than anyone can have expected a hundred years ago. Scientific progress, and a general rise in the level of human comfort and human control over the circumstances of our lives, have had no more effect against it than has the harassment of atheist dictatorships. Religious believers have been unable to provide any plausible argument for their truth claims. Yet this seems to have had no impact whatever on religion. The inference lies near at hand that a religious response to the world, however ill-grounded it may be in reality, is a necessary part of what we are as humans.

It is reasonable that at least part of religion's indispensability lies in its power to open doors to aspects of human experience that otherwise would be closed to most people, to which they could otherwise respond only with repression and with willed ignorance. These aspects certainly belong to the realm of the unconscious, or what I might call the communal unconscious. By this, I do not mean the "collective unconscious" in the Jungian sense, but the body of unconscious perceptions that members of a community are bound to share.[5] It is in this way that we can explain the seem-

5. Whether by virtue of being members of that specific community—ethnic, religious, or cultural—or simply by virtue of being humans. Perceptions of the latter sort will transcend communal boundaries, yet are likely to be shaped by the cultural patterns and historical experience of each community holding them. All humans, for example, are likely to have had the infantile experiences that lie behind the Eden story. Yet there is surely something in the pattern of Judeo-Christian (and perhaps also Muslim) cultures that makes the Bible's mode of expressing these experiences peculiarly meaningful.

ingly unshakable power of religious myths, even over people who know consciously that they ought not to take them seriously. If the story of the Garden of Eden cannot be expunged from our communal awareness, despite the absurdities of its manifest content, this must be because it speaks to us about a crucial aspect of the infantile experience that we all share—and speaks on this subject better than any other discourse in our tradition ever has.

We cannot suppose that the contents of the communal unconscious are necessarily bright and kindly. The contrary is far more likely to be true. There is much there that is dreadful and monstrous, which we nonetheless ignore at our peril. Access to these dark and terrible realms, however indirect, may be a necessary part of what religion means for us. A religious teacher or text that can grant us such access has the potential for doing us great service, as well as enormous injury.

Ezekiel, perhaps, was such a teacher, his book such a text.

The study of Ezekiel's impact on Judaism and Christianity, and thereby on the Western world (and perhaps Islam as well), is a monumental task that has so far barely been attempted.[6] One may argue for the task's importance on the basis of this study. It is hard to imagine an individual as disturbed as Ezekiel being elevated to authoritative status, without this having some deep effect on the societies that canonized him.

I would buttress this argument with a personal observation, from my graduate student days at the Hebrew University of Jerusalem (the mid-1970s). Several series of Bible commentaries sat on the shelves of the library's Judaica Reading Room. In each series, it was invariably the commentary on Ezekiel that showed the most wear and tear. If any volume had to be rebound, it was the Ezekiel volume.

I do not know why the students (or perhaps the male students?) at the Hebrew University were so deeply interested in Ezekiel. It is possible that many of them shared his ambivalent feelings toward images of male power (first and foremost, God), or his far less ambivalent dread and loathing of female sexuality. If this is so, it seems very likely that Ezekiel helped to reinforce these feelings. At least as far as female sexuality is concerned, we must regard this as a profoundly negative outcome. This is what I meant

---

6. A few beginnings have been made: Wilhelm Neuss's *Das Buch Ezechiel in Theologie und Kunst* [215]; my own *Faces of the Chariot* [125]; and now Michael Lieb's *The Visionary Mode: Biblical Prophecy, Hermeneutics, and Cultural Change* (Cornell University Press, 1991).

when I spoke of the enormous injury that can be done by access to the darker side of the communal unconscious. I think it very probable that the Book of Ezekiel, by its existence and by its canonical status, has wreaked such injury on generation after generation of Western men and women.

Yet an apocryphal saying, attributed to Jesus in one early manuscript of Luke 6:4, may help us put the matter in a different light. "When on the same day he saw a man doing work on the Sabbath, he said to him: Man! if thou knowest what thou doest, blessed art thou! But if thou knowest not, thou art cursed and a transgressor of the law" [141]. C. G. Jung quotes this passage in support of his view that "unconsciousness is not only no excuse [for wrongdoing] but is actually one of the most heinous sins" [355]. Whatever else of Jung's we may believe or disbelieve, we must surely agree with him on this point. The unconscious messages of the Book of Ezekiel are likely to be dangerous and destructive to us, precisely as long as we do not permit ourselves to become conscious of what they are.

Once we allow ourselves this consciousness, Ezekiel's positive value may become available to us, whether inside or outside a religious context. He may serve as guide to gloomy and dreadful regions of the mind, in which we nonetheless have the most vital interest. Not the least of these, as I have tried to indicate throughout, is the breeding place of the sexual antagonism between the two halves of our species, which continues, day by day and year by year, to sour one of the dearest comforts we have in this unkind universe.

It is for this reason that I urge the reader not to recoil from the sheer ugliness of what a psychoanalytic examination has to reveal about the prophet Ezekiel. Nor may we concentrate all the ugliness in Ezekiel, deluding ourselves that we can make ourselves beautiful by casting him out—perhaps with a label of "paranoid schizophrenic," perhaps with some less clinical epithet. We share his sickness too intimately for this process to have any good effect. On the contrary, we must learn from him how to recognize his disease in our mirrors. We may thereby work toward healing this ancient illness: symbolically, in Ezekiel; in reality, in ourselves.

The healing of Ezekiel may thus become for us a symbol of hope.

Taken literally, it is of course impossible. Ezekiel is gone forever. We have every reason to suppose that he died as he had lived: wretched, hateful, tormented by rages and longings which he could not possibly have understood.

Yet a person of the past can be transformed into a vessel of meaning for people of the present. George Lyman Kittredge remarks, apropos of the

New England Puritans and their belief in witchcraft, that the effort to do some measure of justice to our ancestors and to their illusions is "a matter . . . of no moment to them, for they have gone to their reward, but, I take it, of considerable importance to us" [410]. These words will apply to Ezekiel, and to our struggle to grasp the meaning of his inner torment.

In this sense, a posthumous redemption of Ezekiel, accomplished by a harrowing of his unconscious hell, becomes an imaginable possibility. It is fraught with redemptive meaning for us all.

In this sense, the insights of psychoanalysis can at last open Ezekiel's mouth. He speaks with us fugitives in the universe. He is dumb no more.

Ezekiel cries with a loud voice across the centuries, out of a pain that is as fresh and as recognizable as our yesterday. Our ears are now opened. We at last can hear him.

Excursus: Ezekiel 12:1–16

Ezekiel 12:1–16 has obvious ties to two of the passages most central to my argument. It is linked with 24:15–27 by the day-evening-morning sequence that Ezekiel uses to describe his actions (verses 3–8), by the question the exiles supposedly have asked him (verse 9), and by his designation of himself as a "token" for them (*mofet*, verses 6 and 11). It is linked no less clearly with 8:7–12, by Ezekiel's act of "digging through the wall" (verses 5, 7, 12). Chapter 12 is therefore plainly relevant to our work. I cannot afford to pass over it in silence. I must offer some explanation, however tentative and conjectural, of its meaning and of its relationship to 8:7–12 and 24:15–27.

The key to its interpretation, I believe, lies in its enigmatic figure of the "prince" (*nasi'*). This character first appears in verse 10, where he is said to be "this burden" (*massa'*; a play on *nasi'*, which is from the same root). Taken at face value, and in its context, "this burden" would seem to refer to the burden, never described more exactly, that Ezekiel carries on his shoulder in verses 6–7, as part of an elaborate symbolic action (*'al katef tissa'* . . . *'al katef nasa'ti*).

In verse 12, however, the "prince" becomes himself the carrier of the burden. Ezekiel's symbolic actions are there represented as foreshadowing the "prince's" future experiences. The Hebrew text states this in remarkably awkward and fumbling language: *wehannasi' 'asher betokham 'el katef yissa' ba'alatah weyese' baqqir yahteru lehosi' bo panaw yekhasseh ya'an 'asher lo' yir'eh la'ayin hu' 'et ha'ares*. We may translate, more or less literally: "And the prince who is in their midst will carry [what?] on [his] shoulder in the darkness, that he may go forth; they shall dig through the wall, to bring [him?] out through it; his face he shall cover, so that he may not see to [?] the eye the ground."

Verse 13 glosses this image, presumably after the fact, as a prophecy of the blinding and exile of Zedekiah. "I will spread my net over him, and he will be taken in my snare, and I will bring him to Babylon, the Chaldean land; yet he will not see it; and he will die there." The gloss, as Greenberg says [111], may well be Ezekiel's own. It is clear, in any case, that Ezekiel's conscious intent was to apply his symbolic behavior to historical (or soon-to-be-historical) events in the real world. I suspect, however, that this historical application cloaks a more elemental unconscious symbolism.

In 44:3, we meet a "prince" who sits within the sealed gate of the Temple, there being passively nourished ("he shall sit in it, to eat bread before Yahweh"). Given the female Temple symbolism that we have estab- lished for Ezekiel, we can hardly doubt the essential truth of the tradi- tional Christian interpretation that took this passage to be a prophecy of the Virgin Mary.[1] The space within the sealed gate is the womb; the "prince" is the fetus within it. Ezekiel 12:12, understood in this way, will describe how the fetus is dragged out of its haven "into exile, into captiv- ity" (verse 11). In both cases, we may imagine that the infant "prince" is Ezekiel himself. In 44:3, he imagines himself cozily ensconced in the womb. In 12:12, he "remembers" himself painfully expelled from it. The context of chapter 12, which represents Ezekiel's actions and the "prince's" as the same, supports this assumption.

We recall that the prince is not only a "carrier"; but, in verse 10, is himself the "burden" to be carried on the shoulder. This will strengthen our interpretation of the "prince" as an infant.

Job 10:18–19 confirms our view that Ezekiel 12:12 is a representation of childbirth. Job here rails at God for having let him be born, in language that strikingly resembles Ezekiel's. "Why did you bring me out of the womb [merehem hose'tani]? I should have perished, without any eye seeing me [we'ayin lo' tir'eni]. I would be as if I had not been, carried straight from womb to grave." The Job passage thus gives us our first possibility for interpreting Ezekiel's lo' yir'eh la'ayin. The verb is to be read as a Niph'al (yera'eh), translated "he shall not be seen to the eye," and understood as expressing a wish like Job's—that Ezekiel had been stillborn, and carried enwrapped ("his face he shall cover") from his mother's womb to the womb of death.

Job's use of the verb hosi' ("bring out") well suits the assumption that the act of "digging through the wall," to bring the "prince" out, represents Ezekiel's imagined "memory" of his birth. But, in the light of 8:7–12, we

1. See Chapter 5, section 5.

may suppose that it simultaneously expresses Ezekiel's yearning for reentry, by means of his penis.[2]

This fantasy is of course strictly taboo. In retribution for it, Ezekiel inflicts upon himself the Oedipal punishment of sightlessness. Understood in this way, the verb of *lo' yir'eh la'ayin* must be taken as active (Qal). The *'ayin*, despite the strange preposition attached to it, will then be the "eye" with which the prince will no longer "see."

His blindness, however, may be protective as well as punitive, in that it prevents him from seeing forbidden sights. Hebrew *'ayin* can mean "spring" or "fountain" as well as "eye," and there is evidence—from a much later period, to be sure—that it can be used as a symbol for the female genitals [132,361]. We may accordingly take the preposition of *la'ayin* as introducing the direct object, and interpret: the prince, his face discreetly covered, will be protected from the arousing and terrifying sight of his mother's genitals.

It will follow, from what I have said so far, that the phrase *lo' yir'eh* [or *yera'eh*] *la'ayin* condenses at least three distinct meanings, at least two of which are likely to have been wholly unconscious. This will no doubt explain the phrase's awkwardness.

If I have correctly interpreted 12:12 as conveying (among other things) a Job-like wish to have been stillborn, we must see it as expressing not only Ezekiel's misery, but an intense rage, which he here turns against himself. (We have seen that he could also turn that rage in other directions.)

This will appear also from verses 14–16: "All [the prince's] helpers that are about him, and all his troops, I will scatter in every direction, and I will empty the sword after them [*wehereb 'ariq 'aharehem*]. They will know that I am Yahweh, when I disperse them among the nations and scatter them among the lands, and I leave of them just a few survivors, from sword, famine, and plague . . ." The language—especially the phrase *hereb 'ariq 'aharehem*—is very suggestive of 5:1–4. Ezekiel there begins by turning his "sword" (actually, a razor) against himself, in an action that is very suggestive of castration.

2. Which may help account for Ezekiel 12:12's remarkable resemblance to the description of the adulterer in Job 24:15–16 (see Chapter 3, section 1). Compare Ezekiel's *ba'alatah . . . baqqir yahteru* with Job's *hatar bahoshekh battim*, Ezekiel's *panaw yekhasseh* with Job's *weseter panim yasim*, Ezekiel's *lo' yir'eh la'ayin* with Job's *lo' teshureni 'ayin*. These associations between Ezekiel and Job will oblige us to modify Millar Burrows's view that there are practically no literary links between the two texts [36]. They are perhaps to be interpreted in the light of the fact that Job is mentioned, outside his own book, only in Ezekiel 14:12–20.

I propose that in 12:14–16, as in 5:1–4, Ezekiel wields his castrating sword (also phallic; note the orgasmic implications of "emptying the sword")[3] against the "prince"; that is to say, himself. He thereby punishes himself for the incestuous wish to "dig through the wall."

Ezekiel's castrating fury is very marked in 21:30–31. Here, as in 5:1–4 and 12:14–16, we may suppose it to have been directed against himself. The context is a wild, at times incoherent, invocation of a "sharpened, polished sword" (21:14), which is to be unsheathed "against all flesh" (verses 9–10).[4] In verses 30–31, Ezekiel seems to turn the "sword" against a specific individual. "And as for you, mutilated man, wicked man, prince of Israel [*ḥalal rashaʿ neśiʾ yiśraʾel*], whose day has come in the time of the iniquity of the end; thus says the Lord Yahweh: Remove the turban, lift off the crown . . ." (verses 30–31).

The commentators agree that this "prince of Israel" is Zedekiah. As far as Ezekiel's conscious intent is concerned, I would not dispute them. What I am suggesting is that the "prince" also functioned unconsciously for Ezekiel as a self-representation, and that it was this figure's unconscious meaning that determined much of the imagery Ezekiel used for it. "Removing the turban" has clear overtones of castration. If we suppose that *ʿaṭarah* ("crown") already had in Ezekiel's time the meaning it was to have in rabbinic Hebrew, of the corona of the penis, the implications of "lifting off the crown" will be clearer still.

All modern commentators have observed that Ezekiel 12:1–16 is an extremely difficult text, riddled with tensions and inconsistencies. Most have been unable to deal with these inconsistencies except by resorting to what Greenberg calls "literary surgery" [111]. A psychoanalytic approach can offer a more satisfying resolution. It fully acknowledges the tensions in the current text. It explains them as rooted in the fundamental tension between the conscious, historical associations of Ezekiel's imagery, and its complex, multivalent, overdetermined unconscious associations.

Ezekiel 12:1–16 and 24:15–27 share the fundamental theme of the loss of a mother or a mother-substitute. In chapter 12, this happens through the child's expulsion from the womb; in chapter 24, through the woman's

3. The idiom is not unique to Ezekiel, but seems to have had a special appeal for him. It occurs seven times in the Hebrew Bible: five times in Ezekiel (5:2, 12, 12:14, 28:7, 30:11), once in H (Leviticus 26:33), once in the Song at the Sea (Exodus 15:9). Its sexual overtones are particularly clear in Ezekiel 28:7.

4. *Baśar;* used specifically for the penis in 16:26, 23:20.

death. In chapter 24, the child turns his pain and rage at his loss against the woman; in chapter 12, against himself. In both passages, Ezekiel tries to attach historical or prophetic significance to his unconscious memories and perceptions. He represents his compulsive behavior as the nexus ("token") between the conscious/historical and unconscious/personal spheres. It will thus begin to be intelligible that the two passages' descriptions of his behavior resemble one another.

In the light of these parallels, we may suspect that the "fugitive" who leaves Jerusalem in chapter 24 has the same unconscious meaning for Ezekiel as the "prince" who leaves the city in chapter 12.[5] Job 21:10, which uses the Pi'el of *plṭ* to describe a cow's giving birth (*tefalleṭ parato welo' teshakkel*), confirms that *paliṭ* is an appropriate word for a newly born (= newly expelled) infant. So, perhaps, does the rabbinic usage of Qal *plṭ* for a woman's discharge of the semen that had earlier been ejaculated into her (Mishnah, Berakhot 3:6). Anticipating the arrival of this "fugitive," from a womb both detested and longed for, Ezekiel anticipated his own coming. Hence his certainty that the "fugitive's" journey would take no time at all. "Your mouth shall be opened with the fugitive." The infant who long ago cried unheard, and his adult counterpart, will both speak together, "and shall be dumb no more."

5. I am speaking, of course, only of the *anticipated* fugitive of 24:25–27, who was a creature of Ezekiel's fantasy. The *real* fugitive of 33:21–22, a historical individual of whom we will never know anything, is of no importance to our inquiry.

Reference List

A. ANCIENT NEAR EASTERN, BIBLICAL, JUDAIC

In citing commentaries, I specify page numbers only where I judge that the reader will not be able to locate the precise reference on the basis of the context of the citation. If, for example, I refer in the text to the commentaries of Cooke, Greenberg, and Zimmerli [56,104,297] on Ezekiel 8:12, the reader can find the passages I am drawing on simply by looking up Ezekiel 8:12 in each commentary. Page numbers will be unnecessary.

[1] Abramsky, Shula. "He'aneq Dom Metim 'Ebel Lo' Ta'aśeh (Yeḥezqel 24:13)." *Bet Mikra* 27 (1981): 15.
[2] Abusch, Tzvi. "Ishtar's Proposal and Gilgamesh's Refusal: An Interpretation of The Gilgamesh Epic, Tablet 6, Lines 1–79." *History of Religions* 26 (1986): 143–87. I owe this reference to Jack M. Sasson.
 [3] Page 168.
[4] Albright, William Foxwell. *Archaeology and the Religion of Israel: The Ayer Lectures of the Colgate-Rochester Divinity School, 1941*, pages 165–68. Baltimore: Johns Hopkins University Press, 1942.
[5] Aletti, Jean-Noel. "Séduction et Parole en Proverbes I–IX." *Vetus Testamentum* 27 (1977): 129–44. This reference is known to me only through its citation in Camp [37].
[6] Alster, Bendt. *Dumuzi's Dream: Aspects of Oral Poetry in a Sumerian Myth.* Vol. 1 of *Mesopotamia: Copenhagen Studies in Assyriology.* Copenhagen: Akademisk, 1972.
 [7] Pages 10–14.
 [8] Pages 115–16.
[9] Alt, Albrecht. "Die Weisheit Salomos." In *Kleine Schriften zur Geschichte des Volkes Israel*, vol. 2, pages 90–99. Munich: C. H. Beck, 1953. Originally appeared in *Theologische Literaturzeitung* 76 (1951), cols. 139–44.
[10] Amiet, Pierre. *La Glyptique Mésopotamienne Archaïque*, figs. 847, 849, 1203. *Thèses Présentées a la Faculté des Lettres de L'Université de Paris, 3 Mai 1958.* Paris: Centre National de la Recherche Scientifique, 1961.
[11] Andersen, A. A. *The Book of Psalms*, page 899. *New Century Bible.* London: Oliphants, 1972.
[12] Auvray, Paul. *Isaïe 1–39.* Paris: J. Gabalda, 1972.
[13] Avigad, Nahman. *Hebrew Bullae from the Time of Jeremiah: Remnants of a Burnt Archive*, page 118. Jerusalem: Israel Exploration Society, 1986.

[14] Badè, William F. "The Seal of Jaazaniah." *Zeitschrift für die alttestamentliche Wissenschaft* 51 (1933): 150–56.

[15] Baentsch, B. "Pathologische Züge in Israels Prophetentum." *Zeitschrift für wissenschaftliche Theologie* 50 (1908): 52–81.

[16] Balentine, Samuel E. "The Prophet as Intercessor: A Reassessment." *Journal of Biblical Literature* 103 (1984): 161–73.

[17] Becker, Joachim. "Ez 8–11 als einheitliche Komposition in einem pseudepigraphischen Ezechielbuch." In Lust [189], pages 136–50.

[18] Begg, Christopher. "The Non-Mention of Ezekiel in the Book of Jeremiah: An Additional Consideration." *Ephemerides Theologicae Lovanienses* 65 (1989): 94–95.

[19] Betlyon, John W. Review of Tigay [265]. *Catholic Biblical Quarterly* 50 (1988): 516–18.

[20] Blake, Frank R. *A Resurvey of Hebrew Tenses; with an Appendix: Hebrew Influence on Biblical Aramaic*, pages 50–53. Rome: Pontificium Institutum Biblicum, 1951.

[21] Block, Daniel I. "Text and Emotion: A Study in the 'Corruptions' in Ezekiel's Inaugural Vision (Ezekiel 1:4–28)." *Catholic Biblical Quarterly* 50 (1988): 418–42.

[22] Bodenheimer, F. S. "Fauna," page 250. In *The Interpreter's Dictionary of the Bible: An Illustrated Encyclopedia*, vol. 2. New York: Abingdon Press, 1962.

[23] Braude, William G., and Israel J. Kapstein, trans. *Pesikta de-Rab Kahana: R. Kahana's Compilation of Discourses for Sabbaths and Festal Days*, pages 52–53. Philadelphia: Jewish Publication Society, 1975.

[24] Bright, John. *A History of Israel*, page 326. Philadelphia: Westminster Press, 3d ed., 1981.

[25] Bright, John. *Jeremiah: Introduction, Translation, and Notes*. Vol. 21 of *The Anchor Bible*. Garden City, N.Y.: Doubleday, 1965.

    [26] Pages lv–lxxxv.

    [27] Pages 94–95.

[28] Broome, Edwin C. "Ezekiel's Abnormal Personality." *Journal of Biblical Literature* 65 (1946): 277–92.

    [29] Pages 288–89.

[30] Brown, Francis, S. R. Driver, and Charles A. Briggs. *A Hebrew and English Lexicon of the Old Testament*. Oxford: Clarendon Press, 1907.

[31] Brownlee, William H. *Ezekiel 1–19*. Vol. 28 of *The Word Biblical Commentary*. Waco, Tex.: Word Books, 1986.

    [32] Pages xix–xxix.

    [33] Pages 134–35.

[34] Buber, Salomon. *Midrasch Echa Rabbati: Sammlung agadischer Auslegungen der Klagelieder*, pages 8b–9a. Vilna: Romm, 1899.

[35] Buber, Salomon. *Midrasch Tanchuma: Ein agadischer Commentar zum Pentateuch von Rabbi Tanchuma ben Rabbi Abba*, Deuteronomy, pages 21a–b. Israel: Books Export Enterprises, n.d. Originally published Vilna: Romm, 1885.

[36] Burrows, Millar. *The Literary Relations of Ezekiel*, pages 84–85. Philadelphia: Jewish Publication Society, 1925.

[37] Camp, Claudia V. *Wisdom and the Feminine in the Book of Proverbs*. Decatur, Ga.: Almond Press, 1985.

    [38] Pages 115–33.

    [39] Pages 198–207.

[40] Carley, Keith W. *Ezekiel among the Prophets*. Naperville, Ill.: Alec R. Allenson, 1975.
 [41] Pages 13–37.
 [42] Pages 42–45.
 [43] Pages 62–65.
[44] Carroll, Robert P. *Jeremiah: A Commentary*. Philadelphia: Westminster Press, 1986.
 [45] Pages 33–86.
 [46] Page 221.
 [47] Page 233.
[48] Carroll, Robert P. *When Prophecy Failed: Cognitive Dissonance in the Prophetic Traditions of the Old Testament*, pages 50–52. New York: Seabury Press, 1979.
[49] Cassem, Ned H. "Ezekiel's Psychotic Personality: Reservations on the Use of the Couch for Biblical Personalities." In *The Word in the World: Essays in Honor of Frederick L. Moriarty, S.J.*, ed. Richard J. Clifford and George W. MacRae, pages 59–70. Cambridge, Mass.: Weston College Press, 1973.
[50] Chomsky, William. *David Ḳimḥi's Hebrew Grammar (Mikhlol): Systematically Presented and Critically Annotated*, part 1, pages 85–87, 98–99. Philadelphia: Dropsie College Press, 1933.
[51] Chomsky, William. *David Ḳimḥi's Hebrew Grammar (Mikhlol): Systematically Presented and Critically Annotated*, part 2, pages 171, 213–14. New York: Bloch, 1952.
[52] Claburn, W. Eugene. "The Fiscal Basis of Josiah's Reforms." *Journal of Biblical Literature* 92 (1973): 11–22.
[53] Clements, R. E. *The New Century Bible Commentary: Isaiah 1–39*. Grand Rapids, Mich.: Eerdmans, 1980.
[54] Cogan, Morton. *Imperialism and Religion: Assyria, Judah and Israel in the Eighth and Seventh Centuries B.C.E.* Missoula, Mont.: Society of Biblical Literature and Scholars Press, 1974.
 [55] Pages 77–83.
[56] Cooke, G. A. *A Critical and Exegetical Commentary on the Book of Ezekiel*. International Critical Commentary, no. 21. Edinburgh: T. & T. Clark, 1951. Originally published 1936.
 [57] Page 122.
[58] Cureton, William. *Spicilegium Syriacum: Containing Remains of Bardesan, Meliton, Ambrose, and Mara bar Serapion*, page 44. London: Rivington, 1855.
[59] Davies, G. I. Review of Tigay [265]. *Journal of Theological Studies*, n.s., 40 (1989): 143–46.
[60] Davis, Ellen F. *Swallowing the Scroll: Textuality and the Dynamics of Discourse in Ezekiel's Prophecy*. Sheffield, U.K.: Almond Press, 1989.
 [61] Page 27.
 [62] Page 37.
 [63] Pages 48–58.
 [64] Pages 63–71.
 [65] Pages 101–2.
 [66] Pages 113–14.
 [67] Pages 134–35.
[68] Day, John. *Molech: A God of Human Sacrifice in the Old Testament*. University of Cambridge Oriental Publications, no. 41. Cambridge: Cambridge University Press, 1989.

[69]   De Vaux, Roland. *Ancient Israel: Its Life and Institutions*, page 337. London: Darton, Longman & Todd, 1961.

[70]   Dhorme, E. *A Commentary on the Book of Job*. Translated from the French by Harold Knight. London: Nelson, 1967. Originally published Paris: J. Gabalda, 1926.

[71]   Dieckhoff [no first name or initial given]. "Der Prophet Ezechiel." *Zeitschrift für Religionspsychologie* (1908): 193–206.

Eissfeldt, Otto. *The Old Testament: An Introduction*. Translated from the German by Peter R. Ackroyd. New York: Harper & Row, 1965.

    [72]   Pages 316–17.

    [73]   Pages 346–65.

[74]   E[merton], J. A. Review of Tigay [265]. *Vetus Testamentum* 37 (1987): 509–10.

[75]   Fewell, Danna Nolan, and David M. Gunn. "Controlling Perspectives: Women, Men, and the Authority of Violence in Judges 4 & 5." *Journal of the American Academy of Religion* 58 (1990): 389–411.

[76]   Finkelstein, Louis. *The Pharisees: The Sociological Background of Their Faith*, vol. 1, page 319; vol. 2, page 688n. Philadelphia: Jewish Publication Society, 1940.

Fishbane, Michael. *Biblical Interpretation in Ancient Israel*. Oxford: Clarendon Press, 1985.

    [77]   Pages 312–14.

    [78]   Pages 321–22.

[79]   Fishbane, Michael. "Sin and Judgment in the Prophecies of Ezekiel." *Interpretation* 38 (1984): 131–50.

[80]   Fohrer, Georg. *Das Buch Jesaja*, vol. 1. Stuttgart: Zwingli, 1960.

[81]   Fohrer, Georg. "Die Glossen im Buche Ezechiel." *Zeitschrift für die Alttestamentliche Wissenschaft* 63 (1951): 38.

[82]   Fohrer, Georg. *Die Hauptprobleme des Buches Ezechiel*, pages 164–77. Beihefte zur ZAW, no. 72. Berlin: A. Töpelmann, 1952. I am using Greenberg's summary of Fohrer's arguments [115].

[83]   Fowler, Jeaneane D. *Theophoric Personal Names in Ancient Hebrew: A Comparative Study*. Journal for the Study of the Old Testament, Supplement Series, no. 49. Sheffield, U.K.: JSOT Press, 1988.

Frankfort, Henri. *Stratified Cylinder Seals from the Diyala Region*. University of Chicago Oriental Institute Publications, no. 72. Chicago: University of Chicago Press, 1955.

    [84]   Page 38.

    [85]   Figure 559.

[86]   Freedman, David Noel. "The Structure of Psalm 137," pages 311–12. In *Pottery, Poetry, and Prophecy: Studies in Early Hebrew Poetry*. Winona Lake, Ind.: Eisenbrauns, 1980.

[87]   Freedy, K. S., and D. B. Redford. "The Dates in Ezekiel in Relation to Biblical, Babylonian and Egyptian Sources." *Journal of the American Oriental Society* 90 (1970): 462–85.

    [88]   Page 468.

[89]   Friedmann, M. *Pesikta Rabbati: Midrasch für den Festcyclus und die ausgezeichneten Sabbathe*, page 26b. Tel Aviv, 1963. Originally published Vienna, 1880.

[90]   Gadd, C. J. "Some Contributions to the Gilgamesh Epic." *Iraq* 28 (1966): 177. Quoted in Abusch [2], page 162.

[91] Galambush, Julie. *Jerusalem in the Book of Ezekiel: The City as Yahweh's Wife.*
      SBL Dissertation Series, no. 130. Atlanta: Scholars Press, 1992.
[92] Garfinkel, Stephen. "Another Model for Ezekiel's Abnormalities." *Journal
      of the Ancient Near Eastern Society* 19 (1989): 39–50.
      [93] Pages 39–43.
[94] Garfinkel, Stephen. "Of Thistles and Thorns: A New Approach to Ezekiel
      II 6." *Vetus Testamentum* 4 (1987): 421–37.
      [95] Pages 435–36.
[96] Gaster, Theodor. "Ezekiel and the Mysteries." *Journal of Biblical Literature*
      60 (1941): 289–310.
[97] Gelb, Ignace J., et al., eds. *The Assyrian Dictionary of the Oriental Institute of
      the University of Chicago*, vol. 6, s.v. *ḫā'iru*. Chicago: Oriental Institute, 1956.
      My colleague Jack M. Sasson helped me locate this and the following refer-
      ence.
[98] Gelb, Ignace J., et al., eds. *The Assyrian Dictionary of the Oriental Institute of the
      University of Chicago*, vol. 16, s.v. *ṣuḫrētu*. Chicago: Oriental Institute, 1962.
[99] Glueck, J. J. "Proverbs XXX 15a." *Vetus Testamentum* 14 (1964): 367–70.
[100] Good, Edwin M. *In Turns of Tempest: A Reading of Job with a Translation.*
      Stanford: Stanford University Press, 1990.
[101] Goodenough, E. R. *An Introduction to Philo Judaeus*, pages 22–24. Oxford:
      Basil Blackwell, 2d ed., 1962.
[102] Gordis, Robert. *The Book of Job*. New York: Jewish Theological Seminary,
      1978.
[103] Gordis, Robert. " 'The Branch to the Nose': A Note on Ezekiel VIII 17."
      Journal of Theological Studies 37 (1936): 284–88.
[104] Greenberg, Moshe. *Ezekiel 1–20: A New Translation with Introduction and Com-
      mentary.* Vol. 22 of *The Anchor Bible*. Garden City, N.Y.: Doubleday, 1983.
      [105] Pages 7–11.
      [106] Pages 102–3, 120–21.
      [107] Pages 135–37.
      [108] Pages 168–71.
      [109] Page 175.
      [110] Pages 194–202.
      [111] Pages 219–20.
      [112] Pages 297–301.
      [113] Page 387.
[114] Greenberg, Moshe. "On Ezekiel's Dumbness." *Journal of Biblical Literature*
      77 (1958): 101–5.
      Greenberg, Moshe. "Prolegomenon." In Torrey [272], pages xi–xxxv.
      [115] Pages xviii–xxix.
      [116] Page xxxiii.
[117] Greenberg, Moshe. "The Use of the Ancient Versions for Interpreting the
      Hebrew Text: A Sampling from Ezekiel ii 1–iii 11." In *Congress Volume,
      Göttingen 1977* (Supplements to *Vetus Testamentum*, no. 29), pages 131–48.
      Leiden: E. J. Brill, 1978.
[118] Greenberg, Moshe. "What Are Valid Criteria for Determining Inauthentic
      Matter in Ezekiel?" In Lust [189], pages 123–35.
      [119] Pages 131–33.
[120] Greenfield, Jonas. "Shte Miqra'ot le'Or Tequfatan—Yeḥezqel 16:30 u-
      Mal'akhi 3:17." *Eretz Israel* 16 (1982): 56–57.

[121] Gunkel, Hermann. *Das Märchen im Alten Testament*, pages 115–16. Tübingen: J.C.B. Mohr, 1917. Quoted and translated in Greenberg [104], page 300.

[122] Gurney, O. R. "Tammuz Reconsidered: Some Recent Developments." *Journal of Semitic Studies* 7 (1962): 151–57.

[123] Habel, Norman C. *The Book of Job*. Philadelphia: Westminster Press, 1985.

[124] Halperin, David J. "The Exegetical Character of Ezek. x 9–17." *Vetus Testamentum* 26 (1976): 129–41.

[125] Halperin, David J. *The Faces of the Chariot: Early Jewish Responses to Ezekiel's Vision*. Texte und Studien zum Antiken Judentum, no. 16. Tübingen: J.C.B. Mohr, 1988.

    [126] Page 42.
    [127] Pages 190–92.
    [128] Pages 200–201, 393–96.
    [129] Page 330.
    [130] Page 528.

[131] Halperin, David J. *The Merkabah in Rabbinic Literature*, pages 39–59. American Oriental Series, no. 62. New Haven: American Oriental Society, 1980.

[132] Halperin, David J. "A Sexual Image in Hekhalot Rabbati, and Its Implications." In *Proceedings of the First International Conference on the History of Jewish Mysticism: Early Jewish Mysticism*, ed. Joseph Dan, English section, pages 117–32. Jerusalem: Hebrew University, 1987.

[133] Hatch, Edwin, and Henry A. Redpath. *A Concordance to the Septuagint and the Other Greek Versions of the Old Testament*. 3 vols. in 2. Graz: Akademische Druck- u. Verlagsanstalt, 1954. Originally published 1897.

[134] Hayes, John H., and Stuart Irvine. *Isaiah: The Eighth Century Prophet*. Nashville: Abingdon Press, 1987.

[135] Heider, George C. *The Cult of Molek: A Reassessment*. Journal for the Study of the Old Testament, Supplement Series, no. 43. Sheffield, U.K.: JSOT Press, 1985.

    [136] Page 269.
    [137] Pages 282–301, 326–28.
    [138] Pages 336–46.
    [139] Pages 365–75.

[140] Heider, George C. "A Further Turn on Ezekiel's Baroque Twist in Ezek 20:25–26." *Journal of Biblical Literature* 107 (1988): 721–24.

[141] Hennecke, Edgar. *New Testament Apocrypha*. Edited by Wilhelm Schneemelcher. English translation edited by R. McL. Wilson. Vol. 1, *Gospels and Related Writings*, page 89. Philadelphia: Westminster Press, 1963.

[142] Hoffmann, Hans-Detlef. *Reform und Reformen: Untersuchungen zu einem Grundthema der deuteronomistischen Geschichtsschreibung*, pages 264–70. Vol. 66 of *Abhandlungen zur Theologie des Alten und Neuen Testaments*. Zurich: Theologischer Verlag, 1980.

Howie, Carl Gordon. *The Date and Composition of Ezekiel*. Journal of Biblical Literature Monograph Series, no. 4. Philadelphia: Society of Biblical Literature, 1950.

    [143] Pages 69–79.
    [144] Pages 82–83.

[145] Hvidberg, Flemming Friis. *Weeping and Laughter in the Old Testament: A Study of Canaanite-Israelite Religion*. Translated from the Danish by Niels

Haislund. Leiden: E. J. Brill; Copenhagen: Nordisk, 1962. I owe this reference to Daniel Merkur.

    [146]   Pages 66–76.

    [147]   Pages 112–15.

[148]   Jacobsen, Thorkild. "Toward the Image of Tammuz." In *Toward the Image of Tammuz and Other Essays on Mesopotamian History and Culture*, ed. William L. Moran, pages 73–103. Cambridge: Harvard University Press, 1970. The paper originally appeared in *History of Religions* 1 (1961): 189–213.

Jacobsen, Thorkild. *The Treasures of Darkness: A History of Mesopotamian Religion*. New Haven: Yale University Press, 1976.

    [149]   Pages 46–63.

    [150]   Pages 135–43.

    [151]   Page 195.

[152]   Jaspers, Karl. "Der Prophet Ezechiel: Eine pathographische Studie." In Jaspers, *Aneignung und Polemik: Gesammelte Reden und Aufsätze zur Geschichte der Philosophie*, pages 13–21. Munich: Piper, 1968. Originally published 1947.

    [153]   Page 19.

[154]   Jastrow, Marcus. *A Dictionary of the Targumim, the Talmud Babli and Yerushalmi, and the Midrashic Literature*. New York: Pardes, 1950. Originally published 1903.

    [155]   S.v. *šht*.

[156]   Jensen, Joseph. *Isaiah 1–39*. Vol. 8 of *The Old Testament Message: A Biblical-Theological Commentary*. Wilmington, Del.: Michael Glazier, 1984.

[157]   Johnson, Bo. *Hebräisches Perfekt und Imperfekt mit vorangehendem we*, pages 42–46, 64, 78–81. Lund: CWK Gleerup, 1979.

[158]   Kaiser, Otto. *Isaiah 1–12: A Commentary*. Translated by John Bowden from the 5th German ed. (1981). London: SCM Press, 2d English ed., 1983.

[159]   Kaiser, Otto. *Isaiah 13–39: A Commentary*, pages 234–36, 298–304. Translated from the German by R. A. Wilson. London: SCM Press, 2d ed., 1980.

[160]   Kaufman, Stephen A. Review of Tigay [265]. *Journal of Biblical Literature* 107 (1988): 506–7.

Kaufmann, Yehezkel. *The Religion of Israel: From Its Beginnings to the Babylonian Exile*. Translated from the Hebrew [165] and abridged by Moshe Greenberg. Chicago: University of Chicago Press, 1960.

    [161]   Pages 204–5, 280, 423–24.

    [162]   Pages 403–9.

    [163]   Pages 428–32.

    [164]   Page 440.

[165]   Kaufmann, Yehezkel. *Toledot ha-'Emunah ha-Yiśra'elit*, vol. 7 (3/2). Tel Aviv: Mossad Bialik-Dvir, 1956.

    [166]   Pages 382–92.

    [167]   Pages 499–505.

Kautzsch, E. *Gesenius' Hebrew Grammar*. Translated by A. E. Cowley from the 28th German ed. (1909). Oxford: Clarendon Press, 2d English ed., 1910.

    [168]   Page 171.

    [169]   Page 216.

    [170]   Page 296.

[171]   Kilian, Rudolf. *Literarkritische und Formgeschichtliche Untersuchung des Heiligkeitsgesetzes*, pages 180–86. Bonn: Peter Hanstein, 1963.

[172]   Kimhi, David. *Sefer ha-Shorashim* [*The Book of Roots*], page 380, s.v. *šhb*. New York, n.p., 1948. Originally published Berlin, n.p., 1847.

[173] Klostermann, August. "Ezechiel: Ein Beitrag zu besserer Würdigung seiner Person und seiner Schrift." *Theologische Studien und Kritiken* 50 (1877): 391–439.
    [174] Pages 399–403.
    [175] Page 421.
    [176] Pages 424–31.
    [177] Pages 438–39.
[178] Kornfeld, Walter. *Studien zum Heiligkeitsgesetz (Lev 17–26)*, page 47. Vienna: Herder, 1952.
Kramer, Samuel Noah. *The Sacred Marriage Rite: Aspects of Faith, Myth, and Ritual in Ancient Sumer.* Bloomington: Indiana University Press, 1969.
    [179] Pages 49–84.
    [180] Pages 57–62.
    [181] Pages 105–33.
[182] Lambert, W. G. "The Problem of the Love Lyrics." In *Unity and Diversity: Essays in the History, Literature, and Religion of the Ancient Near East*, ed. Hans Goedicke and J.J.M. Roberts, pages 98–125. Baltimore: Johns Hopkins University Press, 1975. I owe this reference to Jack M. Sasson.
Lang, Bernhard. *Ezechiel: Der Prophet und das Buch.* Erträge der Forschung, no. 153. Darmstadt: Wissenschaftliche Buchgesellschaft, 1981.
    [183] Pages 7–12.
    [184] Pages 57–76.
Legrain, L. *Ur Excavations Volume III: Archaic Seal-Impressions.* British Museum and the University Museum, University of Pennsylvania, 1936.
    [185] Figures 268–70.
    [186] Figure 366.
[187] Levine, Baruch A. "Excursus 7: The Cult of Molech in Biblical Israel." In *The JPS Torah Commentary: Leviticus*, pages 258–60. Philadelphia: Jewish Publication Society, 1989.
Lieb, Michael. *The Visionary Mode: Biblical Prophecy, Hermeneutics, and Cultural Change.* Ithaca and London: Cornell University Press, 1991.
[188] Lieberman, Saul. *The Tosefta: According to Codex Vienna, With Variants From Codices Erfurt, London, Genizah Mss. and Editio Princeps (Venice 1521)*. Vol. 2, *Moʿed.* New York: Jewish Theological Seminary of America, 1962.
[189] Lust, J. *Ezekiel and His Book: Textual and Literary Criticism and their Interrelation.* Leuven: University Press, 1986.
[190] Maier, Walter A., III. *'Ašerah: Extrabiblical Evidence.* Atlanta: Scholars Press, 1986.
    [191] Pages 168–72.
[192] Mandelbaum, Bernard. *Pesikta de Rav Kahana, According to an Oxford Manuscript*, vol. 1, page 449. New York: Jewish Theological Seminary of America, 1962.
[193] Margaliot, Ephraim Zalman. *Zeraʿ Ephraim* [commentary on *Pesiqta Rabbati*]. In *Pesiqta Rabbati de-Rab Kahana* [sic], pages 34a–b. New York: Menorah Institute, 1959. Originally published 1893.
[194] Margulies, Mordecai. *Midrash Wayyikra Rabbah: A Critical Edition Based on Manuscripts and Genizah Fragments with Variants and Notes*, pages 387–88. Jerusalem: Wahrmann Books, 1972. Originally published 1953–60.
[195] Mayes, A.D.H. "Deuteronomy 4 and the Literary Criticism of Deuteronomy." *Journal of Biblical Literature* 100 (1981): 23–51.
    [196] Pages 48–51.

[197] Mayes, A.D.H. "King and Covenant: A Study of 2 Kings Chs 22–23." *Hermathena* 125 (1978): 34–47.

[198] Mayes, A.D.H. *The Story of Israel Between Settlement and Exile: A Redactional Study of the Deuteronomistic History.* London: SCM Press, 1983.

[199] McCarthy, Carmel. *The Tiqqune Sopherim and Other Theological Corrections in the Masoretic Text of the Old Testament,* pages 91–97. Freiburg: Universitäts-verlag; Göttingen: Vandenhoeck & Ruprecht, 1981.

[200] McCarthy, Dennis. *Treaty and Covenant: A Study in Form in the Ancient Oriental Documents and in the Old Testament.* Rome: Biblical Institute Press, 2d ed., 1978.

[201] McCullough, W. S. "Rock Badger." In *The Interpreter's Dictionary of the Bible: An Illustrated Encyclopedia,* vol. 4. New York: Abingdon Press, 1962.

[202] McGregor, Leslie John. *The Greek Text of Ezekiel: An Examination of Its Homogeneity,* pages 160–61. Atlanta: Scholars Press, 1985.

[203] McKane, William. *Proverbs: A New Approach.* Philadelphia: Westminster, 1970.
　　　 [204] Pages 285–86.

[205] McKay, John. *Religion in Judah under the Assyrians: 732–609 B.C.* Naperville, Ill.: Alec R. Allenson, 1973.
　　　 [206] Pages 28–44.
　　　 [207] Page 93.

[208] *Midrash Rabbah.* 2 vols. Jerusalem, n.p., 1961. Originally published Vilna: Romm, 1887.

[209] Milgrom, Jacob. "Priestly Terminology and the Political and Social Structure of Pre-Monarchic Israel." *Jewish Quarterly Review,* n.s., 69 (1978): 65–81.

[210] Miller, J. Maxwell, and John H. Hayes. *A History of Ancient Israel and Judah,* page 404. Philadelphia: Westminster Press, 1986.

[211] Miller, John Wolf. *Das Verhältnis Jeremias und Hesekiels sprachlich und theologisch untersucht,* pages 95–96. Van Gorcum's Theologische Bibliothek, no. 28. Assen: Van Gorcum, 1955.

[212] *Miqra'ot Gedolot.* 5 vols. Jerusalem: Etz Hayyim, 1974. Contains the text of the Hebrew Bible, with Targums and a selection of the major medieval commentaries (e.g., Rashi, Kimhi, Ibn Ezra).

[213] Mosca, Paul G. *Child Sacrifice in Canaanite and Israelite Religion: A Study in Mulk and mlk.* Ph.D. dissertation, Harvard University, 1975. I know this work only through Heider's citations [135].

[214] Mulder, M. J. Review of Tigay [265]. *Bibliotheca Orientalis* 45 (1988), cols. 166–68.

[215] Neuss, Wilhelm. *Das Buch Ezechiel in Theologie und Kunst bis zum Ende des XII. Jahrhunderts.* Beiträge zur Geschichte des alten Mönchtums und des Bene-diktinerordens, no. 112. Münster: Aschendorff, 1912.
　　　 [216] Index, s.v. "Maria, Unversehrte Jungfräulichkeit."

Nicholson, E. W. *Deuteronomy and Tradition.* Philadelphia: Fortress Press, 1966.
　　　 [217] Pages 1–17.
　　　 [218] Pages 18–36.

[219] Niehr, Herbert. Review of Tigay [265]. *Biblische Zeitschrift* 33 (1987): 298–99.

[220] Nobile, Marco. "Lo sfondo culturale di Ez 8–11." *Antonianum* 58 (1983): 185–200. I do not read Italian, and am dependent on the summary of this article in *Old Testament Abstracts* 7 (1984): 275.

[221] Noth, Martin. *The Deuteronomistic History,* pages 12–17, 26–35. Journal for the Study of the Old Testament, Supplement Series, no. 15. Translated

from the 2d German ed. (1957) of *Überlieferungsgeschichtliche Studien*. Sheffield, U.K.: JSOT Press, 1981.

[222]   Noth, Martin. *A History of Pentateuchal Traditions*, pages 244–45. Translated from the German (1948) by Bernhard W. Anderson. Englewood Cliffs, N.J.: Prentice-Hall, 1972.

[223]   O'Brien, Mark A. *The Deuteronomistic History Hypothesis: A Reassessment*. Freiburg: Universitätsverlag; Göttingen: Vandenhoeck & Ruprecht, 1989.

[224]   Olyan, Saul M. *Asherah and the Cult of Yahweh in Israel*. Atlanta: Scholars Press, 1988.

      [225]   Page 2.

[226]   Pope, Marvin H. *Job: Introduction, Translation, and Notes*. Vol. 15 of *The Anchor Bible*. New York: Doubleday, 1965.

[227]   Pope, Marvin H. *Song of Songs: A New Translation with Introduction and Commentary*. Vol. 7C of *The Anchor Bible*. Garden City, N.Y.: Doubleday, 1977.

      [228]   Page 503.
      [229]   Page 518.
      [230]   Pages 617–20.

[231]   Pritchard, James B., ed. *Ancient Near Eastern Texts Relating to the Old Testament*. Princeton: Princeton University Press, 3d ed., 1969.

Reiner, Erica. *Your thwarts in pieces, Your mooring rope cut: Poetry from Babylonia and Assyria* (Michigan Studies in the Humanities 5). Ann Arbor: University of Michigan Press, 1985.

      [232]   Pages 29–49.
      [233]   Page 46.

[234]   Rendsburg, Gary A. "The Mock of Baal in 1 Kings 18:27." *Catholic Biblical Quarterly* 50 (1988): 414–17.

[235]   Ringgren, Helmer. *Israelite Religion*, page 166. Translated from the German by David E. Green. Philadelphia: Fortress Press, 1966.

[236]   Robertson, Noel. "The Ritual Background of the Dying God in Cyprus and Syro-Palestine." *Harvard Theological Review* 75 (1982): 313–59.

      [237]   Pages 322, 325, 355.
      [238]   Pages 345–47.

[239]   Rofé, Alexander. "The Monotheistic Argumentation in Deuteronomy IV 32–40: Contents, Composition, and Text." *Vetus Testamentum* 35 (1985): 434–45.

[240]   Rowley, H. H. "The Book of Ezekiel in Modern Study." In *Men of God: Studies in Old Testament History and Prophecy*, pages 169–210. London: Nelson, 1963. The paper originally appeared in the *Bulletin of the John Rylands Library* 36 (1953–54): 146–90. It gives an excellent summary of the major approaches to Ezekiel in the first half of this century. The material on Smith is on pages 175–76.

      [241]   Pages 174–81.
      [242]   Pages 207–9.

[243]   Rowley, H. H. *Job*. In the *Century Bible*. London: Nelson, 1970.

[244]   Saggs, H.W.F. "The Branch to the Nose." *Journal of Theological Studies*, n.s., 11 (1960): 318–29.

      [245]   Pages 324–25.

[246]   Sarna, Nahum M. "Ezekiel 8:17: A Fresh Examination." *Harvard Theological Review* 57 (1964): 347–52.

[247] Sherlock, Charles. "Ezekiel's Dumbness." *Expository Times* 94 (1983): 296–98.

[248] Smith, James. *The Book of the Prophet Ezekiel: A New Interpretation*. London: Society for Promoting Christian Knowledge, 1931.

[249] Smith, Mark S. "The Near Eastern Background of Solar Language for Yahweh." *Journal of Biblical Literature* 109 (1990): 29–39.

[250] Smith, Morton. *Jesus the Magician*, pages 8–16. San Francisco: Harper & Row, 1978.

[251] Smith, Morton. "A Note on Burning Babies." *Journal of the American Oriental Society* 95 (1975): 477–79.

[252] Smith, Morton. "The Veracity of Ezekiel, the Sins of Manasseh, and Jeremiah 44 18." *Zeitschrift für die alttestamentliche Wissenschaft* 87 (1975): 11–16.

Soleh, Aryeh. "Mivneh ha-Ḥazon be-Yeḥezqel 8–11." In *Sefer Doctor Baruch ben Yehudah: Meḥqarim be-Miqra' ube-Maḥshevet Yiśra'el*, ed. B. Z. Luria, pages 281–95. Tel Aviv: The Society for Bible Study in Israel, 1981.
    [253] Page 282.

[254] Speiser, E. A., trans. "Descent of Ishtar to the Nether World." In Pritchard [231], pages 106–9.

[255] Speiser, E. A., trans. "The Epic of Gilgamesh." In Pritchard [231], pages 72–99.

[256] Spiegel, Shalom. "Ezekiel or Pseudo-Ezekiel?" In Torrey [272], pages 123–99. Originally appeared in *Harvard Theological Review* 24 (1931): 245–321.

[257] Spiegel, Shalom. "Toward Certainty in Ezekiel." In Torrey [272], pages 235–61. Originally appeared in *Journal of Biblical Literature* 54 (1935): 145–71.

[258] Stähli, Hans-Peter. *Solare Elemente im Jahweglauben des Alten Testaments*, pages 45–51. Freiburg: Universitätsverlag; Göttingen: Vandenhoeck & Ruprecht, 1985.

[259] Talmage, Frank Ephraim. *David Kimhi: The Man and the Commentaries*, pages 95–96. Harvard Judaic Monographs, no. 1. Cambridge: Harvard University Press, 1975.

[260] Tcherikover, Victor. *Hellenistic Civilization and the Jews*, pages 211–20. Translated from the Hebrew by S. Appelbaum. Philadelphia: Jewish Publication Society of America, 1966.

[261] te Stroete, G. A. "Ezekiel 24:15–27: The Meaning of a Symbolic Act." *Bijdragen: Tijdschrift voor Filosofie en Theologie* 38 (1977): 163–75.

Tigay, Jeffrey H. *The Evolution of the Gilgamesh Epic*. Philadelphia: University of Pennsylvania Press, 1982.
    [262] Pages 125–26, 170–74.
    [263] Pages 130–31.

[264] Tigay, Jeffrey H. "Israelite Religion: The Onomastic and Epigraphic Evidence." In *Ancient Israelite Religion*, ed. Patrick D. Miller, Jr., Paul D. Hanson, and S. Dean McBride, pages 157–94. Philadelphia: Fortress Press, 1987.

[265] Tigay, Jeffrey H. *You Shall Have No Other Gods: Israelite Religion in the Light of Hebrew Inscriptions*. Atlanta: Scholars Press, 1986.
    [266] Pages 26–33.
    [267] Page 36.
    [268] Page 40.

[269] Torczyner, H. "Semel Ha-Qin'ah Ha-Maqneh." *Journal of Biblical Literature* 65 (1946): 293–302.
    [270] Pages 298–99.

[271]   Torrey, Charles Cutler. "Certainly Pseudo-Ezekiel." In Torrey [272],
        pages 205–34. Originally appeared in *Journal of Biblical Literature* 53 (1934):
        291–320.

[272]   Torrey, Charles Cutler. *Pseudo-Ezekiel and the Original Prophecy.* New York:
        Ktav Publishing House, 1970. Originally published New Haven: Yale Uni-
        versity Press, 1930. The Ktav edition includes the debate between Torrey
        and Shalom Spiegel that followed the original publication of *Pseudo-Ezekiel*
        [256,257,271], and an excellent prolegomenon by Moshe Greenberg.
        [273]   Pages 45–57.

[274]   Tov, Emanuel. "Recensional Differences Between the MT and LXX of
        Ezekiel." *Ephemerides Theologicae Lovanienses* 62 (1986): 94.

[275]   Toy, Crawford H. *A Critical and Exegetical Commentary on the Book of Prov-
        erbs.* International Critical Commentary, no. 16. Edinburgh: T. & T. Clark,
        1970. Originally published 1899.

Unterman, Jeremiah. *From Repentance to Redemption: Jeremiah's Thought in Transition.*
        Journal for the Study of the Old Testament, Supplement Series, no. 54.
        Sheffield, U.K.: JSOT Press, 1987.
        [276]   Pages 55–74.
        [277]   Page 169.

[278]   Van Buren, E. Douglas. "The Scorpion in Mesopotamian Art and Reli-
        gion." *Archiv für Orientforschung* 12 (1937–39): 1–28. I owe this reference to
        Jack M. Sasson.

[279]   Van der Toorn, Karel. "Female Prostitution in Payment of Vows in Ancient
        Israel." *Journal of Biblical Literature* 108 (1989): 193–205.

Van Nuys, Kelvin. "Evaluating the Pathological in Prophetic Experience (Particu-
        larly in Ezekiel)." *Journal of Bible and Religion* 21 (1953): 244–51.
        [280]   Page 250.

[281]   Van Seters, John. *In Search of History: Historiography in the Ancient World and
        the Origins of Biblical History*, pages 277–91. New Haven: Yale University
        Press, 1983.

[282]   Vanstiphout, H.L.J. "Inanna/Ishtar as a Figure of Controversy." In *Strug-
        gles of Gods: Papers of the Groningen Work Group for the Study of the History of
        Religions*, ed. H. G. Kippenberg, H.J.W. Drijvers, and Y. Kuiper, pages
        225–38. Berlin, New York, and Amsterdam: Mouton, 1984.

Vogt, Ernst. *Untersuchungen zum Buch Ezechiel.* Rome: Pontifical Biblical Institute
        Press, 1981.
        [283]   Page 40.
        [284]   Pages 92–106.

[285]   Ward, J. M. "Jaazaniah." In *The Interpreter's Dictionary of the Bible: An Illus-
        trated Encyclopedia*, vol. 2. New York: Abingdon Press, 1962.

[286]   Ward, James M. *The Prophets*, pages 101–2. Nashville: Abingdon Press,
        1982.

[287]   Weinfeld, Moshe. *Deuteronomy and the Deuteronomic School*, pages 69–74.
        Oxford: Clarendon Press, 1972.

[288]   Weinfeld, Moshe. "The Worship of Molech and of the Queen of Heaven
        and Its Background." *Ugarit-Forschungen* 4 (1972): 133–54.

[289]   Weiser, Artur. *Das Buch Hiob.* Das Alte Testament Deutsch, no. 13. Göt-
        tingen: Vandenhoeck & Ruprecht, 1974.

[290]   Wilson, Robert R. "An Interpretation of Ezekiel's Dumbness." *Vetus Testa-
        mentum* 22 (1972): 91–104.

[291] Wolkstein, Diane, and Samuel Noah Kramer. *Inanna, Queen of Heaven and Earth: Her Stories and Hymns from Sumer.* New York: Harper & Row, 1983.
    [292] Page 12.
    [293] Page 37.
    [294] Pages 52–89.
    [295] Page 59.
    [296] Pages 155–63.
[297] Zimmerli, Walther. *Ezekiel: A Commentary on the Book of the Prophet Ezekiel.* Translated from the German (1969) by Ronald E. Clements (vol. 1) and James D. Martin (vol. 2). Philadelphia: Fortress Press, 1979–83.
    [298] Vol. 1, pages 18–19.
    [299] Vol. 1, pages 36–43.
    [300] Vol. 1, pages 160–61, 508.
    [301] Vol. 1, page 209.
    [302] Vol. 1, pages 233–34.
    [303] Vol. 1, page 245.
    [304] Vol. 1, pages 334–39, 348–53.
    [305] Vol. 1, page 480.
    [306] Vol. 2, pages 191–94.

B. MEDICAL, PSYCHOANALYTIC, ETHNOGRAPHIC

[307] Adams, Kenneth Alan. "Arachnophobia: Love American Style." *Journal of Psychoanalytic Anthropology* 4 (1981): 173–79.
[308] Adams, Kenneth Alan. "Family and Fantasy: Dread of the Female and the Narcissistic Ethos in American Culture." Ph.D. dissertation, Brandeis University, 1980.
[309] Arlow, Jacob. "The Consecration of the Prophet." *Psychoanalytic Quarterly* 20 (1951): 374–97.
    [310] Pages 391–94.
[311] Aronson, Arnold E. "Speech Pathology and Symptom Therapy in the Interdisciplinary Treatment of Psychogenic Aphonia." *Journal of Speech and Hearing Disorders* 34 (1969): 321–41.
    [312] Pages 328–33.
Aronson, Arnold E. *Clinical Voice Disorders: An Interdisciplinary Approach.* New York: Thieme, 2d ed., 1985.
    [313] Pages 141–45.
    [314] Pages 347–59.
[315] Aronson, Arnold E., Herbert W. Peterson, Jr., and Edward M. Litin. "Psychiatric Symptomatology in Functional Dysphonia and Aphonia." *Journal of Speech and Hearing Disorders* 31 (1966): 115–27.
[316] *Biographical Directory of Fellows & Members of the American Psychiatric Association.* New York: R. R. Bowker, 1977. S.v. "Cassem, Edwin Hughes."
Bogoras, Waldemar. "Shamanistic Performance in the Inner Room." In *Reader in Comparative Religion: An Anthropological Approach,* ed. William A. Lessa and Evon Z. Vogt, pages 454–60. New York: Harper & Row, 2d ed., 1965. I owe this reference to my colleague James Sanford.
    [317] Page 459.

[318] Bouhdiba, Abdelwahab. *La Sexualité en Islam*, pages 247–48. Paris: Presses Universitaires de France, 1975.

[319] Buckley, Thomas, and Alma Gottlieb, eds. *Blood Magic: The Anthropology of Menstruation*. Berkeley and Los Angeles: University of California Press, 1988.

[320] Buckley, Thomas, and Alma Gottlieb. "A Critical Appraisal of Theories of Menstrual Symbolism." In Buckley and Gottlieb [319], pages 1–50.

[321] Crewdson, John. *By Silence Betrayed: Sexual Abuse of Children in America*. Boston: Little, Brown, 1988.

[322] De Silva, Regis A., and Bernard Lown. "Ventricular Premature Beats, Stress, and Sudden Death." *Psychosomatics* 19:11 (November 1978): 649–61.

[323] Dement, William, and Edward A. Wolpert. "Relationships in the Manifest Content of Dreams Occurring on the Same Night." *Journal of Nervous and Mental Disease* 126 (1958): 568–78. I owe this reference to Daniel Merkur.

[324] Dinnerstein, Dorothy. *The Mermaid and the Minotaur: Sexual Arrangements and Human Malaise*. New York: Harper & Row, 1976.

[325] Dodds, E. R. *The Greeks and the Irrational*, pages 110–16. Berkeley and Los Angeles: University of California Press, 1951.

[326] Eilberg-Schwartz, Howard. *The Savage in Judaism: An Anthropology of Israelite Religion and Ancient Judaism*, pages 177–94. Bloomington: Indiana University Press, 1990.

[327] Ellenberger, Henri F. *The Discovery of the Unconscious: The History and Evolution of Dynamic Psychiatry*, pages 427–57, 477–80. New York: Basic Books, 1970.

[328] Elwin, Verrier. "The Vagina Dentata Legend." *British Journal of Medical Psychology* 19 (1943): 439–53.

[329] Engel, George L. "Sudden and Rapid Death During Psychological Stress: Folklore or Folk Wisdom?" *Annals of Internal Medicine* 74 (1971): 771–82.

Farber, Leslie H., and Charles Fisher. "An Experimental Approach to Dream Psychology Through the Use of Hypnosis." *Psychoanalytic Quarterly* 2 (1943): 202–16.
  [330] Pages 213–14.

[331] Feldman, S. S. "Fear of Mice." *Psychoanalytic Quarterly* 18 (1949): 227–30.

Fisher, Charles. "Psychoanalytic Implications of Recent Research on Sleep and Dreaming. Part I: Empirical Findings." *Journal of the American Psychoanalytic Association* 13 (1965): 197–270. I owe this reference to Daniel Merkur.
  [332] Page 215.

[333] Freud, Sigmund. *The Interpretation of Dreams*. Translated from the German and edited by James Strachey. New York: Avon Books, 1965.
  [334] Pages 152–53.
  [335] Pages 318–26.
  [336] Pages 369–70.
  [337] Pages 526–41.
  [338] Pages 608–9.

[339] Freud, Sigmund. *Jokes and Their Relation to the Unconscious*. Translated from the German and edited by James Strachey. New York: W. W. Norton, 1960.
  [340] Page 205.

[341] Freud, Sigmund. *Leonardo da Vinci and a Memory of His Childhood*, page 13. Translated from the German by Alan Tyson. New York: W. W. Norton, 1964.

[342] Freud, Sigmund. *Moses and Monotheism*, pages 107–8, 154–76. Translated from the German by Katherine Jones. New York: Vintage Books, 1939.

[343] Freud, Sigmund. *An Outline of Psycho-Analysis*, page 24. Translated from the German by James Strachey. New York: W. W. Norton, 1969.

[344] Freud, Sigmund. "A Premonitory Dream Fulfilled." Published as an appendix to Freud [333], pages 661–64.

Freud, Sigmund. "Psychoanalytic Notes Upon an Autobiographical Account of a Case of Paranoia (Dementia Paranoides) (1911)." In Freud, *Three Case Histories*, pages 103–86. New York: Collier Books, 1963.
　　[345] Pages 142–43.

[346] Gay, Peter. *Freud: A Life for Our Time*, pages 30–37, 496. New York: W. W. Norton, 1988.

[347] Gay, Peter. "Six Names in Search of an Interpretation." In Gay, *Reading Freud: Explorations & Entertainments*, pages 54–73. New Haven: Yale University Press, 1990.

Goitein, S. D. "The Sexual Mores of the Common People." In *Society and the Sexes in Medieval Islam*, ed. Afaf Lutfi Al-Sayyid-Marsot, pages 43–61. Malibu, Calif.: Undena Publications, 1979.
　　[348] Pages 46–47.

Gregor, Thomas. *Anxious Pleasures: The Sexual Lives of an Amazonian People*. Chicago: University of Chicago Press, 1985.
　　[349] Page 142.
　　[350] Pages 162–66.

[351] Hays, H. R. *The Dangerous Sex: The Myth of Feminine Evil*. New York: G. P. Putnam's Sons, 1964.
　　[352] Pages 173–74.

[353] Horney, Karen. "The Dread of Woman." *International Journal of Psychoanalysis* 13 (1932): 348–60.

[354] Jaspers, Karl. *General Psychopathology*, page 729. Translated from the 7th German ed. (1959) by J. Hoenig and Marian W. Hamilton. Chicago: University of Chicago Press, 1963. I owe this reference to Daniel Merkur.

[355] Jung, C. G. *Flying Saucers: A Modern Myth of Things Seen in the Skies*, pages 60–61. Translated from the German by R.F.C. Hull. New York: New American Library, 1969. Originally published Zurich, 1958.

[356] Kinzl, Johann, Wilfried Biebl, and Hermann Rauchegger. "Functional Aphonia: A Conversion Symptom as Defensive Mechanism against Anxiety." *Psychotherapy and Psychosomatics* 49 (1988): 31–36.

Kroll, Jerome, and Bernard Bachrach. "Visions and Psychopathology in the Middle Ages." *Journal of Nervous and Mental Disease* 170 (1982): 41–49.

[357] Lawrence, Denise L. "Menstrual Politics: Women and Pigs in Rural Portugal." In Buckley and Gottlieb [319], pages 117–36.

[358] Lederer, Wolfgang. *The Fear of Women*. London: Grune & Stratton, 1968.
　　[359] Pages 44–52.

[360] Legman, Gershon. *Rationale of the Dirty Joke: An Analysis of Sexual Humor, Second Series*, pages 415, 429–30. New York: Breaking Point, 1975.

Levy, Ludwig. "Sexualsymbolik in der Simsonsage." In Spiegel [396], pages 75–93.
　　[361] Pages 87–88.

[362] Lown, Bernard. "Mental Stress, Arrhythmias and Sudden Death." *American Journal of Medicine* 72 (February 1982): 177–80.

[363] Lown, Bernard. "Reflections on Sudden Cardiac Death: Brain and
       Heart." *Transactions & Studies of the College of Physicians of Philadelphia* 10
       (1988): 63–80.
          [364] Pages 70–72.
[365] Lown, Bernard. "Sudden Cardiac Death: Biobehavioral Perspective." *Circu-
       lation* 76, suppl. 1 (July 1987): 186–96.
[366] Lown, Bernard, John V. Temte, Peter Reich, Charles Gaughan, Quentin
       Regestein, and Hamid Hai. "Basis for Recurring Ventricular Fibrillation in
       the Absence of Coronary Heart Disease and its Management." *New England
       Journal of Medicine* 294:12 (18 March 1976): 623–29.
[367] Masson, Jeffrey Moussaieff. *The Assault on Truth: Freud's Suppression of the
       Seduction Theory.* New York: Farrar, Straus & Giroux, 1984.
[368] McCue, Elspeth C., and Peter A. McCue. "Hypnosis in the Elucidation of
       Hysterical Aphonia: A Case Report." *American Journal of Clinical Hypnosis*
       30 (1988): 178–82.
[369] Merkur, Daniel. *Becoming Half Hidden: Shamanism and Initiation among the
       Inuit*, pages 95–101. Stockholm: Almqvist & Wiksell, 1985.
[370] Merkur, Daniel. "Prophetic Initiation in Israel and Judah." *Psychoanalytic
       Study of Society* 12 (1988): 37–67.
          [371] Pages 51–73.
[372] Miller, Alice. *Thou Shalt Not Be Aware: Society's Betrayal of the Child.* Trans-
       lated from the German by Hildegarde Hannum and Hunter Hannum.
       New York: New American Library, 1984.
          [373] Pages 237–38.
Neumann, Erich. *The Great Mother: An Analysis of the Archetype.* Bollingen Series,
       no. 47. Translated from the German by Ralph Manheim. Princeton: Prince-
       ton University Press, 1963. I thank Robert Segal for directing me toward
       this valuable resource.
          [374] Page 138.
          [375] Pages 147–208.
          [376] Pages 153, 181; plates 67, 84b.
          [377] Page 171.
[378] Newman, Richard, Jay Katz, and Robert Rubinstein. "The Experimental
       Situation as a Determinant of Hypnotic Dreams: A Contribution to the
       Experimental Use of Hypnosis." *Psychiatry* 23 (1960): 63–73.
[379] Offenkrantz, William, and Allan Rechtschaffen. "Clinical Studies of Se-
       quential Dreams. I. A Patient in Psychotherapy." *Archives of General Psychia-
       try* 8 (1963): 497–508. I owe this reference to Daniel Merkur.
          [380] Pages 505–6.
[381] Paige, Karen Ericksen, and Jeffery M. Paige. *The Politics of Reproductive
       Ritual*, pages 240–45. Berkeley and Los Angeles: University of California
       Press, 1981.
[382] Perepel, E. "On the Physiology of Hysterical Aphonia and Mutism." *Inter-
       national Journal of Psycho-Analysis* 11 (1930): 185–92.
[383] Reich, Peter, Regis A. DeSilva, Bernard Lown, and Benjamin J. Murawsky.
       "Acute Psychological Disturbances Preceding Life-Threatening Ventricular
       Arrhythmias." *Journal of the American Medical Association* 246:3 (17 July 1981):
       233–35.
[384] Rubinstein, Robert, Jay Katz, and Richard Newman. "On the Sources and

Determinants of Hypnotic Dreams." *Canadian Psychiatric Association Journal* 2 (1957): 154–61.

[385] Sapir, Shimon, and Arnold E. Aronson. "The Relationship Between Psychopathology and Speech and Language Disorders in Neurologic Patients." *Journal of Speech and Hearing Disorders* 55 (1990): 505.

[386] Satow, Roberta. "Where Has All the Hysteria Gone?" *Psychoanalytic Review* 66 (1979): 463–77.

[387] Schnier, Jacques. "Morphology of a Symbol: The Octopus." *American Imago* 13 (1956): 23.

[388] Shengold, Leonard. *Soul Murder: The Effects of Childhood Abuse and Deprivation.* New Haven: Yale University Press, 1989.

[389] Pages 26, 28, 99.

[390] Page 143.

[391] Page 316.

[392] Silverman, Julian. "Shamans and Acute Schizophrenia." *American Anthropologist* 69 (1967): 21–31. I owe this reference to Robert Segal.

[393] Skoda, Joseph. "Geschichte einer durch mehrere Monate anhaltenden Katalepsis." *Zeitschrift der kaiserlich königliche Gesellschaft der Ärzte zu Wien* 8 (1852): 404–19.

[394] Page 418.

[395] Slater, Philip E. *The Glory of Hera: Greek Mythology and the Greek Family.* Boston: Beacon Press, 1968.

[396] Spiegel, Yorick, ed. *Psychoanalytische Interpretationen biblischer Texte.* Munich: Christian Kaiser, 1972.

[397] Spiro, Melford E. *Oedipus in the Trobriands.* Chicago: University of Chicago Press, 1982.

[398] Stephens, William N. *The Oedipus Complex: Cross-Cultural Evidence.* New York: Free Press of Glencoe, 1962.

[399] Pages 85–123.

[400] Tauber, Edward S. "Certain Psychic Mechanisms in Aphonia: A Case Illustration." *Psychoanalytic Review* 34 (1947): 469–84.

[401] Page 483.

Terr, Lenore. *Too Scared to Cry: Psychic Trauma in Childhood.* New York: Harper & Row, 1990.

[402] Pages 63–64.

[403] Page 181.

[404] Pages 235–80.

[405] Trosman, Harry, Allan Rechtschaffen, William Offenkrantz, and Edward Wolpert. "Studies in Psychophysiology of Dreams. IV. Relations Among Dreams in Sequence." *Archives of General Psychiatry* 3 (1960): 602–7.

[406] Veith, Ilza. *Hysteria: The History of a Disease,* pages 15–20. Chicago: University of Chicago Press, 1965.

[407] Verrier, Richard L., Eric L. Hagestad, and Bernard Lown. "Delayed Myocardial Ischemia Induced by Anger." *Circulation* 75:1 (January 1987): 249–54.

[408] Walton, D., and D. A. Black. "The Application of Modern Learning Theory to the Treatment of Chronic Hysterical Aphonia." *Journal of Psychosomatic Research* 3 (1959): 303–11.

[409] Ziegler, Frederick J., and John B. Imboden. "Contemporary Conversion

Reactions. II. A Conceptual Model." *Archives of General Psychiatry* 6 (1962): 279–87.

C. OTHER

[410]   Kittredge, George Lyman. *Witchcraft in Old and New England*, page 330. New York: Atheneum, 1972. Originally published 1929.

[411]   Kretzmer, Herbert. "At the End of the Day." Lyrics in *A Musical: Les Misérables* by Alan Boublil and Claude-Michel Schoenberg. Cameron Mackintosh (RSC) production; recorded at CTS Studios, Wembley (England), between October 28 and November 12, 1985. First Night Records, 1985.

[412]   Mahfouz, Naguib. *Palace Walk*, chapter 25. Translated from the Arabic by William Maynard Hutchins and Olive E. Kenny. New York: Doubleday, 1990.

[413]   McPherson, James M. *Battle Cry of Freedom: The Civil War Era*, page 802. New York: Oxford University Press, 1988.

[414]   Milton, John. *The Complete English Poems of John Milton*, pages 125–26. Edited by John D. Jump. New York: Washington Square Press, 1964.

[415]   Orwell, George. "Rudyard Kipling." In Orwell, *A Collection of Essays*, page 138. Garden City, N.Y.: Doubleday, 1954.

[416]   Steinbrunner, Chris, and Burt Goldblatt. *Cinema of the Fantastic*, pages 177–98. New York: Saturday Review Press, 1972. With photographs. Dexter Hall located this resource for me.

[417]   Updike, John. *Rabbit Is Rich*, page 451. New York: Alfred A. Knopf, 1981.

[418]   Updike, John. *Rabbit Redux*, page 127. Greenwich, Conn.: Fawcett, 1971.

[419]   Von Gunden, Kenneth. *Flights of Fantasy: The Great Fantasy Films*, pages 170–74. Jefferson, N.C.: McFarland, 1989. This resource, too, I owe to Dexter Hall.

Indexes

Index of References

Index of Hebrew Words and Phrases

Index of Modern Authors

Subject Index

Made in the USA
Coppell, TX
10 January 2021

47883712R00164